# SHOULD ALL SPEAK WITH TONGUES?

## MAC WARD SYMES

WESTBOW
PRESS
A DIVISION OF THOMAS NELSON

*WestBow Press books may be ordered through booksellers or by contacting:*

*WestBow Press*
*A Division of Thomas Nelson*
*1663 Liberty Drive*
*Bloomington, IN 47403*
*www.westbowpress.com*
*1-(866) 928-1240*

*ISBN: 978-1-4497-6800-3 (sc)*
*ISBN: 978-1-4497-6801-0 (e)*

*Library of Congress Control Number: 2012921485*

*Printed in the United States of America*

*WestBow Press rev. date: 6/12/2013*

# TABLE OF CONTENTS

I wish to express my thanks and deep appreciation to my marvelous wife, Margaret Elizabeth Symes, for her expert assistance in working with me during the editing process of this book. She is due special recognition for her patience during the long hours I have spent in the research and writing of the manuscript. She shares my burden for the message which is needed for the perfecting of the church in these last days. She is a God-given companion, sweetheart, and wife.
Both of her names, Margaret and Elizabeth, are Queen's names. She is more than a Queen to me.

# PREFACE

It is the author's desire to participate in the perfecting of the church that will doubtless occur in the last days. He also aspires to help set men free from the traditions and doctrines of men that have crept into the doctrinal fabric of Christianity over the past years and centuries. These doctrines have entangled people in many things that are not founded in New Testament truth as revealed by Christ and the early apostles, and that were not believed and practiced by the early New Testament church.

- *EPH 2: 20 And are built upon the foundation of the apostles and prophets, Jesus Christ himself being the chief corner stone;*

Today all doctrinal beliefs and practices of the church must come from the New Testament, with Christ, the apostles, and the early church as our foundation and pattern. This does not mean that the Old Testament is to be abolished. The truth is, the Old Testament by types and shadows portrayed and foretold of things that actually were to be revealed and occur in the New Testament.

- *HEB 10:1 For the law having a shadow of good things to come, and not the very image of the things, can never with those sacrifices which they offered year by year continually make the comers thereunto perfect.*

  *8 ... Above when he said, Sacrifice and offering and*

> *burnt offerings and offering for sin thou wouldest not,*
> *neither hadst pleasure therein; which are offered by*
> *the law;*
> *9 Then said he, Lo, I come to do thy will, O God. He*
> *taketh away the first, that he may establish the second.*
> *10 By the which will we are sanctified through the*
> *offering of the body of Jesus Christ once for all.*

The Old Testament contains prophesies yet to be fulfilled, and its historical information regarding God's dealings with Israel – and mankind in general--is invaluable, but that which has been abolished as Old Testament doctrine are the works and ordinances of the Law of Moses which were given to Israel and not to the church. The New Testament is very clear on the fact that the *ordinances of the law* were *"slain," "nailed to the cross," "abolished,"* and *"done away"* when Christ became their fulfillment.

- *EPH 2:15 Having **abolished** in his flesh the enmity, even the law of commandments contained in **ordinances**; for to make in himself of twain one new man, so making peace;*
  *16 And that he might reconcile both unto God in one body **by the cross**, having **slain** the enmity thereby:*
- *COL 2:14 Blotting out the handwriting of **ordinances** that was against us, which was contrary to us, and took it out of the way, **nailing it to his cross**;*

One must forsake all ordinances (*works*) of the law of Moses (GAL 2:16). For instance, we no longer sacrifice lambs because Jesus became the Lamb of God slain for us. One must hold unswervingly to the truth which says we have been made able ministers of the New Testament, and not to the *"letter"* of the law. This firm conviction is based on many scriptures such as the following:

- *2CO 3:6 Who also hath made us able ministers of the new testament; not of the letter, but of the spirit: for the letter killeth, but the spirit giveth life.*

> *11 ... For if that which is **done away** was glorious, much more that which remaineth is glorious.*

Therefore, we must base all doctrines of the New Testament church on that which is revealed in the New Testament and refuse to carry forward anything from the Mosaic law *("the letter")* that was *"abolished"* by the cross of Christ.

God's plan was to bring Jews and Gentiles together into one body called the church. This was accomplished when Christ died on the cross, whereby all the works, ordinances, ceremonies, rituals, requirements, and commandments of the law were made obsolete. The offering of Christ's body and blood as the supreme and total sacrifice forever satisfied and fulfilled all those works and ordinances that were required by the law of Moses. Since that time the resurrection of Christ has completely confirmed God's acceptance of that sacrifice on our behalf. Today the only way men can be saved is by accepting the gift of God's Son and believing in him through faith; and therefore, it is impossible for justification to be obtained through keeping the works of the law.

Sad to say, down through the centuries, besides carrying forward into the church several Mosaic laws, men have invented new ordinances and traditions that are just as binding, and that require obedience, just as did the ordinances of the Mosaic law. These new religious inventions are many and are incorporated in a multitude of church dogmas, rituals, sacraments, sacerdotal orders, and membership requirements that have no basis in the New Testament.

Many of these practices have permeated Christianity even outside the confines of major organized Christian religions, and have become an indelible part of the portrait of churchanity as it exists in the so-called Christian world today. It is distressing that these deformed appendages which have been added to the church body are most of what the world outside the church sees when they look at Christianity today. That is, they see the characteristic differences that mark the divisions within the body of Christ...and it leaves a

hungry world confused, perplexed, and reluctant to get involved...
not knowing which church is right, nor which one to join.

It is the author's opinion that there exist serious problem-areas
where deviations from the central truth of the gospel of Christ have
occurred. A major component of true preaching and teaching must
be remedial through exhorting and even reproving in love.

- *EPH 5:11 And have no fellowship with the unfruitful
  works of darkness, but rather reprove them.*
- *2TI 4:1 I charge thee therefore before God, and the Lord
  Jesus Christ, who shall judge the quick and the dead at
  his appearing and his kingdom;*
  *2 Preach the word; be instant in season, out of season;
  reprove, rebuke, exhort with all longsuffering and
  doctrine.*

The fact is, if a minister truly loves those to whom he is
ministering, he will not ignore, overlook, or refuse to deal with
religious ideologies that may be spiritually fatal to those involved.

A primary objective must be to preach the gospel and save the
lost from eternal destruction. The author believes he is directly
involved in preaching a salvation message in two ways:

(1) The first being, the deliverance of the Lord's sheep that have
become entangled in religious traditions and rudiments that will
cause their destruction. Rudiments are religious rules and tenets
of faith that do not come from the Bible, but from other religious
sources...namely the religious world, which has its authority from
man, but not from God.

- *COL 2:20 Wherefore if ye be dead with Christ from the
  rudiments of the world, why, as though living in the
  world, are ye subject to ordinances,*
  *21 (Touch not; taste not; handle not;*
  *22 Which all are to perish with the using;) after the
  commandments and doctrines of men?*

Make no mistake, the world of religion is much larger in scope than the true church, and multiplied millions of people are involved and entangled in it.

(2) The author's second objective is, to present the gospel of Christ in such truth that it will deter new converts from becoming entangled in doctrines and traditions of men. Therefore, the author declares that, while he is dealing with many issues through a corrective approach, he is a gospel preacher bearing the good news that "Jesus saves."

While we all want to hear about that which is right with the church, we must realize that a major portion of Paul's writings have to do with that which was wrong with the church, therefore must be corrected to strengthen and edify the church collectively and individually through truthful and loving preaching and teaching. Paul warned as follows:

- *ACT 20:30 Also of your own selves shall men arise, speaking perverse things, to draw away disciples after them.*

  *31 Therefore watch, and remember, that by the space of three years I ceased not to warn every one night and day with tears.*

  *32 And now, brethren, I commend you to God, and to the word of his grace, which is able to build you up, and to give you an inheritance among all them which are sanctified.*

The author sincerely believes Christ is in the process of perfecting his church in preparation for his second coming, Therefore he must have true ministers of the New Testament who are able to preach the word with such power and authority that it will wash out and purge away the blemishes and impurities spiritually, doctrinally, emotionally, theologically, and traditionally, so that the church can be presented to Christ at his second coming as a wife that is perfected, holy, and without blemish. Speaking of the church as the wife of Christ, Paul said:

- *EPH 5:26 That he might sanctify and cleanse it with the washing of water by the word,*
*That he might present it to himself a glorious church, not having spot, or wrinkle, or any such thing; but that it should be holy and without blemish.*
*32 ... This is a great mystery: but I speak concerning Christ and the church.*

The cleansing of the church will certainly not harm the church but will bring glory and honor to God through his Son.

- *EPH 3:21 Unto him be glory in the church by Christ Jesus throughout all ages, world without end.*

A call goes out to all who are in Christian service to work with Christ with the objective to edify his church.

- *EPH 4:12 For the perfecting of the saints, for the work of the ministry, for the edifying of the body of Christ:*

Now, listen carefully to this next verse:

*13 Till we all come in the unity of the faith, **and of the knowledge of the Son of God**, unto a perfect man, unto the measure of the stature of the fulness of Christ:*

Can the church dare to take this literally...*Till we all come to the one faith that is given to the church?*
Remember, there is only one faith:

- *EPH 4:5 One Lord, **one faith**, one baptism,*

Do we want *"the knowledge of the Son of God"*...his knowledge about truth?

- *PHI 3:8 Yea doubtless, and I count all things but loss for the excellency of the knowledge of Christ Jesus my Lord:*

Do we believe it is God's will and plan to perfect his church... until it becomes fully grown in stature that befits the Head, which is Christ?

- *EPH 5:25-27 ...even as Christ also loved the church, and gave himself for it; That he might sanctify and cleanse it with the washing of water by the word, That he might present it to himself a glorious church, not having spot, or wrinkle, or any such thing; but that it should be holy and without blemish.*

This author believes it and is preaching and teaching truth concerning the perfecting of the church wherever and anywhere.

- *EPH 4:14 That we henceforth be no more children, tossed to and fro, and carried about with every wind of doctrine, by the sleight of men, and cunning craftiness, whereby they lie in wait to deceive;*
  *15 But speaking the truth in love, may grow up into him in all things, which is the head, even Christ:*

May God bless,

Mac Ward Symes, Author

# INTRODUCTION

Most Christians individually and denominationally are divided by a major issue. That issue has to do with the baptism in the Holy Ghost, and more particularly, that of speaking in other tongues.

The labels "Pentecostal" and "Non-Pentecostal" have identified the opposing sides, and no other issue has divided the church so distinctly as that of speaking in other tongues. There is no gray area or middle ground, and all are definitely on one side or the other. This issue has separated neighbors, friends, family, relatives, churches, husbands and wives. No other line so distinct exists between major and minor denominations than that of being either Pentecostal or Non-Pentecostal.

This polarization does not have so much to do with the validity of the person of the Holy Ghost as with the operation of the various gifts, or ministries, of the Holy Ghost. These gifts of the Spirit have no way of manifestation except through believers who are the temple, or dwelling place of the Holy Ghost (2CO 6:16).

The terms "Holy Ghost" and "Holy Spirit" are synonymous, and are often designated with the masculine pronoun "He." In this writing they both may appear, used interchangeably on the same page, in the same paragraph, or even in the same sentence. I am often oblivious to which is used.

This book is written for the benefit of anyone interested in the subject of the Holy Spirit, and if anyone reads carefully, they will gain fresh Biblical information and perspective. Lack of information and misinformation concerning the Holy Spirit are serious problems within the church.

Great spiritual benefits accompany a literal interpretation of the Bible pertaining to the Baptism with the Holy Spirit, and all the gifts, manifestations, and fruit that accompany the experience. It is imperative that one study the subject thoroughly so their faith can be based only on the word of God...and I stress "*only.*"

The author truly believes that information contained in this book will unite Pentecostals and Non-Pentecostals...at least on this one vital issue. This can be a stepping stone toward unity on other vital matters of doctrine and faith. Hopefully, both sides will return to the Biblical point of simply being "Christians."

The Bible teaches that Christ will bring his church together in the last days prior to his second coming, and the above issue is one which should be clarified. It is Christ's desire that we all come into the unity of the faith.

- *EPH 4:12 For the perfecting of the saints, for the work of the ministry, for the edifying of the body of Christ:*
  *13 Till we all come in the unity of the faith, and of the knowledge of the Son of God, unto a perfect man, unto the measure of the stature of the fulness of Christ:*
  *14 That we henceforth be no more children, tossed to and fro, and carried about with every wind of doctrine, by the sleight of men, and cunning craftiness, whereby they lie in wait to deceive;*
  *15 But speaking the truth in love, may grow up into him in all things, which is the head, even Christ:*

The answer to the question posed by the title of this book, "*Should all speak with tongues?*", is not difficult to answer Biblically, but the answer finds its difficulty in the many doctrines that exist among the many divided churches which exist in the world today. Hopefully, this book will shed some important and Biblically true light on this question.

The undergirding truth is much broader than speaking in tongues, and has to do with the person of the Holy Spirit. Primary emphasis focuses on him and his ministry to the church as the body of Christ. The Holy Spirit was sent to the church soon after the ascension of Christ, and he is the designated administrator of the continuing ministry of Christ as he functions as the Head of the church.

The Holy Spirit brought to the church various **fruits** of the Spirit listed in Galatians 5:22-23, and he operates within the church through the **gifts** of the Spirit listed in First Corinthians 12:8 thru 10.

Even though speaking with tongues is the specific subject of this book, the author also gives appropriate attention to the person of the Holy Spirit and to all the gifts of the Spirit. Keep in mind that "Tongues" is listed as one of these gifts.

This book presents a fresh approach to the subject of the infilling of the Holy Spirit, the accompanying fruit, and the gifts of the Spirit. This approach is not from the traditional Pentecostal or Non-Pentecostal view, but from a Biblical viewpoint that does not divide the body into separate doctrinal segments, but into a unity of the faith that is *"sound doctrine"* scripturally. We must all pursue the following guidelines of truth:

- *TIT 2:1 But speak thou the things which become **sound doctrine**:*
- *TIT 1:9 Holding fast the faithful word as he hath been taught, that he may be able by **sound doctrine** both to exhort and to convince the gainsayers.*

God bless as you read.

Mac Ward Symes, Author

# CHAPTER 1

# TRUTH UNITES

Christianity, as a faith has long been fragmented by many divisive factors which have splintered the body of believers into a multitude of different theological camps. This book is not about division but is about unity among Christians. A deep commitment by the author to the unity of the body of Christ in the earth undergirds the writing of this book.

All Christians have long sung the rousing hymn, "Onward, Christian Soldiers." It is now time to march to the words of the song.

> **"Like a mighty army moves the church of God;**
> **Brothers, we are treading where the saints have trod;**
> **We are not divided; All one body we,**
> **One in hope and doctrine, One in charity."**

- *JUD 1:3 Beloved, when I gave all diligence to write unto you of the common salvation, it was needful for me to write unto you, and exhort you that ye should earnestly contend for <u>the faith</u> which was once delivered unto the saints.*

*"The faith"* was once delivered to the saints--the early church--in a pure form through the ministry of Christ, and through the early apostles. Some of these apostles were instruments through which a major portion of the New Testament was given to the church by the Holy Ghost. We are truly challenged to tread where saints have trod. The original revelation provides a foundation on which the church must be built throughout succeeding generations.

- *EPH 2:20 And are built upon the foundation of the apostles and prophets, Jesus Christ himself being the chief corner stone;*
  *21 In whom all the building fitly framed together groweth unto an holy temple in the Lord:*
  *22 In whom ye also are builded together for an habitation of God through the Spirit.*

The things which happened to, and through, the early apostles are given as examples and patterns for the church to follow. The apostles were filled with the Holy Spirit, and lived and walked in the Spirit, which means they were continually guided and taught by the Spirit. Their bodies became temples or dwelling places for the Holy Ghost, who lived within their spirit, mind, and body, exerting great control over their thoughts, actions, and emotions.

Jesus promised his disciples that when he returned back into heaven, he would ask the heavenly Father to send the Holy Ghost to dwell within his followers. I have selected a series of verses, all of them containing words spoken by Jesus during his last few days on earth. They show the emphasis Jesus placed on the Holy Spirit.

- *JOH 14:16 And I will pray the Father, and he shall give you another Comforter, that he may abide with you for ever;*
  *17 Even the Spirit of truth; whom the world cannot receive, because it seeth him not, neither knoweth him: but ye know him; for he dwelleth with you, and shall be in you.*
  *26 ...But the Comforter, which is the Holy Ghost, whom*

the Father will send in my name, he shall teach you all things, and bring all things to your remembrance, whatsoever I have said unto you.

- JOH 15:26 But when the Comforter is come, whom I will send unto you from the Father, even the Spirit of truth, which proceedeth from the Father, he shall testify of me:
- JOH 16:7 Nevertheless I tell you the truth; It is expedient for you that I go away: for if I go not away, the Comforter will not come unto you; but if I depart, I will send him unto you.

8 And when he is come, he will reprove the world of sin, and of righteousness, and of judgment:

12 ...I have yet many things to say unto you, but ye cannot bear them now.

13 Howbeit when he, the Spirit of truth, is come, he will guide you into all truth: for he shall not speak of himself; but whatsoever he shall hear, that shall he speak: and he will shew you things to come.

14 He shall glorify me: for he shall receive of mine, and shall shew it unto you.

- ACT 1:4 And, being assembled together with them, commanded them that they should not depart from Jerusalem, but wait for the promise of the Father, which, saith he, ye have heard of me.

5 For John truly baptized with water; but ye shall be baptized with the Holy Ghost not many days hence.

8 ...But ye shall receive power, after that the Holy Ghost is come upon you: and ye shall be witnesses unto me both in Jerusalem, and in all Judaea, and in Samaria, and unto the uttermost part of the earth.

These verses will provide a platform of Biblical support for the things contained in this book. Since they came directly from Christ, they shall be the chief cornerstone support for the foundation of the apostles and prophets of the early New Testament church on which we are to build the church today.

Prior to the beginning of Christ's ministry John the Baptist, the forerunner of Christ, introduced Jesus as the one who would baptize believers in the Holy Ghost. This should indicate the importance of this truth, and alert all who believe in Christ that they must be baptized in the Holy Ghost. John the Baptist said,

- *MAT 3:11 I indeed baptize you with water unto repentance: but he that cometh after me is mightier than I, whose shoes I am not worthy to bear: **he shall baptize you with the Holy Ghost, and with fire:***

## Traditions of men

During the time since that original revelation concerning the Holy Ghost, carnal minds have veered from the truth, having substituted many doctrines and traditions of men in place of the gospel of the kingdom and the doctrines of Christ. During the centuries which followed the time of Christ and the early church, history reveals that men gradually replaced the truth with their religious traditions, and an institutionalized church evolved, which gained control over the masses who embrace Christianity.

The church today is in a struggle to become un-entangled from doctrines which were derived...not from Christ, neither from the apostles, nor the Bible...but from traditions invented by men. Only that which may be learned from Christ can be valid, and if any doctrine of the church today does not connect directly back to Christ and the apostles, it should not be tasted, handled or touched.

- *COL 2:21 (Touch not; taste not; handle not; 22 Which all are to perish with the using;) after the commandments and doctrines of men?*
- *EPH 4:20 But ye have not so learned Christ; If so be that ye have heard him, and have been taught by him, as the truth is in Jesus:*

What a powerful statement --*"the truth is in Jesus." Back to the basics* should be the watchword of the church in these last days prior to the second coming of Christ. A constant preoccupation of the church should be to rediscover truth which was once delivered to the saints (JUD 1:3).

Much of the truth which was delivered to the saints in the early church has been smothered by traditions of men.

• *MAR 7:13 Making the word of God of none effect through your tradition, which ye have delivered: and many such like things do ye.*

The truth will set believers free from the division and denominational fragmentation that has the church so fractured over the matter of the Holy Spirit. Christ, as the Prince of Peace is working on this problem with haste. The Holy Spirit is revealing truth to whomever he can find that will take what the word of God says over what their tradition says, or what they want to believe.

Before the turn of the twentieth century, hardly any emphasis had been placed upon the indwelling of the Holy Spirit. But, in the mid-eighteen-nineties people began to claim experiences of being baptized in the Holy Ghost, just as it occurred on the day of Pentecost, complete with speaking in other tongues as the Spirit gave the utterance.

Opposing doctrines began to crystallize. Since that time, a major doctrinal rift has divided the church over the issue of the baptism in the Holy Ghost and the manifestation of the gifts of the Spirit, especially speaking in other tongues (foreign languages).

At the turn of the century, for most Christians the Holy Spirit was like a new discovery since their churches and ministers had not given any information about him. The reality of the Holy Spirit became an exciting discovery which was enthusiastically and evangelistically shared by many. The new enthusiasts claimed that the infilling with the Holy Spirit was, according to the Bible, supposed to be accompanied by manifestations which had not been evident in the lives of Christians or in the church. In reply to this outbreak of what many people thought to be fanatical preoccupation with the Holy Ghost baptism, traditional theologians settled on the opinion that they had received the Holy Spirit when they were saved and had possessed him all along.

Those involved in the new movement rejected the claim that one receives the Holy Spirit at conversion. Their contention was that they had only been saved, but had not been baptized in the Holy Spirit because they had ignored, overlooked, or did not understand the truth about him. Furthermore, they took the position that speaking in tongues was the "initial evidence" of the indwelling of the Spirit, therefore, all who had not spoken in tongues had not received the Spirit.

This position was claimed to be the "full gospel," and new churches sprang up which were known as full gospel churches. The term "Pentecostal" became the identifier of the new movement. This name was derived from the day of Pentecost--the day on which the Holy Ghost was first given to the church. The terms, *Pentecostal, full gospel, spirit filled,* and *holiness*, became terms and titles identifying the new movement. These were thorns in the side of the old-line traditionalists because it was as if Pentecostals were saying, "we are full gospel and you are not," or "we are spirit filled and you are not," etc.

## Charismatics

Beginning in the nineteen-sixties, a secondary Pentecostal movement occurred. Those involved in this movement were mainly constituents of the old-line denominations. They identified themselves as *Charismatic*, and speaking in other tongues was given a new identifier..."glossalalia." While they had become convinced regarding the Biblical authenticity of the baptism in the Holy Spirit--complete with speaking in tongues, prophesying, the word of knowledge, the gift of healing, etc.,--they did not particularly want to be associated with the old-line Pentecostals. This only enlarged the division which already existed among God's people...the family of God, because we now had a new branch of Pentecostals.

Many tried to hang onto their old denominational connections by terming themselves as *spirit-filled Baptists, spirit-filled Catholics, spirit-filled Methodist,* etc., right down the entire denominational line. Most were forced out of their denominational churches if they became too obvious or outspoken. Thousands of Charismatic churches sprang up all over the country and around the world. This movement had an impressive growth in a short period of time, and soon became a thorn in the side of traditionalism because of the emphasis on the operation of the gifts of the Spirit. Among Charismatics more emphasis was placed on "prophesy" and the "word of knowledge" than in the first outpouring in the late nineteenth century and early twentieth century. Strong emphasis was placed on speaking in tongues, while avoiding being identified as "Pentecostal."

## Truth that can unite

The question facing the church today is, "what central, or basic truth could there possibly be that would unite brethren who are divided over man-made doctrinal issues?" Is it a hopeless cause? Are we too far gone?

I think not. The answer is in the word of God...if one can find and accept it? It is the Holy Spirit's job to guide us into *"all truth."* He will not teach different things to different people! Can he guide us into this truth? A deeper question is, "do we want to be guided into truth that will unite us?" Or, are we afraid we might be forced to give up something having to do with our church ideas or doctrinal opinions?

## Both sides must budge

The author comes from a strong traditional Pentecostal background, and yet, he has made adjustments to accommodate the word of God, without any loss of truth, but rather gaining insight into essential truths. He believes God has revealed to him basic truth that can unite divided brethren--Pentecostal and Non-Pentecostal.

It will be necessary for both sides of the issue to first listen, and then be willing to study and accept the word of God over tradition. All men will have to come to a better knowledge of truth. They will all be happier for having done so...as they see truth that is in the word of God.

## The final authority

The first basic principle that must be established is, **the Bible is the word of God, and is the final authority on all matters of doctrinal truth.**

- *2TI 3:16 All scripture is given by inspiration of God, and is profitable for doctrine, for reproof, for correction, for instruction in righteousness:*
  *17 That the man of God may be perfect, throughly furnished unto all good works.*

The willingness to listen helps one to always be open for what *"thus sayeth the Lord."* All must believe that Christ intends to perfect his church, and to wash it with water by the word. This prevents one from closing their mind to revelation and the understanding of more truth.

- *EPH 5:26 That he might sanctify and cleanse it with the washing of water by the word,*
  *27 That he might present it to himself a glorious church, not having spot, or wrinkle, or any such thing; but that it should be holy and without blemish.*

Pentecostals and Non-Pentecostals have been so set in their ways doctrinally that there has been little room for dialogue or discussion. The time has come that both sides must discuss this issue openly and thoroughly. When there are two different doctrinal opinions, one has to be wrong…and maybe both. At this point, let's say that both sides have been partially right. Hopefully, this book will be a timely contribution to the unity of the faith by helping both sides come to agreement concerning the one faith.

- *EPH 4:2 With all lowliness and meekness, with longsuffering, forbearing one another in love;*
  *3 Endeavouring to keep the unity of the Spirit in the bond of peace.*
  *4 There is one body, and **one Spirit**, even as ye are called in one hope of your calling;*
  *5 One Lord, <u>one faith</u>, one baptism,*
  *6 One God and Father of all, who is above all, and through all, and in you all.*

# CHAPTER 2

# OPINIONS ABOUT SPEAKING IN OTHER TONGUES

Everyone must analyze the sources which have influenced their opinions concerning the baptism with the Holy Ghost and speaking in tongues, plus other gifts of the spirit, such as divine healing, or prophesy. One must determine if their opinions have been formed by opinions of others, rather than by the word of God. Opinions of friends, relatives, and favorite ministers can easily dominate what one believes.

Of course, there will be those who have never heard anything concerning this subject, and it will all be new to them. Reading this book will bring them up-to-date in a constructive way.

I will here repeat a statement which I made in the Introduction to this book:

"The terms "Holy Ghost" and "Holy Spirit" are synonymous, and are often designated with the masculine pronoun "He." In this writing they both may appear, used interchangeably on the same page, in the same paragraph, or even in the same sentence. I am often oblivious to which is used."

## Expedient

What the Bible has to say about the Holy Spirit is very clear and easily understood, and yet there are divergent opinions about him and his ministry within the church ... and within the individual believer. Jesus considered information regarding the Holy Spirit as being so important that he used the word, *"expedient,"* when speaking of the necessity for the Holy Ghost to be sent from heaven to dwell within the followers of Christ.

- *JOH 16:7 Nevertheless I tell you the truth; It is **expedient** for you that I go away: for if I go not away, the Comforter will not come unto you; but if I depart, I will send him unto you.*

The Holy Spirit receives truth from Christ and reveals it to those who believe in him. The Holy Spirit never teaches anything that does not agree with the Bible. The only way one can truly know and understand Christ is through the ministry of the Holy Spirit.

- *JOH 16:14 He shall glorify me: for he shall receive of mine, and shall shew it unto you.*

One's attention must be drawn to the Holy Spirit in such a way that they will appreciate the extreme urgency (expediency) Christ placed upon the Holy Spirit's ministry. One must *receive* the Holy Spirit by faith in the same fullness, readiness, and open-mindedness that they receive Christ.

It is also necessary that *all* Christians receive the Biblical truth concerning the Holy Ghost with the same obedience that the disciples manifested when they remained in Jerusalem on the strength of Christ's promise that he would send them the Holy Spirit after he returned to heaven. Jesus explained very little about the Spirit, and even though they waited and tarried in prayer for ten days, they had little or no idea about what they were expecting to receive.

Speaking in tongues was doubtless a total surprise. And,

evidently God did it that way so they could have no preconceived input into the supernatural manifestation. Speaking in tongues was just as supernatural as the sound of a rushing mighty wind, and the appearance of cloven tongues of fire which sat upon each of them.

I am amazed at the unique ingenuity of God in his selection of tongues as a manifestation of the Spirit. There is no logical explanation for it. It completely surpasses human reasoning and intellect. It requires total faith in God's purposes and will. It requires total surrender of pride and ego. One must forego personal opinions and submit totally to God's will and plan. The opinions of others must hold no power nor generate fear. A commitment to Christ as the baptizer requires total trust in his integrity, and also requires unswerving confidence in his word.

Jesus had told his disciples just prior to his ascension that *"these signs shall follow them that believe...they shall speak with new tongues"* (MAR 16:17). At the time they probably did not comprehend the significance of what he had said.

## The refreshing

The disciples knew the Old Testament quite well, and only after the Holy Ghost had been given, did they fully understand ancient prophesies concerning the Spirit which had been given hundreds of years before.

- *ISA 28:11 For with stammering lips and another tongue will he speak to this people.*
  *12 To whom he said, This is the rest wherewith ye may cause the weary to rest; and **this is the refreshing**: yet they would not hear.*

Isaiah said prophetically *"this is the refreshing."* Peter made reference to this Old Testament passage soon after the Holy Spirit was given on the day of Pentecost.

- *ACT 3:19 Repent ye therefore, and be converted, that your sins may be blotted out, when the **times of refreshing** shall come from the presence of the Lord.*
- *ACT 2:33 Therefore being by the right hand of God*

*exalted, and having received of the Father the promise*
*of the Holy Ghost, **he hath shed forth this, which ye***
***now see and hear.***

## The Great Teacher

It is not required that one understands the Holy Spirit before receiving him, because he is the teacher. One receives a teacher so they can be taught.

In the Tyndale House Book by Grace Livingston Hill entitled <u>Duskin</u>, (Soft Back Edition), we pick up the text on page 195 where Carol Berkley was reading her Bible seriously, which had not been her normal practice:

> **"She spent a good deal of the afternoon reading**
> **her Bible, and was amazed to find how interesting**
> **it had become. She knew nothing of the revealing**
> **power of the great Teacher the Holy Spirit, whom**
> **Christ promised should reveal the truth to the**
> **seeking heart."**

It is the Holy Spirit who helps believers to understand God, Christ, and the gospel as revealed in the New Testament. Even Jesus knew his disciples would be unable to comprehend truth concerning the church and the ministry of the Holy Spirit prior to receiving the Holy Spirit as an in-dwelling teacher, guide and comforter. Jesus said the following:

- *JOH 16:12 I have yet many things to say unto you, but ye cannot bear them now.*
  *13 Howbeit when he, the Spirit of truth, is come, he will guide you into all truth: for he shall not speak of himself; but whatsoever he shall hear, that shall he speak: and he will shew you things to come.*

Many truths which Christ intended to impart to his church did not come directly in fullness through Christ personally. They were later revealed by the Holy Spirit through apostles who were chosen of God for this purpose. Jesus gave no detailed instructions concerning the structure of the church and how it was to function. He however made two important references to his church: (1) that he was going to build his church: *"on this rock I will build my church"* (MAT 16:18), and (2) that this church would have a framework of spiritual authority and organized social structure:

- *MAT 18:15 Moreover if thy brother shall trespass against thee, go and tell him his fault between thee and him alone: if he shall hear thee, thou hast gained thy brother.*
  *16 But if he will not hear thee, then take with thee one or two more, that in the mouth of two or three witnesses every word may be established.*
  *17 And if he shall neglect to hear them,* **tell it unto the church***: but if he neglect to hear the church, let him be unto thee as an heathen man and a publican.*
  *18 Verily I say unto you, Whatsoever ye shall bind on earth shall be bound in heaven: and whatsoever ye shall loose on earth shall be loosed in heaven.*

The understanding of these things came after the Holy Ghost was given, and information came to, and through, the apostles as it was needed, and as the Holy Ghost led. Paul was caught up to the third heavens and he conversed directly with Christ who revealed to him the mystery concerning the church...especially that it would consist of both Jews and Gentiles.

- *EPH 3:1 For this cause I Paul, the prisoner of Jesus Christ for you Gentiles,*
  *2 If ye have heard of the dispensation of the grace of God which is given me to you-ward:*
  *3 How that by revelation he made known unto me the mystery; (as I wrote afore in few words,*
  *4 Whereby, when ye read, ye may understand my knowledge in the mystery of Christ)*

*6 ... That the Gentiles should be fellowheirs, and of the same body, and partakers of his promise in Christ by the gospel:*

There is no way the disciples would have understood this prior to the death, resurrection, and ascension of Christ. It was only after the church began to function under the tutorship of the Holy Spirit that answers could be understood as they were needed. Jesus said the Holy Ghost would show them things to come:

- *JOH 16:13 Howbeit when he, the Spirit of truth, is come, he will guide you into all truth: for he shall not speak of himself; but whatsoever he shall hear, that shall he speak: and **he will shew you things to come.***

While the apostle Paul was clearly given the ministry as the foundation builder for the church, he shared these truths with the other apostles, and they sorted out the will of God through the guidance of the Holy Spirit. As a result, today we have the part of the New Testament which follows the four gospels...which was given to men by the Holy Spirit...and which contains the blueprint and guidelines for the church to understand as the established will of God.

This takes nothing away from Christ as the head of the church, but adds to the relationship as we see his promise to the apostles fulfilled. This is why Paul gave a picture of the church as a structure built upon Christ as the only foundation.

- *1CO 3:10 According to the grace of God which is given unto me, as a wise masterbuilder, I have laid the foundation, and another buildeth thereon. But let every man take heed how he buildeth thereupon.*
*11 For other foundation can no man lay than that is laid, which is Jesus Christ.*

And yet, Paul understood fully the part the apostles were playing in the laying of this foundation. It was systematically developed by the Holy Spirit through the ministry of the apostles and prophets of the New Testament church. In another distinctly separate and different analogy Paul depicted the foundation as consisting of the apostles and prophets with Christ being the chief corner stone.

- *EPH 2:20 And are built upon the foundation of the apostles and prophets, Jesus Christ himself being the chief corner stone;*
  *21 In whom all the building fitly framed together groweth unto an holy temple in the Lord:*
  *22 In whom ye also are builded together for an habitation of God through the Spirit.*

The last phrase of the above passage says, *"through the Spirit."* This is one of many scriptures which confirms the Holy Spirit's involvement in the development and understanding of truth which Christ revealed after he had returned to his throne in heaven.

## The Holy Spirit wrote the book

The reason that the Holy Spirit is designated as the Teacher of Biblical truth is because he wrote the book.

- *2PE 1:20 Knowing this first, that no prophecy of the scripture is of any private interpretation.*
  *21 For the prophecy came not in old time by the will of man: **but holy men of God spake as they were moved by the Holy Ghost.***

My brother was a student at the University of Illinois. He said that many of their textbooks had been written by the professor teaching the class. The brother said, "If you want a great teacher, study under the professor who wrote the book."

This is why it is so important today for believers to be walking in the fullness of the Spirit. This means walking in all the ways the Spirit manifests himself to and through believers. The main emphasis of this book has to do with speaking in other tongues and its significance and importance. An all-out effort is being put forth to explain Biblically why one should...and must...speak in tongues. But, it is necessary to include many other aspects of the indwelling of the Holy Spirit.

The first, and most simple reason to believe is, that Jesus said *"these signs shall follow them that believe ... they shall speak with new tongues" (MAR 16:17)*. Speaking in new tongues was included in the list of spiritual signs. There is no reason to believe that this does not apply to all believers...that some would, and some would not. If there are any intrinsic benefits in speaking in tongues, then Jesus meant them for the good of *all* Christians.

There must be some beneficial reason that Paul spoke in tongues.

- *1CO 14:18 I thank my God, I speak with tongues more than ye all:*

When one speaks in tongues they are speaking to God. While the one speaking does not understand what is being said, the Spirit is, nonetheless communicating with God through them...making intercession for them according to the will of God. In later chapters we will go into this in great detail, but at this point let it suffice to say that, if Christ thought it *"expedient"* that the Holy Ghost should come, then all believers must hold the matter as significantly important.

Even though speaking in tongues is not necessarily the initial evidence, speaking in tongues is a know-for-sure sign that the Holy Spirit has taken up his abode within a believer's body.

- *1CO 14:22 Wherefore tongues are for a sign ...*
- *1CO 6:19 What? know ye not that your body is the temple of the Holy Ghost which is in you, which ye have of God ...*

## As the Spirit gave them utterance

No one should down-play, deny, or reject speaking in other tongues...as the Spirit gives the utterance. If speaking in tongues comes from any other source, even the speakers own mind, then it is not by the Spirit.

- *ACT 2:4 And they were all filled with the Holy Ghost, and began to speak with other tongues, **as the Spirit gave them utterance**.*

It is incumbent upon ministers of Christ today to keep this truth alive and in the forefront of doctrinal values. One should hunger for the full manifestation of speaking in other tongues as a sign which gives evidence of the infilling of the Holy Spirit. Jesus said,

- *MAT 5:6 Blessed are they which do hunger and thirst after righteousness: for they shall be filled.*

The nearer we get to the second coming of Christ and to the intense world conditions politically, socially, economically, and spiritually that are prophetically predicted to be associated with that time, the need for the baptism in the Holy Ghost intensifies greatly.

## The great last day outpouring of the Spirit

The day of Pentecost was a great outpouring that continues today, but the greatest outpouring (prophesied by Joel) is yet to come, and will occur shortly before the second coming of Christ…a very intense time which will bring about a world-wide harvest of souls and a mass uniting of Christianity as the body of Christ.

Peter was able to quote from Joel, who had prophesied concerning a great outpouring of the Holy Spirit which would take place in the last days. The day of Pentecost was not the complete fulfillment of Joel's prophesy because it did not take place during the end-time which Peter called *"the last days"* which immediately precedes the day when the Lord comes to earth again:

- *ACT 2:17 And it shall come to pass in **the last days**, saith God, I will pour out of my Spirit upon all flesh: and your sons and your daughters shall prophesy, and your young men shall see visions, and your old men shall dream dreams:*
  *18 And on my servants and on my handmaidens I will pour out in those days of my Spirit; and they shall prophesy:*
  *19 And I will shew wonders in heaven above, and signs in the earth beneath; blood, and fire, and vapour of smoke:*
  *20 The sun shall be turned into darkness, and the moon*

*into blood, before the great and notable **day of the Lord come:***

Many Christians today, who seem to have little interest in the Holy Ghost and the gifts of the Spirit, will at that time welcome the spiritual power and help of the Holy Ghost. When they are so distressed because of world conditions spiritually and politically, and they do not know what or how to pray, they will welcome the intercession of the Holy Spirit as he prays in other tongues for them and their needs.

- *ROM 8:26 Likewise the Spirit also helpeth our infirmities: for we know not what we should pray for as we ought: but the Spirit itself maketh intercession for us with groanings which cannot be uttered.*
  *27 And he that searcheth the hearts knoweth what is the mind of the Spirit, because he maketh intercession for the saints according to the will of God.*

Why wait until distressing times come? Everyone needs the help and comfort of the Holy Spirit daily. Doesn't it seem reasonable that one should be learning about the fullness of the experience right now, rather than wait?

It is to this assumption that the author directs this book because he believes he has already experienced many marvelous events in his life that have resulted from the working of the Holy Ghost. Also, the manifestation of the gift of speaking in other tongues has been confirmed as a truly miraculous operation of the Spirit that has incalculable benefits to the believer. This will all come out as these matters are woven into the fabric of this text.

# CHAPTER 3

# ADMINISTRATIONS, OPERATIONS, MANIFESTATIONS

Scripturally there are *"diversities of gifts,"* or different kinds of gifts, but they all come from the same, one-and-only Holy Spirit. These diversities are found in First Corinthians, Chapter twelve, and are referred to as *"administrations," "operations,"* and *"manifestations of the Spirit."* These three words are used frequently in this writing, and find their scriptural source in the following verses:

- *1CO 12:4 Now there are diversities of gifts, but the same Spirit.*
  *5 And there are differences of administrations, but the same Lord.*
  *6 And there are diversities of operations, but it is the same God which worketh all in all.*
  *7 But the manifestation of the Spirit is given to every man to profit withal.*

These are ways the Holy Spirit works through individual

Christians as members of the body of Christ…He administers, He operates, He manifests.

It is incumbent upon all believers to accept all the "administrations," "operations," and "manifestations," as being in full force and operational in the church today including the gift of healing, working of miracles, prophesy, speaking in tongues, the interpretation of tongues, plus the rest. The list is given in the verses which follow the above text:

- *1CO 12:8 For to one is given by the Spirit the word of wisdom; to another the word of knowledge by the same Spirit;*

  *9 To another faith by the same Spirit; to another the gifts of healing by the same Spirit;*

  *10 To another the working of miracles; to another prophecy; to another discerning of spirits; to another divers kinds of tongues; to another the interpretation of tongues:*

  *11 But all these worketh that one and the selfsame Spirit, dividing to every man severally as he will.*

  *12 For as the body is one, and hath many members, and all the members of that one body, being many, are one body. so also is Christ.*

Verse 12 is extremely important because it places the functioning of all the gifts within the body of Christ which is the church. Verse 12 is so important because it involves every single member of the body. Yes, every member, and none is exempted, therefore every person who has been placed into Christ should embrace the truth regarding all gifts of the Spirit. This answers the question, *"should all speak with tongues?,"* as a resounding "YES."

This outlines God's plan concerning the place of the Holy Spirit and his gifts within the body of Christ. The church is not a denomination, nor a combination of denominations. The church consists of every person on the face of the earth who has been placed into Christ…Jew or Gentile, male or female, bond or free.

- *1CO 12:13 For by one Spirit are we all baptized into one body, whether we be Jews or Gentiles, whether we be bond or free; and have been all made to drink into one Spirit.*
- *GAL 3:28 There is neither Jew nor Greek, there is neither bond nor free, there is neither male nor female: for ye are all one in Christ Jesus.*

## Non-Pentecostals

Denominations and individuals, who consider themselves as Non-Pentecostals, usually do not accept or practice all of the above gifts of the Spirit. Their favorite gifts are wisdom, knowledge, and prophesying, with prophesying equated to preaching. Endowments of wisdom and knowledge, whether natural or acquired through educational processes, meet their qualifications for the gifts of wisdom and knowledge. For them, applying this wisdom and knowledge through preaching, or public speaking, is equated to prophesying...with no supernatural endowments required.

All true gifts of the Spirit are manifestations of the Spirit, and are not displays of human intelligence or ability. Emphasis must be placed on their *supernatural* qualities. In this book *speaking in tongues* serves as a focal point which is illustrative of all the other gifts. A sincere attempt is being made to rightly divide the word of truth so clearly and accurately that anyone can see precisely what the Bible says on this subject.

## Love is the glue

Christian love for Christ can be demonstrated only to, and through, those around us. Jesus said, *"when you do it* (show love and kindness) *to the least of my disciples, ye do it unto me."* We are told that *"charity is the bond of perfectness"* (COL 3:14)--thus, is the glue (*"bond"*) that binds the Children of God in fellowship around Christ.

The spiritual force behind this unity is the Holy Spirit. Christians have been called to the **vocation** of functioning in life as a member of the body of Christ. One must walk in a way-of-life that befits this lifestyle...worthy of participating in the united fellowship of the saints. A conscious effort must be made by all disciples of Christ to endeavor, or put forth, whatever effort it takes to see that the bond of love is not broken, nor the fellowship divided and fragmented by doctrines of men, or for any other reason.

- *EPH 4:1 I therefore, the prisoner of the Lord, beseech you that ye walk worthy of **the vocation** wherewith ye are called,*
  *2 With all lowliness and meekness, with longsuffering, forbearing one another in love;*
  *3 Endeavouring to keep the unity of the Spirit in the bond of peace.*
  *4 There is one body, and one Spirit, even as ye are called in one hope of your calling;*

## God's last day gift

God's answer to the pressures and temptations of *"the last days"* is to give the gift of the Spirit to every believer. It is imperative that this relationship be active and not dormant, alive and not dead, positive and not negative, real and not a pretense.

## The gospel of the kingdom

When Jesus gave his dissertation concerning the end-times, He concluded with this statement:

- *MAT 24:14 And this gospel of the kingdom shall be preached in all the world for a witness unto all nations; and then shall the end come.*

Consider the phrase, *"this gospel of the kingdom."* This means the truth...the gospel truth...shall be preached throughout the world. One should have no greater aspiration than to be a preacher of the gospel truth. The gospel is the truth as Jesus knows it...the gospel of Christ.

The gospel of the kingdom is the truth about the objectives of Christ concerning his kingdom...both now and in the future--that of ruling his kingdom from the vantage point of his Father's throne in heaven. This unseen kingdom does not come at the present time *"with observation"* (visibly), but is within the believers (LUK 17:20). It will come literally and visibly when Jesus returns to earth to reign for a duration of one thousand years.

## Fear of the truth

Many people have been programmed to be so negative concerning truth that, every time they hear the word "truth," they become defensive, and retort, "what is truth?" I heard a person make the statement, "most people freak out when someone uses the word *truth*." We must believe that truth will be revealed to the church on a larger scale than we ever dreamed possible. In fact, God promised through Christ,

- *JOH 8:32 And ye shall know the truth, and the truth shall make you free.*

## The Pentecostal/Non-Pentecostal Grand Canyon

A serious chasm divides Christianity into two religious orders identified as "Pentecostals" and "Non-Pentecostals." This remains today as the most dominant point of division within Christianity, comparable to the Catholic/Protestant separation.

The Non-Pentecostals consist primarily of all the major old-line denominations which have historically taken a firm stand against the Pentecostal persuasion. Since the turn of the twentieth century several denominations have developed over Pentecostalism and the rift has become set in doctrinal concrete. Today all churches are classified as either Pentecostal or Non-Pentecostal.

## Like-minded

One might think the author has deviated from the title and subject of this book, but this is not at all true. We are right on course. It is necessary to deal with the many divisions that have separated the children of God from one another. Especially tragic has been the mistake of dividing the church right down the middle over the matter of the baptism of the Holy Ghost and speaking with other tongues.

The objective of the author is to look at why and how divisions came, and to find truth in the word of God that will unite us.

When people all believe the same truth, it unites them on that point. If allowed to do so, the Holy Spirit will teach us all the same thing.

> • *ROM 15:4 For whatsoever things were written aforetime were written for our learning, that we through patience and comfort of the scriptures might have hope.*
> *5 Now the God of patience and consolation grant you to be likeminded one toward another according to Christ Jesus:*
> *6 That ye may with one mind and one mouth glorify God, even the Father of our Lord Jesus Christ.*
> *7 Wherefore receive ye one another, as Christ also received us to the glory of God.*

This is a New Testament command from Jesus given to the church through the apostle Paul. Such terms as *"like-minded," "one mind," "one mouth,"* and **"receive ye one another,"** are precious nuggets of truth to those who embrace the idea of unity and fellowship in the church as the one body of Christ.

## Adopted sons and daughters

Rather than separating one's self from other believers over the issue of Pentecostalism, believers who know the truth about the church will rally around verse seven above, and will hold as precious truth the admonition to receive all other Christians on the basis that Christ has received them.

Paul draws an analogy of sons and daughters being adopted into a family. It is incumbent upon every child who is adopted to receive the others who have also been adopted in the same way. It is the Father's will that everyone do so. It is tragic that the family of God has been so divided while they all have been adopted into the same family by the same Father. It is not consistent with the Biblical spirit of Christianity, and yet this divided condition has been presented worldwide as the normal state of Christendom. But this will change as Christ perfects his church in the last days ... as he prepares her for the time when he will present the church to himself at his second coming.

- *EPH 5:26 That he might sanctify and cleanse it with the washing of water by the word,*
  *That he might present it to himself a glorious church, not having spot, or wrinkle, or any such thing; but that it should be holy and without blemish.*

## The same mind

To those who love the truth regarding the Holy Spirit, scriptures such as the following will leap off the page:

- *1CO 1:10 Now I beseech you, brethren, by the name of our Lord Jesus Christ, that ye all speak the same thing, and that there be no divisions among you; but that ye be perfectly joined together in the same mind and in the same judgment.*

It is God's will that the church be *"perfectly joined together in the same mind and in the same judgment"* concerning the Holy Spirit. As stated earlier, Christianity has been split right down the middle on this issue, particularly concerning speaking in other tongues. But as the prophetic reality and fulfillment of the last days intensifies, the truth concerning the abiding of the Holy Spirit in all believers will become a treasured common denominator for the unity of the body of Christ.

This is why Paul said, *"endeavoring to keep the unity of the Spirit in the bond of peace"* (EPH 4:3). It is significant that *"Spirit"* is capitalized. The phrase, *"the unity of the Spirit"* is most significant, and lets us know that the Holy Spirit is the spiritual force behind the unity of the body of Christ. The Holy Spirit will teach the same truth to all who hunger for righteousness. During the process of perfecting the saints, the Holy Spirit will not endorse division on one hand, and then condemn it on the other. Neither will he teach one person one thing and teach another person something else.

Paul's next statement in support of his admonition for unity is

*"There is one body* (church), *and one Spirit* (Holy Spirit), *even as ye are called in one hope of your calling"* (one heaven). This is reason enough for endeavoring to *"keep the unity of the Spirit in the bond of peace"* (Christ's love).

## Start by stopping

A good starting place could be for the entire body of Christ to discontinue the practice of designating themselves as "Pentecostal" or "Non-Pentecostal." It is incumbent upon both sides to discover common ground in the scripture that will bring both factions into one union with God through truth found only in the word of God, and not in the traditions of either side.

Many will jump at the chance to refute this by saying, "you will never find two men who see exactly alike." This may be true in a natural sense, but the Holy Spirit will be able to find many who see alike on spiritual things…as he teaches them all the same thing. We already have a great starting point, for there are millions who already see alike concerning Jesus--who he is, what he is, and what he will do. Our common ground is Jesus. We are commanded--based on the name of Jesus--to *"all speak the same thing."*

- *1CO 1:10 Now I beseech you, brethren, <u>by the name of our Lord Jesus Christ</u>, that ye all speak the same thing, and that there be no divisions among you; but that ye be perfectly joined together in the same mind and in the same judgment.*

This common ground can be found only in the scripture as we are all taught the same thing…by the Holy Spirit. If one looks anywhere else other than the scripture they will not find it. This is what Jesus said the Holy Spirit would do; *"he will guide you into all truth"* (JOH 16:13). The natural mind says this is impossible, but one must not be controlled by the natural mind.

- *1CO 2:12 Now we have received, not the spirit of the world, but the spirit which is of God; that we might know the things that are freely given to us of God.*
  *13 Which things also we speak, not in the words which*

*man's wisdom teacheth, but which the Holy Ghost*
*teacheth; comparing spiritual things with spiritual.*
*14 But the natural man receiveth not the things of*
*the Spirit of God: for they are foolishness unto him:*
*neither can he know them, because they are spiritually*
*discerned.*

All must use the spiritual mind which was given when they were
"*born of the Spirit,*"…at the time of their new birth.

## They that understand shall instruct many

Daniel saw people who would instruct others in the last days. It
is not too much for one to hope to be one of those instructors? Being
a pioneer for truth is not easy…and has never been easy. But, it is
worth it if one understands the truth and can share it with others.

- *DAN 11:32 …but the people that do know their God shall*
  *be strong, and do exploits.*
  *33 And they that understand among the people shall*
  *instruct many:*

# CHAPTER 4

# UNITY OF THE SPIRIT

The author sincerely believes his prayerful thirty-five-year study of issues that have divided God's people, has led him into understanding Biblical truth that can be welcomed by both sides. As has been stated, a major cause for disunity has been over the matter of the gift of tongues. Granted, many claim to be filled with the Holy Spirit, yet they omit the manifestation of most of the gifts of the Spirit, and particularly, speaking in other tongues.

It seems appropriate that this should be a major area for striving for unity? Paul called upon the church to humbly demonstrate meekness toward one another, putting forth an extreme effort (endeavoring) to maintain the unity of the Spirit. Paul made his appeal on the basis that there is only *"one body"* (one church), and *"one hope of your calling"* (heaven), plus other important *"ones"* that should be reason enough to unite believers in the *"one faith"* under the *"one Lord"* and the *"one God"* who is the *"one Father"* of all his spiritual family. Here are the exact words of Paul:

- *EPH 4:4 There is one body, and one Spirit, even as ye are called in one hope of your calling;*
  *5 One Lord, one faith, one baptism,*

*6 One God and Father of all, who is above all, and*
*through all, and in you all.*

It is high time that all of Christendom be confronted over factions regarding the Holy Spirit. Both sides have held part of the truth and it seems that never the twain should meet, but this cannot continue to apply to children in the same family of the same heavenly Father, and who are in the same body, his church.

## One body

Paul makes an appeal for unity by pointing out that every member in the body of Christ has the same Holy Spirit, and it is this one-and-only Spirit that places all believers into the one-and-only church...the body of Christ.

- *1CO 12:13 For by one Spirit are we all baptized into*
  *one body, whether we be Jews or Gentiles, whether we*
  *be bond or free; and have been all made to drink into*
  *one Spirit.*
  *14 For the body is not one member, but many.*

Just as the members of our human body--hands, feet, eyes, ears, etc.--are interconnected into one unit, so is the church with all its members. If my hand claimed it was not a part of my body, or claimed to be a part of some other body, it would not make it so.

Paul said he suffered the loss of all things, which included all his Jewish background and traditions in order to gain the excellent knowledge of Christ.

- *PHI 3:8 Yea doubtless, and I count all things but loss for*
  *the excellency of the knowledge of Christ Jesus my Lord:*
  *for whom I have suffered the loss of all things, and do*
  *count them but dung, that I may win Christ,*

Today the vast majority of Christians believe traditions rooted mainly in Non-Pentecostal denominational doctrines. Regardless of how powerful they are, Non-Pentecostal traditions are giving way to the unity of the Spirit which is working in the church today throughout the world. A few decades back many people in formal and traditional nominal churches had little or no knowledge about the Holy Spirit because they rarely heard any mention of him in their church. But with the advent of the Charismatic movement many people right in their midst began broaching the subject, and the exposure to the subject has been effective. Today many more references are being heard regarding the Holy Spirit, even from their pulpits. Non-Charismatics in defense began to claim to be filled with the Holy Spirit while discounting speaking in other tongues.

A vast majority of Christians have believed only those things which have come forth from man's wisdom, but as these things are rectified through the truth that the Holy Ghost teaches, drastic changes are coming about within Christianity.

- *1CO 2:13 Which things also we speak, not in the words which man's wisdom teacheth, but which the Holy Ghost teacheth; comparing spiritual things with spiritual.*

It is imperative that we think of the Holy Spirit as the teacher of truth, and as the promoter of unity within the body of Christ. All of his ministries are important. If we can emphasize the unity of the brotherhood, we will see the Holy Spirit manifesting himself greatly within that fellowship of love. Doctrinal antagonism prevents the full and free flowing of the Spirit as the anointing oil of God.

We must think of the church strictly within scriptural guidelines, and not in terms of its traditional present-day divided format. We must strive for unity within this body, and hold fast to the fact that Jesus has only one church. He said, "my church" and it is evident he has only one. Paul asked the question, *"is Christ divided?"* meaning, is Christ the head over two or more bodies (1CO 1:13)? One must get beyond believing doctrines based on what "their church" believes. Hearing Jesus say, *"my church"* will become increasingly endearing.

This writing is not grinding a Pentecostal axe, neither is it attacking Non-Pentecostal believers, but is preaching unity of the body of Christ, the light of truth must be shined into every crevasse of the church. That which is not sound doctrine must be manifested by the light.

- *EPH 5:13 But all things that are reproved are made manifest by the light: for whatsoever doth make manifest is light.*
  *14 Wherefore he saith, Awake thou that sleepest, and arise from the dead, and Christ shall give thee light.*

The truth is, the division that exists within the ranks of Christianity today is soundly condemned by the word of God. In spite of this, this author is very optimistic about the future of the church. There is more common ground within professing Christianity than one might think.

While I strongly believe the terms *Pentecostal* and *Non-Pentecostal* are Biblical misnomers, I use them reluctantly in this book because they have become coined words in our religious vernacular, and for the purpose of exposing their divisive connotation. The very fact their use is scripturally unsound and divisive should let us know that something is wrong and out of order.

I actually feel a sense of guilt if I refer to myself as a Pentecostal, because I am admitting to being different from some others in the family of God; or saying that some believers are different from me. I refrain from using the terms in normal conversation, but for purposes set forth in this book, I cannot deny the strong doctrinal differences which are implied by each term. I want to magnify the erroneous idea behind the reasons that some believers identify themselves as Pentecostal while others as Non-Pentecostal. This does not conform to the truth that there is only one faith. This idea did not come from the gospel of Christ.

- *PHI 1:27 Only let your conversation be as it becometh the gospel of Christ: that whether I come and see you, or else be absent, I may hear of your affairs, that ye stand fast in one spirit, with one mind striving together for the faith of the gospel;*
- *PHI 2:2 Fulfil ye my joy, that ye be likeminded, having the same love, being of one accord, of one mind.*

Many believers are discarding the practice of referring to

themselves as Pentecostal because they see that it is a designator which divides brethren. By the same token, believers must discontinue referring to themselves as Non-Pentecostal. To the Jews, Pentecost meant the fiftieth day after Passover. It was on this Jewish feast day that the Holy Ghost fell on the church.

The term "Pentecostal" has come to mean "I believe in the Holy Ghost just as he came on the day of Pentecost, complete with speaking in other tongues." "Non-Pentecostal" has come to mean "I believe in the Holy Ghost just as he came on the day of Pentecost, except that tongues are not for the church today."

## Baptism in the Spirit at the time of the new birth

Most who call themselves "Non-Pentecostals" believe they receive the Holy Ghost when they get saved, but, for the most part, they shy away from any literal operation, or manifestation of the gifts of the Holy Spirit in their life personally, or in their church... frequently teaching that the supernatural gifts are no longer operative in the church.

The important truth regarding this matter is that all believers should find unity in knowing they are all Christians, and should stay away from calling themselves Pentecostal Christians or Non-Pentecostal Christians.

## Tongues as the initial evidence

Those who identify themselves as "Pentecostals" believe that one does not receive the baptism of the Holy Ghost until such time as one speaks in other tongues, which is said to be "the initial evidence" that the Holy Ghost has taken up residence within a believer.

The baptism with the Holy Ghost is believed by Pentecostals to be an experience, separate from, and subsequent to the experience of salvation. It is accepted that both experiences can, and might, occur within practically the same time frame, or the same prayer session, but are two distinctly separate experiences. These ideas will be explored in depth before we are through.

## One faith

Since the Bible teaches there is only one Father, only one Jesus, one Holy Ghost, one heaven, one church and one faith, let's believe that God can lead us all into that one faith concerning the Holy Spirit.

There must be a central truth hidden somewhere within the scripture that will bring the church into unity on this issue. Let's go on a treasure hunt together. Treasures we will hope to uncover scripturally are answers to the following questions: "Does one receive the Holy Ghost when they are saved?" "Do all speak in tongues?" "Is speaking in other tongues the initial evidence of receiving the Holy Ghost?" "Has speaking in tongues ceased?" "Are *other tongues* actual known human languages?"

## You shall receive

Let's attempt to settle the issue now. Does one receive the gift of the Holy Ghost when they are born again, meaning when they are placed into Christ ... which Paul described as being *"baptized into Christ?"* It is at the moment when one receives *"remission of sins"* that they also *"receive the gift of the Holy Ghost."*

- *ACT 2:38 Then Peter said unto them, Repent, and be baptized every one of you in the name of Jesus Christ for the <u>remission of sins</u>, and ye **shall receive the gift of the Holy Ghost**.*
  *39 For the promise is unto you, and to your children, and to all that are afar off, even as many as the Lord our God shall call.*
- *GAL 3:26 For ye are all the children of God by faith in Christ Jesus.*
  *27 For as many of you as have been baptized into Christ have put on Christ.*

# CHAPTER 5

# OTHER TONGUES

To *"speak with <u>other tongues</u>"* is a phrase found in the Bible.

* *ACT 2:4 And they were all filled with the Holy Ghost, and began to <u>speak with other tongues</u>, as the Spirit gave them utterance.*

It is one of nine gifts of the Holy Spirit named in the twelfth chapter of First Corinthians. It means to speak by <u>supernatural utterance</u> in a language unknown to the person speaking.. but is a valid foreign language (other tongues) spoken and understood somewhere in the world.

Scriptural proof that speaking in tongues is speaking in foreign languages can be found in the following passage:

* *ACT 2:5 And there were dwelling at Jerusalem Jews, devout men, out of every nation under heaven.*
*6 Now when this was noised abroad, the multitude came together, and were confounded, because that every man heard them speak in his own **<u>language</u>**.*
*7 And they were all amazed and marvelled, saying one to another, Behold, are not all these which speak Galilaeans?*

> *8 And how hear we every man in our own __tongue__,*
> *wherein we were born?*

Speaking in other tongues was one of the supernatural gifts manifested on the day of Pentecost when the divine person, the Holy Ghost, or Holy Spirit came to live in omnipresence within all Christians.

## Jesus shall baptize you

The matter of the Holy Ghost has profound doctrinal importance. John the Baptist was sent by God to be the forerunner of Christ, and he introduced Jesus as the one who would baptize in the Holy Ghost. John the Baptist had this knowledge because God himself had told him about it.

God had revealed many things to John by direct conversations with him. John knew he would be the one who baptized the Messiah in water, and he knew that when he baptized him, the Holy Ghost would come upon the Messiah to empower him for his earthly ministry.

- *John 1:33 And I knew him not: but he that sent me to baptize with water, the same said unto me, Upon whom thou shalt see the Spirit descending, and remaining on him, __the same is he which baptizeth with the Holy Ghost__.*

If God instructed John the Baptist to introduce Jesus as the one who would baptize in the Holy Ghost, it must be important, and worthy of special attention. Those who have given little attention to the Holy Ghost should seriously consider this matter as worthy of special attention.

## Born of the Spirit

A careful study of the ministry of Christ reveals that he came to earth to accomplish many things. One of these important things was that he would provide the means, through his death and resurrection, whereby men could be reconciled to God. The Holy Spirit would become the force from God which would enter into man, regenerating him into a new creature in Christ Jesus...born again...born of the Spirit. It is by the infilling of the Spirit that one is born again.

This is exactly what Jesus explained to Nicodemus.

- *JOH 3:6 That which is born of the flesh is flesh; and **that which is born of the Spirit is spirit**.*
  *7 Marvel not that I said unto thee, Ye must be born again.*

At what precise moment does the Holy Spirit take up his abode within a newly born again believer in Christ? This is the crux issue. Before the Holy Ghost was given on the day of Pentecost, Jesus told his disciples the Holy Ghost was *"with"* them, but the time would come when he would be *"in"* them. When does he come in?

- *JOH 14:17 Even the Spirit of truth; whom the world cannot receive, because it seeth him not, neither knoweth him: but ye know him; for he dwelleth <u>with</u> you, and shall be <u>in</u> you.*

At the time Jesus spoke this, The Holy Spirit was dwelling within *him*. The disciples had not received the Holy Ghost as an indwelling Spirit, and he only dwelled *"with"* them at that present time. He was with them in the fact that he was *"in"* Christ who was with them. He was also with them as an outside omnipresent force, but would soon take up his abode *"in"* them as a dynamic spiritual force. This was confirmed in the book of Acts.

- *ACT 2:4 And they were all filled with the Holy Ghost, and began to speak with other tongues, as the Spirit gave them utterance.*

Notice that they were *"<u>all</u> filled with the Holy Ghost."* Jesus said the Holy Ghost would be a teacher and guide that would lead those who received him into all truth. Many years after Pentecost John had this to say:

- *1JO 2:27 But the anointing which ye have received of him abideth in you, and ye need not that any man teach you: but as the same anointing teacheth you of all things,*

*and is truth, and is no lie, and even as it hath taught you,*
*ye shall abide in him.*

The Holy Spirit is involved in all phases of one's spiritual relationship with God, from the very first prick of conviction for sin…all the way through conversion…and the subsequent life and walk in the Spirit.

• *JOH 16:8 And when he is come, he will reprove the world of sin, and of righteousness, and of judgment:*

Jesus became our example in all things, especially concerning being filled with the Spirit. If it was necessary for Jesus in his humanity as an ordinary man to be empowered by the Holy Spirit in order to do the work of God, how much more important is it for us today?

## Fell on them

God said to John the Baptist, *"Upon whom thou shalt see the Spirit descending, and remaining on him."* The example is closely followed at Cornelius' house. While Peter was relating to them *"how God anointed Jesus of Nazareth with the Holy Ghost, who went about doing good"* (ACT 10:38), the Holy Ghost *"fell on all them which heard the word"* (v. 44).

## Remained on them

This is an exact parallel of what happened to Jesus in the Jordan River. Furthermore, it says that the Spirit *"remained on him."* Jesus told his disciples the Holy Ghost would *"abide with them forever"* (JOH 14:16).

## Saved but not baptized in the Spirit

It is traditionally taught by most Pentecostals that one can be saved without receiving the Holy Spirit. It is contended that this is what happens to Non-Pentecostals who do not embrace the entire Pentecostal doctrine including speaking in other tongues. It is also believed that this is what happens to all who are saved but do not speak in other tongues at that time.

The above is primarily how the Pentecostal and Non-Pentecostal theologies stand currently and are presented to the world today. I hope the reader of this book will take a fresh look with me at the matter of the Holy Spirit to see if there is not some room for improvement in Biblical interpretation on both sides. It is believed that a fresh study of this subject can be beneficial in uniting the two distinctly divided theological groups.

The theme of this book can be stated very simply, and then we will go into detail to show the scriptural proof of that which is stated.

**Statement No. 1.** The Holy Ghost is given to every believer at the time of the new birth...immediately upon God's acceptance of their acknowledgment of Christ through confession and repentance. When God is satisfied with their sincere approach to him through Jesus as their Mediator, Redeemer, Savior and Lord, he forgives them, washes away their sins by the blood of Jesus, regenerates them into new creatures, places them into Christ, adds them to his family--the church--and places the Holy Spirit within them immediately and without fail. The Spirit becomes their comforter, guide, teacher, reprover, and empowers them for Christian life and service in the kingdom of God.

**Statement No. 2.** The Holy Ghost is given to believers as God's sign, or proof that he has received them into his family. The gift of the Holy Spirit is God's initial response to one's confession, repentance, and declared faith in Christ.

**Statement No. 3.** When a person decides to receive Christ, they must accept that the sign for knowing they have been received by Christ is that Christ has given them the Holy Spirit.

**Statement No. 4.** The indwelling of the Holy Spirit gives every believer the potential for the manifestation of all fruit of the Spirit and all the gifts of the Spirit including speaking in other tongues.

## Meet for repentance

John the Baptist introduced the New Testament plan of salvation which would come through Christ. He preached that one must first bring forth fruit *"meet for"* repentance, and the consequence would be that Jesus would baptize them with the Holy Ghost. It is significant to note that Jesus was introduced as the baptizer in the Holy Ghost.

*"Meet for"* means "sufficient for" or "meeting the requirement." God knows whether or not one's repentance is sincere, and if one's sorrow for sin is genuine. God knows the thoughts and intents of the heart, and only God knows when repentance meets his requirements according to his plan of justification and redemption.

- *MAT 3:8* **Bring forth therefore fruits <u>meet for</u> repentance:**
  *9 And think not to say within yourselves, We have Abraham to our father: for I say unto you, that God is able of these stones to raise up children unto Abraham.*
  *10 And now also the axe is laid unto the root of the trees: therefore every tree which bringeth not forth good fruit is hewn down, and cast into the fire.*

This new plan of salvation by grace through faith in Christ applies to all men. The Jews could no longer boast of any special advantage with God because they were descendants of Abraham. Religious pride would be a hindrance in this new dispensation.

## Christ's response to repentance

- *MAT 3:11 I indeed baptize you with water unto repentance: but he that cometh after me is mightier than I, whose shoes I am not worthy to bear: he shall baptize you with the Holy Ghost, and with fire:*

John's baptism in water was symbolic of repentance (changing directions), dramatically portraying the process of the death, burial, and resurrection of Christ, which every sinner must manifest in their own life. Repentance and the new birth are not a reference to the experience of "water" baptism, or an experience which is brought about by water baptism, but a "spiritual" baptism which must occur before water baptism is celebrated. This spiritual baptism is elsewhere called the *"new birth"* which was also called *"being born of the Spirit,"* and *"baptized into Christ."*

## Saved

One would be hard put to Biblically separate the salvation experience from baptism in the Holy Spirit. What does it mean to be saved? This was the reason for which Jesus came into the world.

- *LUK 19:10 For the Son of man is come to seek and to save that which was lost.*

Paul and Silas were imprisoned in Philippi. God sent an earthquake and set them free. The jailer thought everyone had escaped and was about to take his own life when Paul let him know they were all there. The jailer knew God had done this and was so convicted he wanted to get saved right then. Notice his question concerning how to be saved. Also notice carefully Paul's answer.

- *ACT 16:29 Then he called for a light, and sprang in, and came trembling, and fell down before Paul and Silas,*
  *30 And brought them out, and said, Sirs, what must I do to be saved?*
  *31 And they said, Believe on the Lord Jesus Christ, and thou shalt be saved, and thy house.*

When one truly believes on the Lord Jesus Christ he immediately accomplishes his saving work in response to their believing by placing them into the Holy Ghost, and placing the Holy Ghost into them. This is termed a baptism in the Holy Ghost. One is saved by being born of the Spirit.

One is saved as a result of believing on the Lord Jesus Christ. One is also baptized in the Holy Ghost through believing on Jesus. This is why Paul's question to the disciples of John the Baptist in Ephesus is so significant.

- *ACT 19:2 He said unto them, Have ye received the Holy Ghost since ye believed? And they said unto him, We have not so much as heard whether there be any Holy Ghost.*

Today it should be expected that anyone who truly believes in Jesus receives the Holy Spirit as the first response of God to this believing. All other aspects of regeneration and the new birth are accomplished by the acts and ministry of the Holy Spirit as he applies Christ's provisions through his life, death, burial, resurrection, and intercession. Jesus most definitely told Nicodemus that being born again was a work of the Spirit.

- *JOH 3:7 Marvel not that I said unto thee, Ye must be born again.*
  *8 The wind bloweth where it listeth, and thou hearest the sound thereof, but canst not tell whence it cometh, and whither it goeth: so is every one that is born of the Spirit.*

The Holy Spirit was sent to the church ten days after Christ returned back to heaven. The purpose for which the Holy Ghost came was that he might indwell all believers. The Holy Spirit would administer all the benefits of Christ to those who believed on him, and the salvation process would be realized by each individual as the Holy Spirit magnified Christ to them. According to verse 6 below, this gift of the Holy Spirit was <u>abundantly</u> shared with believers by Christ.

- *TIT 3:5 Not by works of righteousness which we have done, but according to his mercy he saved us, by the washing of regeneration, <u>and renewing of **the Holy Ghost**</u>;*
  *6 Which he shed on us <u>abundantly</u> through Jesus Christ our Saviour;*
  *7 That being justified by his grace, we should be made heirs according to the hope of eternal life.*

Justification and regeneration involve the operation of the Holy Ghost. The Holy Ghost cannot be left out of the equation. He is a vital and irreplaceable connection to Jesus and the heavenly Father. Carefully read again the above verses. It was clear in Paul's mind that one shall receive the Holy Ghost after they believe. Peter had this same belief which he stated on the day of Pentecost.

- *ACT 2:38 Then Peter said unto them, Repent, and be*

*baptized every one of you in the name of Jesus Christ
for the remission of sins, <u>and ye shall receive the gift of
the Holy Ghost.</u>
39 For the promise is unto you, and to your children,
and to all that are afar off, even as many as the Lord
our God shall call.*

These scriptures give no indication that any delay in receiving the Holy Ghost should be expected. It was an automatic operation of grace in the experience of those who believe in Jesus Christ. Therefore one should accept by faith the fact that they have been baptized in the Holy Ghost. They should also expect by faith to see immediate evidence of the converted life and the empowered life, just as Jesus said:

- *ACT 1:8 But <u>ye shall receive power,</u> after that the Holy
  Ghost is come upon you: and ye shall be witnesses unto
  me both in Jerusalem, and in all Judaea, and in Samaria,
  and unto the uttermost part of the earth.*

The fruit of the Spirit should become evident as a result of the indwelling of the Spirit. The old sinful man is crucified with Christ and it becomes his nature to live a new life.

- *GAL 5.22 But the fruit of the Spirit is love, joy, peace,
  longsuffering, gentleness, goodness, faith,
  23 Meekness, temperance: against such there is no law.
  24 And they that are Christ's have crucified the flesh
  with the affections and lusts.
  25 If we live in the Spirit, let us also walk in the Spirit.*

All of the gifts of the Spirit, including speaking in tongues, should be accepted by faith as potentially possible and probable as needed in the spiritual life and warfare of the believer. Not one single manifestation can be logically deleted, neglected, or omitted. Speaking in tongues as a means of worshipping, praying, and giving messages in tongues to be interpreted for the entire church, should all be embraced and accepted by faith.

- *1CO 12:7 But the manifestation of the Spirit is given to every man to profit withal.*

This passage will never change. Every member in the body of Christ should expect to manifest the gifts of the Spirit as he directs. Read verse eleven in the NIV which says:

- *1CO 12:11 (NIV) All these are the work of one and the same Spirit, and he gives them to each one, just as he determines.*

The outcome depends on whether or not one accepts and believes the Bible to be the authoritative word of God. If so, one must not delete, ignore, or change anything to suit their interpretations or desires. One must bury all prejudice and past traditions which reject the fullness of the Spirit as being resident in every born again child of God, and walk in the truth which says they received the Holy Spirit when they believed for salvation. The above passage begins with the statement, *"to each one the manifestation of the Spirit is given."* Since the day of Pentecost, the Holy Spirit has been given to each one who has received Christ into their heart.

## The Spirit of Christ

In the eighth chapter of Romans it is clear that the indwelling Holy Spirit was the Spirit that empowered Christ in his earthly ministry, and it is this same spirit which dwells within all Christians today. In fact, if one does not have this Spirit within them, then the clear summary is that they do not belong to Christ, meaning *"he is none of his."*

- *ROM 8:9 But ye are not in the flesh, but in the Spirit, if so be that the Spirit of God dwell in you. Now if any man have not the Spirit of Christ, <u>he is none of his</u>.*

The *"Spirit of Christ"* was the Holy Ghost. Christ came to earth as an ordinary man, and it was necessary for him to be filled with the Holy Spirit in order to fulfill his ministry. He was baptized with the Holy Spirit while standing in the Jordan River. From that moment on he was led of the Spirit. Peter had this to say about this matter.

- *ACT 10:38 How God anointed Jesus of Nazareth with the Holy Ghost and with power: who went about doing good, and healing all that were oppressed of the devil; for God was with him.*

It is in this context that the terms *"Spirit of Christ"* and *"Spirit of God"* are making reference to the Holy Ghost personally, since he is the agency of the Godhead that administers the will of the Father and the Son in the earth. The important point to see in this is that *"if any man have not the Spirit of Christ, he is none of his."* This means that every person who belongs to Christ does have the Holy Ghost; otherwise they do not belong to Christ. With this in mind, all believers must be careful about saying they do not have the Holy Ghost. One must realize that if they are saved, they do have the Holy Ghost dwelling within them. He may be so highly suppressed and quenched that his indwelling is not obvious, but this is why every believer must stir up the gift which is within them.

- *2TI 1:6 Wherefore I put thee in remembrance that thou stir up the gift of God, which is in thee...*

One must be aware of traditional church beliefs that will deny anyone the right to receive the Holy Spirit if it does not agree with their prescribed doctrinal guidelines. One's prejudicial doctrines will exclude those who do not meet standards set by their peers. This includes the traditional Pentecostal doctrinal requirement that one should speak in other tongues before they can claim to be a temple of the Holy Ghost. The word declares that one receives the Holy Spirit at the moment they are born again by the Spirit.

The indwelling of the Holy Spirit should be accepted by faith as a fact, based on the premise that God gives the Holy Spirit to everyone who obeys him. One's claim to having the Holy Ghost must be based on a sincere belief that they have experienced the new birth. Anyone who has been saved can rest assured that the Holy Spirit abides within their body as his temple. This assurance should be acknowledged and accepted even before one speaks in tongues.

- *1CO 6:19 What? know ye not that your body is the temple of the Holy Ghost which is in you, which ye have of God, and ye are not your own?*
  *20 For ye are bought with a price: therefore glorify God in your body, and in your spirit, which are God's.*

We can know for sure that Jesus also abides within us because we have the indwelling of the Spirit. The gift of the Spirit is the confirmation of salvation.

- *1JO 3:24 And he that keepeth his commandments dwelleth in him, and he in him. And hereby we know that he abideth in us, by the Spirit which he hath given us.*

A sincere believer should desire to experience supernatural manifestations of the indwelling Holy Spirit. Every member of the body of Christ must accept this by faith, and be willing to allow new believers to move on into the deeper things of the Spirit from the point of conversion. This includes all the manifestations and gifts of the Spirit...including speaking in other tongues. No single gift should be omitted or considered unnecessary ... or forbidden.

Paul covered all this in his advice and admonitions:

- *1CO 14:1 Follow after charity, and desire spiritual gifts, but rather that ye may prophesy.*
- *1CO 14:39 Wherefore, brethren, covet to prophesy, and <u>forbid not to speak with tongues</u>.*
  *40 Let all things be done decently and in order.*

The manifestations of the gift of prophesy is where the Holy Spirit speaks through a believer in the native language of both the speaker and the hearers. Let me say at this point that it is marvelous when the Holy Spirit speaks through a believer in a supernatural manifestation of a foreign language that is unknown to the speaker, but equally marvelous is when the Holy Spirit empowers a believer to supernaturally speak prophetically in his own native language.

- *1CO 14:3 But he that prophesieth speaketh unto men to edification, and exhortation, and comfort.*

## Spirit of God...Spirit of Christ...Holy Spirit...Holy Ghost

The designation, *"Holy Ghost"* is found in the King James Version 89 times, while *"Holy Spirit"* is found 7 times. Other versions use *"Holy Spirit"* exclusively. To some people, *"Holy Spirit"* seems more refined, since the term *ghost* has often carried a spooky, Halloween type association. This is not the way with me, and I am hardly aware of which designation I use. The preponderance of my Bible study has been from the King James Version; therefore I use the designation *"Holy Ghost"* without being aware. The terms *"Holy Ghost"* and *"Holy Spirit"* are the same, just as are the terms *"ghost"* and *"spirit."*

Many become confused concerning the identity of the Spirit, thinking that, perhaps, he is not a distinct spiritual being, but just an extension of God, because, as mentioned above, he is sometimes called *"the Spirit of God,"* and sometimes, *"the Spirit of Christ."* Therefore, some conclude that the Holy Spirit is just a spiritual extension of God, but not a person who is distinctly separate from God or Christ. But the truth is, the Holy Spirit is a distinct divine person, and so are the Father and the Son. Other Biblical identifiers of the Holy Ghost are the *"Holy Spirit,"* the *"Spirit,"* the *"Spirit of God,"* and the *"Spirit of Christ."*

This is because he is the Spirit through which God and Jesus operate in the earth today. He is the administrator of God's will, and of Christ's will. Before the birth of Jesus on earth, all three operated from the vantage point of heaven. When the Son came to earth, The Father and Holy Spirit remained in heaven. When Jesus returned to heaven, the Holy Spirit was sent to earth to dwell within the bodies of all Christians. The Father and the Son are presently in heaven, and the Holy Spirit who indwells all born again Christians gets his directions and instructions from the Father and the Son.

• *JOH 16:13 (NIV) But when he, the Spirit of truth, comes, he will guide you into all truth. He will not speak on his own; he will speak only what he hears, and he will tell you what is yet to come.*

*14 He will bring glory to me by taking from what is mine
and making it known to you.*

The Spirit abides within the church by dwelling within each
individual member that makes up the church. The Father and the
Son are in constant communication with the Holy Spirit who dwells
within each believer, while he makes intercession for their needs.
The Holy Spirit is always in touch with the needs of those in whom
he dwells.

- *ROM 8:26 (NIV) In the same way, the Spirit helps us in
  our weakness. We do not know what we ought to pray
  for, but the Spirit himself intercedes for us with groans
  that words cannot express.*
  *27 And he who searches our hearts knows the mind of
  the Spirit, because the Spirit intercedes for the saints in
  accordance with God's will.*

*"He who searches our hearts"* is God in heaven. He is watching
over us and looking out for our best interest. The Son is sitting with
the Father in his throne and is also observing the saints on earth along
with his Father...*searching our hearts*. The Holy Spirit which dwells
within our body-temple is in constant communication with God
(the Father and the Son) on our behalf. The Spirit never asks amiss
because he always asks in keeping with the will of God *"because
the Spirit intercedes for the saints in accordance with God's will"*
(v. 27 above). It is no wonder that Paul exclaimed in verse 31,*"if God
be for us, who can be against us?"*

## Resurrection life

The Holy Spirit brings about resurrection into a new life by
taking up his abode in the newly converted believer. This is how
the new birth comes about. Just as the Holy Spirit raised Jesus from
the dead, he also raises the now crucified--dead and buried--sinner
unto newness of life.

- *ROM 8:11 But if the Spirit of him that raised up Jesus
  from the dead dwell in you, he that raised up Christ from*

*the dead shall also quicken your mortal bodies by his*
*Spirit that dwelleth in you.*

This is precisely when the Holy Spirit takes up his abode in a newly born again believer. The same Holy Spirit which indwelled Christ (the Spirit of Christ) now dwells in all who are thus resurrected by his power, just as Jesus became alive again while laying in the grave.

- *ROM 6:5 For if we have been planted together in the likeness of his death, we shall be also in the likeness of his resurrection:*
  *6 Knowing this, that our old man is crucified with him, that the body of sin might be destroyed, that henceforth we should not serve sin.*
  *7 For he that is dead is freed from sin.*
  *8 Now if we be dead with Christ, we believe that we shall also live with him:*

During the experience of regeneration, the sinful creature, called "the old man," must be crucified with Christ. A literal experience occurs wherein the sinful, lustful, hateful desires and works of the flesh die and are buried in identification with Christ's baptism into death. At this point, as an inseparable part of the new birth, the Holy Spirit is given to everyone who becomes so identified with Christ. Study carefully the following scriptures:

- *2TH 2:13 But we are bound to give thanks alway to God for you, brethren beloved of the Lord, because God hath* **from the beginning** *chosen you to salvation through sanctification of the Spirit and belief of the truth:*
- *1CO 12:7 But the manifestation of the Spirit is given to every man to profit withal.*
- *2CO 1:22 Who hath also sealed us, and given the earnest of the Spirit in our hearts.*
- *2CO 5:5 Now he that hath wrought us for the selfsame thing is God, who also hath given unto us the earnest of the Spirit.*

- *1JO 3:24 And he that keepeth his commandments dwelleth in him, and he in him. And hereby we know that he abideth in us, by the Spirit which he hath given us.*
- *1JO 4:13 Hereby know we that we dwell in him, and he in us, because he hath given us of his Spirit.*

## Baptized into Christ

Scriptural references to "baptism into Christ" have been mistakenly applied to "water baptism". One must realize that the spiritual experience of <u>Baptism into Christ</u> is not the same as baptism in water. The term "baptism" means *to be placed into.* It is exactly what it says, a baptism "into" Christ…which means the precise time when one is placed into Christ.

One must maintain a distinct understanding of "baptism into Christ" without thinking of water when reading such scriptures as the following:

- *ROM 6:3 Know ye not, that so many of us as were baptized into Jesus Christ were baptized into his death?*
  *4 Therefore we are buried with him by baptism into death: that like as Christ was raised up from the dead by the glory of the Father, even so we also should walk in newness of life.*

When these scriptures are taken to mean water baptism, serious doctrinal errors occur, making water baptism the means by which one is saved, thus becomes essential to salvation. This mistaken interpretation means that one is saved by the blood…plus water. This cannot be true because one is saved by the blood plus nothing.

Catch this: *"Baptized into Christ"* simply means to be "placed into Christ." A close study of the rest of the above chapter will convince one that a spiritual baptism wherein one is placed into Christ is the issue, and not a physical experience of baptism in water.

Jesus used the statement, *"abide in me,"* which is also analogous to being placed into Christ. There are many scriptures which speak of being "in" Christ.

- *JOH 15:7 If ye abide <u>in me</u>, and my words abide in you, ye shall ask what ye will, and it shall be done unto you.*

Baptism into Christ brings about the new birth. In fact, water baptism is a symbolic act which depicts the baptism into Christ, and should occur only after one has been baptized into Christ. The rite of water baptism cannot bring about the new birth. Only baptism into Christ can do that. This is the baptism that is essential to salvation.

Understanding this enables one to distinguish between scriptures which are speaking concerning baptism in water and baptism into Christ. Both baptisms are scripturally authentic but are distinctly different. One is a physical action of the flesh and the other is a spiritual work in the heart.

## The precise Moment

During the spiritual process of the new birth several things occur. The first occurs when one is spiritually crucified and buried with Christ. It is at this precise moment when the Holy Spirit comes in as a resurrection force...bringing forth a new creature in Christ Jesus. This is why the Biblical terminology is used which says *"baptized with the Holy Ghost."*

John the Baptist said:

- *MAR 1:8 I indeed have baptized you with water: but he shall **baptize you with the Holy Ghost**.*

Jesus said:

- *ACT 1:5 For John truly baptized with water; but ye shall be **baptized with the Holy Ghost** not many days hence.*

Water baptism is symbolic of the death, burial, and resurrection of Christ. It is also symbolic of the spiritual death and resurrection of the carnal man which occurs when one is born again by being baptized with the Holy Spirit.

Being baptized with the Holy Ghost at the moment of obtaining salvation is a prerequisite for baptism in water. One is not baptized in water in order to be saved, but because they have been saved. Water baptism is an outward statement of an inner experience. It is a public statement of identification with Christ as one's Savior and Baptizer in the Holy Ghost. Notice how much the Spirit is involved in the process of the new birth.

- *ROM 8:9 But ye are not in the flesh, but in the Spirit, if so be that the Spirit of God dwell in you. Now if any man have not the Spirit of Christ, he is none of his.*
  *10 And if Christ be in you, the body is dead because of sin; but the Spirit is life because of righteousness.*
  *11 But if the Spirit of him that raised up Jesus from the dead dwell in you, he that raised up Christ from the dead shall also quicken your mortal bodies by his Spirit that dwelleth in you.*

Because of this resurrection, we are no longer in bondage to the flesh, but can now live the Christian life through the power of the Spirit which makes it possible to overcome the flesh.

> *12 Therefore, brethren, we are debtors, not to the flesh, to live after the flesh.*
> *13 For if ye live after the flesh, ye shall die: but if ye through the Spirit do mortify the deeds of the body, ye shall live.*

- *GAL 2:20 I am crucified with Christ: nevertheless I live; yet not I, but Christ liveth in me: and the life which I now live in the flesh I live by the faith of the Son of God, who loved me, and gave himself for me.*

## Baptized into his death

- *ROM 6:3 Know ye not, that so many of us as were **baptized into Jesus Christ** were baptized into his death?*

This is why Paul continues with the following statements which explain "baptism into Christ":

- *ROM 6:7 For he that is dead is freed from sin.*

*8 Now if we be dead with Christ, we believe that we shall also live with him:*

*9 Knowing that Christ being raised from the dead dieth no more; death hath no more dominion over him.*

*10 For in that he died, he died unto sin once: but in that he liveth, he liveth unto God.*

*11 Likewise reckon ye also yourselves to be dead indeed unto sin, but alive unto God through Jesus Christ our Lord.*

*12 Let not sin therefore reign in your mortal body, that ye should obey it in the lusts thereof.*

*13 Neither yield ye your members as instruments of unrighteousness unto sin: but yield yourselves unto God, as those that are alive from the dead, and your members as instruments of righteousness unto God.*

The above is totally descriptive of spiritual death with Christ, and resurrection-living *"unto God"* (v. 10) in the Holy Spirit, which includes all who have been born again, which Jesus called *"born of the Spirit"* (JOH 3:6, 8). The possession of the Holy Spirit, and being led by him, is the factor which identifies the children of God. Biblically, the ones who can rightfully call God "Father" are those who possess the Holy Spirit. It is by the work of the Spirit that one is adopted into the Father's family.

*   *ROM 8:14 For as many as are led by the Spirit of God,* ***they are the sons of God.***
    *15 For ye have not received the spirit of bondage again to fear; but ye have received the Spirit of adoption, whereby we cry, Abba, Father.*

Notice that the *Spirit* of adoption uses a capital S, confirming that the Holy Spirit is the agency which administers the adoption into God's family. God, himself, has born witness to his adopted children that they are truly his children by giving them the Spirit.

*16 The Spirit itself beareth witness with our spirit, that we are the children of God:*

How can one definitely know--without any shadow of a doubt--that they are saved? The Biblical answer is, "By knowing that God has given them the Holy Spirit."

- *1JO 3:24 And he that keepeth his commandments dwelleth in him, and he in him. And hereby we know that he abideth in us, by the Spirit which he hath given us.*

## Inseparable works of grace

Receiving the Holy Ghost is not a second, or third work of grace, but an *initial* work of grace, inseparable from the new birth. It is the incoming of the Holy Spirit into a person's being, his body, mind, soul, and spirit that brings about the birth of a new creature in Christ. It is the Spirit that quickeneth, making one alive in Christ.

One must realize the importance of Mary, the mother of Jesus, being overshadowed by the Holy Spirit. Carefully notice what the angel said to Joseph:

- *MAT 1:20 But while he thought on these things, behold, the angel of the Lord appeared unto him in a dream, saying, Joseph, thou son of David, fear not to take unto thee Mary thy wife: for that which is conceived in her is of the Holy Ghost.*

It was the Holy Ghost that brought spontaneous new life into existence within Mary, which would provide the body in which Jesus would live and minister. This event demonstrated to the world the power of the Spirit to generate a new creature into existence within every believer.

- *2CO 5:17 Therefore if any man be in Christ, he is a new creature: old things are passed away; behold, all things are become new.*

## Born of the flesh before born of the Spirit

The birth of the new man (the new creature in Christ Jesus) is accomplished by a work of the Holy Spirit in the heart, mind, soul, and spirit of the old man (the unregenerate creature). Therefore, the close coordination between being saved and filled with the Holy

Spirit is scripturally evident. Jesus made this clear to Nicodemus in the following statements. Jesus explained that a man must first be born of his mother (*"born of water"*) and then must be *"born of the Spirit."* Follow the sequence in these four verses while remembering that Jesus was answering Nicodemus' question regarding entering his mother's womb and being born the second time:

- *JOH 3:5 Jesus answered, Verily, verily, I say unto thee, Except a man be **born of water** (human birth) **and of the Spirit**, he cannot enter into the kingdom of God.*
  *6 That which is **born of the flesh is flesh**; and that which is **born of the Spirit** is spirit.*
  *7 Marvel not that I said unto thee, **Ye must be born again**.*
  *8 The wind bloweth where it listeth, and thou hearest the sound thereof, but canst not tell whence it cometh, and whither it goeth: so is every one that is **born of the Spirit**.*

## New birth evidence

Without doubt, the scriptural evidence of being filled with the Spirit is *the new life in Christ Jesus.* The sign that one has been baptized in the Spirit is the *new birth.* If one claims to have experienced the new birth, they should manifest the change this brings about by walking and living in the Spirit. There are multitudes of scriptures to support this.

Remember that Jesus told the woman taken in adultery to go and sin no more:

- *JOH 8:11 ...And Jesus said unto her, Neither do I condemn thee: go, and sin no more.*

The Holy Spirit does not come in after salvation has been accomplished and acquired, but salvation comes about because the Holy Spirit has come in, initiating the resurrection unto newness of life. Receiving the Holy Spirit is not a subsequent consequence, but is the initiator of the new birth experience. He comes into those who are ready to die with Christ, and then live with him.

- *ROM 6:5  For if we have been planted together in the likeness of his death, we shall be also in the likeness of his resurrection:*
  *6  Knowing this, that our old man is crucified with him, that the body of sin might be destroyed, that henceforth we should not serve sin.*
  *22  ...But now being made free from sin, and become servants to God, ye have your fruit unto holiness, and the end everlasting life.*

It has already been shown how this transformed life, and the continuing overcoming life is the result of receiving the Holy Spirit. It is the same Holy Spirit that raised Jesus from the dead that raises a sinner to newness of life while they are still in their mortal body.

- *ROM 8:11 But if the Spirit of him that raised up Jesus from the dead dwell in you, he that raised up Christ from the dead shall also quicken your mortal bodies by his Spirit that dwelleth in you.*

This is solid scriptural evidence that it is the Holy Spirit that enables one's mortal body to be quickened unto new life in Christ. This means in the here-and-now, while we are in these human bodies.

## Turning from the Law of Moses to Christ

Paul knew that when one turns to Christ for justification and righteousness, they must cease from observing the law of Moses in any form. Paul is so emphatic that he calls them foolish for allowing anyone to persuade them to turn back to the works of the law.

There was great pressure on Jewish Christians to turn back to the law. They had been convinced concerning the reality of Christ because of the amazing signs and wonders they had experienced, but it was difficult for them to refrain from trying to mix law and grace. Converted Jews came under relentless pressure from their friends, relatives, and spiritual leaders because they no longer looked to the law of Moses for justification, but trusted Christ fully. The pressure would not be so relentless if those thus converted would just keep doing the works of the law along with their new-found faith in Christ.

These Jews had been filled with the Spirit because of their faith in Christ. Something so great had never happened to them when they were looking to the law. They had experienced great miracles, and this had not happened while they were under the law.

## Having begun in the Spirit

Then Paul makes an extremely significant statement which lets us know that receiving the Holy Spirit occurs at the very <u>beginning</u> of the salvation experience, and not as a second, or third work in a progressive process. Carefully and slowly read the following passage.

- *GAL 3:1 O foolish Galatians, who hath bewitched you, that ye should not obey the truth, before whose eyes Jesus Christ hath been evidently set forth, crucified among you?*

  *2 This only would I learn of you, <u>Received ye the Spirit</u> by the works of the law, or by the hearing of faith?*

  *3 Are ye so foolish? <u>having begun in the Spirit,</u> are ye now made perfect by the flesh?*

  *5 ...He therefore that ministereth to you the Spirit, and worketh miracles among you, doeth he it by the works of the law, or by the hearing of faith?*

  Look closely at verse three: *"Are ye so foolish? having **begun** in the Spirit, are ye now made perfect by the flesh* (doing the works of the law)*?"* This identifies the receiving of the Spirit as the *"beginning"..."having begun in the Spirit."* This is the beginning point of salvation.

- *2TH 2:13 But we are bound to give thanks alway to God for you, brethren beloved of the Lord, because God hath <u>from the beginning chosen you to salvation through sanctification of the Spirit</u> and belief of the truth:*

One does not become a candidate for the filling with the Holy

Spirit because they got saved, but they got saved because the Holy Spirit filled their heart, mind, soul, and spirit in response to their repentant faith in Jesus and acceptance of him.

Oh, how desperately the entire church needs to hear this truth. It is sad to see hungry souls come forward for salvation and never be told the truth about the ministry the Holy Spirit can, and should do for them. It is through the Spirit that one is crucified with Christ, and is raised up through a new birth as Jesus told Nicodemus. This is how one becomes saved ... born again ... regenerated ... washed.

- *TIT 3:5 Not by works of righteousness which we have done, but according to his mercy he saved us, by the washing of regeneration, and* **renewing of the Holy Ghost***;*
- *ROM 8:13 ...but if ye* **through the Spirit** *do mortify the deeds of the body, ye shall live.*

It is sad to see how the church is divided over the Baptism in the Holy Spirit – divided as Pentecostals and Non-Pentecostals. How wonderful it would be if all who believe in Christ could see and acknowledge that the process of salvation in every person is a work of the Holy Spirit who immediately takes residence in each individual believer because of their faith in Christ.

The subsequent effect of this indwelling is that one is changed, born again, and becomes a new creature in Christ. A further effect is that the Holy Spirit brings the fruit of the Spirit with him and also the gifts of the Spirit. When a person is saved they have the potential for producing the fruit of the Spirit and manifesting all the gifts of the Spirit as they are needed. This brings spiritual growth and maturity as one learns to *"live in the Spirit ...* and *also walk in the Spirit."* And, one cannot leave speaking in other tongues out of the salvation equation.

# CHAPTER 6

# ABOUT THOSE WHO RECEIVED "SINCE" THEY BELIEVED?

At this point a major question must be discussed. What about all the Pentecostal people who say they received the Holy Ghost later, after they were saved…maybe a week, or month, or long after, even years later?

In light of what the Bible says, the answer is simple. They did not actually receive the Holy Ghost at a later time, because the impartation of the Spirit happened at the time they were born again (which Jesus called being born of the Spirit JOH 3:3-8).

They were led to believe when they finally spoke in tongues that this event was the initial, or first reception of the Holy Ghost. But, this experience was actually the first time the Holy Ghost was able to manifest himself openly, and was a delayed first experience for speaking in other tongues. The Holy Ghost had been indwelling them all the time but had remained suppressed or partially dormant due to a variety of reasons, perhaps because of ignorance concerning what the Bible has to say about the matter.

Because of the teaching under which they had been schooled, their beliefs became a barrier to a spontaneous, sovereign outpouring of God along with Biblical manifestations of the indwelling Spirit which had taken up residence within their body temple when they were saved. If they had been taught differently, it is more than likely there would not have been any lapse of time...in fact they would have desired and welcomed the manifestations of the Spirit, especially if they looked upon it as confirmation of obtaining salvation.

Perhaps the manifestation had come upon the first occasion where the Holy Spirit was allowed to utter praises in other tongues. This was the first time the believer actually believed their body had become the temple of the Holy Ghost. Before that time, they did not actually believe they had been given the Holy Ghost because under such circumstances the seeker does not profess the Holy Ghost has come in until they have spoken in tongues. Only after that experience were they able to believe that he had taken up his abode in their body temple.

One must accept by faith what the word of God says, and believe the Holy Ghost is given when they are born again. After one accepts by faith that the Holy Spirit has come in, then it becomes easier to believe for the manifestation of tongues, as well as all other gifts of the Spirit.

When Jesus breathed upon his disciples and said, *"receive ye the Holy Ghost,"* he was anticipating their initial baptism which would come on the day of Pentecost. The disciples did not receive the Holy Ghost at the time Jesus breathed on them, because he clearly told them they would receive him *"not many days hence."* They were instructed to wait in Jerusalem until the Holy Ghost came upon them.

One must not reject the truth concerning the Holy Ghost, but receive it with an open mind and an open heart. Receiving the Holy Ghost begins with spiritual acceptance of what the Bible says about him, regardless of what one's negative tradition has taught them. While one can be hard-put to deny what the Bible says about the Holy Ghost, they can treat him like the proverbial step-child...ignore him, reject him, dislike him, mistreat him, and in general, get along without him, as if he does not exist.

When one *"receives"* and acknowledges the Holy Ghost, they accept and treat him like a dear friend or relative who is welcomed into their home, given the guest room and encouraged to stay as long as he likes, meaning indefinitely and permanently. Excitement fills the air over his presence. No extra effort is too much for such a wonderful guest.

## One baptism--Many fillings

There is an initial baptism, or "receiving" of the Holy Ghost, and many fillings thereafter. Regarding the Holy Spirit, Jesus told the woman at the well:

- *JOH 4:14 But whosoever drinketh of the water that I shall give him shall never thirst; but the water that I shall give him shall be in him a well of water springing up into everlasting life.*
  *23 ...But the hour cometh, and now is, when the true worshippers shall worship the Father in spirit and in truth: for the Father seeketh such to worship him.*
  *24 God is a Spirit: and they that worship him must worship him in spirit and in truth.*

The Spirit is exactly as Jesus said when he cried out to the spiritually thirsty Jews at the feast:

- *JOH 7:37 In the last day, that great day of the feast, Jesus stood and cried, saying, If any man thirst, let him come unto me, and drink.*
  *38 He that believeth on me, as the scripture hath said, out of his belly shall flow rivers of living water.*
  *39 (But this spake he of the Spirit, which they that believe on him should receive: for the Holy Ghost was not yet given; because that Jesus was not yet glorified.)*

When one draws the water down to a low level in a well, it soon fills back up, because there is a running stream or spring in the bottom of the well which keeps replenishing the supply. A flowing river is the same way. Jesus used a springing well, and a flowing river to illustrate the refreshing nature of the Holy Spirit.

After Peter was filled with the Holy Ghost occasions came for him to stand and preach concerning what had happened to them, and to magnify Christ as the crucified and risen Lord. Peter was unable to stand for Jesus prior to being filled with the Spirit, but instead, denied him. He became a different person after being filled with the Spirit, and was able to stand boldly before those same people. Special fillings for special occasions were given, such as when a crippled man was healed at the gate of the Temple:

- *ACT 4:8 Then Peter, filled with the Holy Ghost, said unto them, Ye rulers of the people, and elders of Israel,*
  *9 If we this day be examined of the good deed done to the impotent man, by what means he is made whole;*
  *10 Be it known unto you all, and to all the people of Israel, that by the name of Jesus Christ of Nazareth, whom ye crucified, whom God raised from the dead, even by him doth this man stand here before you whole.*

Now, do not miss this important point. Peter was filled with the Holy Ghost in the second chapter of Acts. Now, here in the fourth chapter he is said to be again *"filled with the Holy Ghost"* (v. 8).

Peter had the boldness to accuse them of crucifying Jesus, and to also declare that God had raised him from the dead. Peter was no longer bound by fear. This is one of the important functions of the Holy Ghost. He is the force behind spiritual power, and of love, and of a sound mind.

- *2TI 1:7 For God hath not given us the spirit of fear; but of power, and of love, and of a sound mind.*

Peter made it clear that receiving the Holy Spirit was not just a one-time filling, but there would be many refillings and refreshings that would follow.

- *ACT 3:19 Repent ye therefore, and be converted, that*

> *your sins may be blotted out, when the times of refreshing*
> *shall come from the presence of the Lord.*

Peter was definitely making reference to the refilling of the Holy Ghost--one baptism...many fillings..."*the times of refreshing shall come.*" Peter was making reference to a prophesy of Isaiah concerning the Holy Ghost.

- *ISA 28:11 For with stammering lips and another tongue*
  *will he speak to this people.*
  *12 To whom he said, This is the rest wherewith ye may*
  *cause the weary to rest; and this is the refreshing:*

This refreshing had to do specifically with receiving the Holy Ghost into one's life. Peter's use of the word *"when"* means *at which time*. Notice (in Acts 3:19 above) the sequence of events involved, which occur in conjunction with the coming of this time of refreshing which comes from the presence of the Lord: (1) Repent; (2) Be converted; (3) Sins blotted out. These things happen in conjunction with, or at the time (4) one receives the initial refreshing from the presence of the Lord ... that refreshing being the baptism with the Holy Ghost.

## My cup runneth over

A short time after the day of Pentecost, the disciples were sorely persecuted by the Jewish religious leaders. They were put in jail, brought before the council, severely threatened, and commanded not to speak at all, nor teach in the name of Jesus (ACT 4:17-18). When they were released they *"went to their own company, and reported all that the chief priests and elders had said unto them."*

Jesus had said that the Holy Ghost would be the "comforter."

- *JOH 14:16 And I will pray the Father, and he shall give*
  *you another Comforter, that he may abide with you for*
  *ever;*
- *JOH 14:26 But the Comforter, which is the Holy Ghost,*
  *whom the Father will send in my name, he shall teach*

*you all things, and bring all things to your remembrance,*
*whatsoever I have said unto you.*

A wonderful example of the comforting of the Holy Ghost was experienced by the disciples after they left the Jewish council. The disciples had a right to be discouraged and spiritually drained, but instead, the well of the Spirit began to spring up until it became a flowing river. Instead of complaining, they began to pray one of the most outstanding prayers in the Bible. Without a doubt, the Holy Ghost made intercession for them with prayers they could not have uttered by themselves.

> *ACT 4:29 And now, Lord, behold their threatenings: and*
> *grant unto thy servants, that with all boldness they may*
> *speak thy word,*
> *30 By stretching forth thine hand to heal; and that signs*
> *and wonders may be done by the name of thy holy child*
> *Jesus.*

The disciples were praying for the exact opposite of what they had been commanded to do. They prayed, *"grant unto thy servants, that with all boldness they may speak thy word."* Notice what happened in the next verse. The refreshing came...the refilling came.

> *31 And when they had prayed, the place was shaken*
> *where they were assembled together; and they were all*
> *filled with the Holy Ghost, and they spake the word of*
> *God with boldness.*

These believers had already been filled with the Holy Ghost just a few days earlier, and yet, here it says, *"they were all filled with the Holy Ghost."* Isaiah had prophesied concerning the New Testament church--who would speak with stammering lips and another tongue--saying:

- *ISA 28:12 To whom he said, This is the rest wherewith ye*
  *may cause the weary to rest; and this is the refreshing:*

The disciples did not suffer spiritual thirst...the well was flowing...they were refreshed by the Spirit--the essence of what

Jesus taught when he used a well...and then a river...to describe the infilling of the Spirit. There is an inexhaustible supply of spiritual power available to the believer through the Holy Ghost.

It is obvious that the disciples had already been filled with the Holy Ghost, and he was resident within each of them, therefore the subsequent statement, *"they were all filled with the Holy Ghost,"* indicates that the anointing of the Spirit will rise up at times of need for special ministry, spiritual warfare, operation of the gifts of the Spirit, or for comfort and peace during times of stress, duress, trouble and turmoil.

One can think of it in terms of renewing, or replenishing the supply. One's spiritual cup is filled and refilled continually. This is making reference to the repeated overflowing manifestations of the Spirit which will follow as needed for special anointing to minister and to utilize the gifts of the Spirit. This is how our inner man is renewed day by day (2CO 4:16). This is why Jesus told the Samaritan woman at the well that those who drink of the water that he gives will never thirst, meaning they will always have an abundant supply.

- *JOH 4:14 But whosoever drinketh of the water that I shall give him shall never thirst; but the water that I shall give him shall be in him a well of water springing up Into everlasting life.*

David used oil to describe the way God keeps filling and refilling one's cup. Oil typified the Holy Spirit in the Old Testament. This is what David meant when he wrote the following:

- *PSA 23:5 Thou preparest a table before me in the presence of mine enemies: thou anointest my head with oil; my cup runneth over.*

This is what happened to the disciples. They were *"filled with the Holy Ghost"* again and again. The prophetic word concerning the Holy Ghost had become a reality in the lives of the believers who were going through *"the valley of the shadow of death."*

Jesus had told his disciples they would be given special power to be witnesses for him after the Holy Ghost had come upon them.

- *ACT 1:8 But ye shall receive power, after that the Holy Ghost is come upon you: and ye shall be witnesses unto me both in Jerusalem, and in all Judaea, and in Samaria, and unto the uttermost part of the earth.*

**One of God's major objectives in sending his Son was that he might baptize believers with the Holy Ghost.**

## The great divide

Neither traditional Pentecostals nor Non-Pentecostals have been able to comprehend the full Biblical truth concerning the Holy Ghost because they have been so inflexible in the positions they have taken on opposite sides of two main points. One point has to do with speaking in other tongues, and the other point has to do with the question, "when does one receive the Holy Ghost...is it at the time of conversion, or at a subsequent time?"

The Holy Spirit will have to de-program many minds in order to remove the old traditions before the truth can be fully received. Jesus warned that one cannot put new wine into old wineskins (bottles made from animal skins which would burst when the new wine expanded). Neither can one put new fabric into an old garment because stress on the seam where the two are sewn together will tear the old fabric while the new holds firm and inflexible.

Most of us will need to become new bottles in order to accept the enlargement doctrinally, spiritually, and ministerially, that this *old-but-new* truth will bring to the body of Christ. The truth is that one does receive the Holy Spirit when they are saved. All preaching and teaching regarding salvation should tell the world that when they are saved they will be baptized in the Holy Ghost, therefore they should expect to see a miraculous conversion that produces the fruit of the Spirit, and they should desire Spiritual gifts without excluding any.

**Most of all, everyone should discard identifying themselves as Pentecostal and Non-Pentecostal.**

# CHAPTER 7

# THE SEAL OF
# CHRIST'S SONSHIP

When the Son of God came to be manifested in human flesh he became a human in every respect and was also called *"the Son of man."* God ordained John the Baptist as the one who would introduce his Son. How was John to know exactly who this Son was? God gave John a sure sign. He showed John that after he baptized the Son of God in water, the Holy Spirit would descend in the form of a dove and remain on him. God confirmed his Son to John the Baptist, and to the rest of the world, by baptizing him with the Holy Spirit.

- *JOH 1:32 And John bare record, saying, I saw the Spirit descending from heaven like a dove, and it abode upon him.*
  *33 And I knew him not: but he that sent me to baptize with water, the same said unto me, Upon whom thou shalt see the Spirit descending, and remaining on him, the same is he which baptizeth with the Holy Ghost.*
  *34 And I saw, and bare record that this is the Son of God.*

Keep in mind that Jesus is our pattern and example in all things.

- *1PE 2:21 For even hereunto were ye called: because Christ also suffered for us, **leaving us an example, that ye should follow his steps:***

According to the New Testament plan of salvation, those who become sons of God are confirmed in the same way as was Jesus, by the gift of the Holy Spirit as a sign and seal of God's confirmation of sonship. The gift of the Holy Spirit serves as God's official seal of proof for all whom he adopts into sonship, and serves as confirmation of acceptance into his family. The gift of the Holy Spirit is proof that one has been born again. It proves one is a son of God. The Holy Spirit is the proof of adoption into the family of God, which gives one the right to call God their Father.

- *ROM 8:14 For as many as are led by the Spirit of God, they are the sons of God.*
  *15 For ye have not received the spirit of bondage again to fear; but ye have received the Spirit of adoption, whereby we cry, Abba, Father.*
  *16 The Spirit itself beareth witness with our spirit, that we are the children of God:*

The Holy Spirit is the seal of approval which God gives to everyone after they believe in Christ. It is like a king's official seal stamped on a document, bearing witness to his official approval.

- *EPH 1:13 In whom ye also trusted, after that ye heard the word of truth, the gospel of your salvation: <u>in whom also **after that ye believed**, ye were sealed with that holy Spirit of promise,</u>*

There is no reason to believe there will be any delay in receiving this confirmation from God ... or that it might not happen expeditiously to those who believe on the Lord Jesus Christ.

An interesting song which used to be popular compared the human body to "This Old House." Picture in your mind three people walking over an old home-place. They come upon an old house that once knew life and occupancy. They determine to make it livable again, and to move into it themselves. They renew it, inside and out, repairing, painting, scrubbing and cleaning. By a cooperative effort they prepare it for residency and soon move in. Each one has done their part, and the goal is accomplished.

This is how regeneration is accomplished in the life of one who has been separated from God through the sin of Adam, and through their own sinfulness. All of the works of grace are accomplished in their body, mind, soul, and spirit. It has all been accomplished by the Father, the Son, and the Holy Spirit. All three should be entitled to full right of occupancy, and each one should be received and appreciated for their unique roll in the redemptive process. There should be no reason for any delay in the moving of each one of the three...including the Holy Spirit. Immediate occupancy upon completion of redemption is the divine plan.

If there is any delay in recognizing, or accepting the reality of the Holy Spirit, it does not make him any less real or any less an occupant. The prevailing Pentecostal doctrine for generations has been that most likely the Holy Spirit will not come in at the time of the new birth, but at a later time as a second or third work of grace.

## Receiving while denying certain gifts

The Non-Pentecostal position has been that one does receive the Holy Spirit when they are born again. And yet, they deny most of the manifestations of the gifts that scripturally confirm the presence and existence of the Spirit in one's life and in the church.

But, the Holy Spirit is very real and dwells in the body-temple of everyone who is saved, even when he is not given the recognition he deserves. The truth that one receives the Holy Ghost immediately upon receiving salvation is based on the following scriptures: Everything that has been said in this book has been taken from these scriptures. (This section is extremely important. Read each passage carefully).

- *MAT 3:11 I indeed baptize you with water unto*

*repentance: but he that cometh after me is mightier than I, whose shoes I am not worthy to bear: he shall baptize you with the Holy Ghost, and with fire:*

- *JOH 7:38 He that believeth on me, as the scripture hath said, out of his belly shall flow rivers of living water. (But this spake he of the Spirit, which they that believe on him should receive ...)*

- *ACT 1:8 But ye shall receive power, after that the Holy Ghost is come upon you: and ye shall be witnesses unto me both in Jerusalem, and in all Judaea, and in Samaria, and unto the uttermost part of the earth.*

- *ACT 2:38 Then Peter said unto them, Repent, and be baptized every one of you in the name of Jesus Christ for the remission of sins, and ye shall receive the gift of the Holy Ghost.*

- *ACT 5:32 And we are his witnesses of these things; and so is also the Holy Ghost, whom God hath given to them that obey him.*

- *ACT 11:15 And as I began to speak, the Holy Ghost fell on them, as on us at the beginning. 16 Then remembered I the word of the Lord, how that he said, John indeed baptized with water; but ye shall be baptized with the Holy Ghost. 17 Forasmuch then as God gave them the like gift as he did unto us, who believed on the Lord Jesus Christ; what was I, that I could withstand God? 18 When they heard these things, they held their peace, and glorified God, saying, Then hath God also to the Gentiles granted repentance unto life.*

- *ACT 15:7 ... Peter rose up, and said unto them, Men and brethren, ye know how that a good while ago God made choice among us, that the Gentiles by my mouth should hear the word of the gospel, and believe. 8 And God, which knoweth the hearts, bare them witness, giving them the Holy Ghost, even as he did unto us;*

*9 And put no difference between us and them, purifying their hearts by faith.*

- *ROM 14:17 For the kingdom of God is not meat and drink; but righteousness, and peace, <u>and joy in the Holy Ghost.</u>*
  *18 For he that in these things serveth Christ is acceptable to God, and approved of men.*
- *ROM 15:16 That I should be the minister of Jesus Christ to the Gentiles, ministering the gospel of God, that the offering up of the Gentiles might be acceptable, <u>being sanctified by the Holy Ghost.</u>*
- *1CO 6:19 What? know ye not that your body is the temple of the Holy Ghost which is in you, which ye have of God, and ye are not your own?*
- *TIT 3:5 Not by works of righteousness which we have done, but according to his mercy he saved us, by the washing of regeneration, and renewing of the Holy Ghost;*
- *HEB 2:4 God also bearing them witness, both with signs and wonders, and with divers miracles, and gifts of the Holy Ghost, according to his own will?*
- *HEB 10.14 For by one offering he hath perfected for ever them that are sanctified.*
  *15 Whereof <u>the Holy Ghost also is a witness to us:</u>*
- *JUD 1:20 But ye, beloved, building up yourselves on your most holy faith, praying in the Holy Ghost,*

## Uninformed and unaware

An actual lack of awareness of him exists on the part of those who are uninformed concerning the Holy Spirit. Without doubt, many local churches have been subjected to misinformed ministries, or denominational creeds which have not given the credulity to the Holy Spirit that he deserves. Of the three in the Godhead, the Holy Spirit has been most rejected and neglected theologically, while he is actually the representative of the Trinity which has been assigned earthly duty, and who dwells within the bodies of all converted believers. Satan has done a good job of keeping many sincere people uninformed concerning the reality of the Holy Spirit and his indwelling presence.

## A positive belief

My father, Rodney Oliver Symes, Sr., was operating a large ranch is central Colorado. Several people who had experienced the manifestation of the gifts of the Holy Ghost were supernaturally led to his house. None had known the others were coming, and, in fact, were not even acquainted.

The day was devoted to Bible study about the Holy Ghost, of which my father knew practically nothing. At the end of the day, dad and one of his hired hands went out to feed the hogs. Dad said to the other man, "well, what do you think about all of this business concerning the Holy Ghost?"

The hired hand replied, "well I don't know," and began to express his reservations. Dad responded, "well, I believe it," and when he did, he felt a surge of supernatural emotional force go through him, and he knew the issue was settled with him. He had chosen to believe, and God had acknowledged that. He knew the Holy Ghost was God's gift to him and he wanted to experience the manifestations of his indwelling.

Needless to say, Dad received the manifestations and fullness of the Spirit a short time later, and the hired hand did not. This is the reason I said a few paragraphs back that "believing is the starting point."

## When light becomes darkness

It is so easy to take a stand against truth. At that point, if Dad had taken the other direction, he probably never would have walked in the truth. Many have done this unwittingly, just falling in line with tradition, or their environment, heritage and background. Once they do this, they become an opponent of the truth, which is a terrible position in which to be, especially if one is sincerely wrong while thinking they are sincerely right.

History has shown that the reality of the Holy Spirit has been easily overlooked for centuries. This is true even among astute Bible Scholars. And then, when the truth regarding the indwelling and manifestations of the Spirit is brought to light, the carnal mind tends to reject it. Satan fights this truth vehemently because he knows how expedient and necessary it is to Christ.

Had Dad only known it, the Holy Spirit had taken up residence within him at the time of his conversion. Although the Holy Spirit is given to everyone who believes, he is immediately quenched in many cases because of ignorance, peer pressure, and even unbelief. Sound teaching is needed almost everywhere.

Rejection of the truth can become one's downfall, in which case, the light in them becomes darkness. They may have been born into this darkness, or have been led into the darkness by others. They may be confronted with opportunities to come out of it, but others will not come out with them, therefore they remain in darkness.

- *LUK 11:35 Take heed therefore that the light which is in thee be not darkness.*
  *36 If thy whole body therefore be full of light, having no part dark, the whole shall be full of light, as when the bright shining of a candle doth give thee light.*

The truth became light in my dad, but it became darkness in the hired hand because he opposed it. The light of truth which we have can become darkness if we take a position opposing that truth. Many people have done this concerning the Holy Ghost and the manifestation of his gifts. This is a terrible tragedy.

- *MAT 6:23 ...If therefore the light that is in thee be darkness, how great is that darkness!*

It is with great concern that I approach the subject of this book, hoping I will not appear as though I think I am more spiritual than someone who has not experienced some gift of the Spirit. I merely want to encourage others to go on to the fullness, and not stop short of tasting all of God's goodness and blessings.

- *EPH 3:16 That he would grant you, according to the*

*riches of his glory, to be strengthened with might <u>by his</u>*
<u>*Spirit in the inner man*</u>*...*
*19 ... And to know the love of Christ, which passeth*
*knowledge, that ye might be filled with all the fulness*
*of God.*

I have a natural tendency to want to share with others anything good that I discover. I am always encouraging my wife to taste something that seems delicious to me, and I believe will taste good to her...if she will try it. When she shares the pleasure with me, it is a great experience to feel I have introduced her to something that adds a little larger dimension to our mutual experience and knowledge. In return, she enjoys the same excitement about sharing with me her blessings and discoveries.

On the other hand, if I offer her something she is already convinced she does not like, or she just does not like the looks of it, her reaction can be completely different. If I continue to urge her to try something new that she is rejecting from prior experience, or sheer visual dislike, it must be done with caution, lest my persistence become irritating.

When I am successful in getting her to go ahead and try anyway, and with eyebrow-raising surprise she registers her approval, I am pleasantly thankful for her being able to override her rejection, and dare to try, even against her will, something that I knew was good, and would be good to her.

There was no pride involved on my part, no ego, no pushiness, and no ulterior motive, nothing to gain on my part except the joy of sharing. I believe there is something wonderful to be shared about the Holy Spirit and speaking in other tongues as the Spirit gives the utterance.

## Turned off

It cannot be denied that some Pentecostals have come across as pushy and egotistical. If anyone reading has ever thought that those who are excited about the baptism in the Holy Ghost feel they are better, or more spiritual, please do not hold that against them. I am sure there are some who feel that way, or at least have given that impression. But, I truly believe, that from my experience with many thousands, almost none truly feel better, or more superior, and they have no intention of giving that impression. Their zeal may have exceeded their wisdom and knowledge.

It is obvious that some feel a compelling responsibility to get out the good news about the fullness of the Spirit. They are so thrilled with their own personal experience, and are so totally convinced concerning its importance to all believers, that they are often received as strong-willed, overbearing, or riding a hobbyhorse.

On the other hand, people have been accused of being pushy and egotistical, when they honestly have not been so. Those who think they are being pushed can be extremely defensive about their religious beliefs. Protectiveness and self-preservation takes over at the mention of anything new, different, or already rejected. Communication is usually broken before any complete or coherent idea can be explained. The result is that the whole story is never allowed to be given, and the whole truth is never heard.

Rudeness, silence, deaf ears, impatience, or being ignored often prevent the truth from being shared. One can also prevent the truth from entering their mind and heart by continually debating and arguing every point that is mentioned. Many walk in darkness because they cannot put themselves into a listening mode.

It is tragic for one to be given the Holy Spirit when they are born again, and yet, through ignorance, or prejudice, fail to walk in the fullness of the Spirit and even argue against it, right while they are quenching the Spirit within them. This is the case with many Christians in the world today. They are living beneath their privileges. In such cases, they are not enjoying all the benefits provided by Christ and given to the New Testament church.

One is not being better-than-thou for speaking out on these issues, any more than the preacher in the pulpit, when he speaks out against shortcomings, and challenges the congregation to go deeper with God.

One must avoid taking a noncommittal position concerning the gifts of the Spirit by saying, "if God wants me to have it he will give it to me." This would be no different than saying, "if God wants me to be saved, he will save me." If one accepts being born again, as a believer, they must accept that God has given them the gift of the Holy Ghost. They must desire spiritual gifts, and believe that God will manifest the gift of tongues to them as a sign. As they read their Bibles they must search for anything that is missing or dormant in their spiritual experience, and ask God for them. Paul said *"desire spiritual gifts"* (1CO 14:1).

## Unreasonable barriers

When one takes the position concerning speaking in tongues that, if God wants me to have it, he will give it to me, this type of commitment is usually followed by "I have asked God for the gift of tongues, but I must be one who is not supposed to have it." They will usually follow with, "Oh, I believe in it, but it is just not for me."

Another angle that can become a barrier to receiving the full manifestation of the Spirit is to use the sovereignty of God as a reason not to request the gifts or manifestations. One can go so far as to adopt the opinion that it is wrong to even ask God for anything pertaining to the Holy Ghost.

I recall an occasion where a person refused to pray with another who believed they had received the Holy Ghost at the time of their new birth, but had never spoken in tongues. They realized they were missing a blessing of God and asked for prayer...that God would manifest this gift and sign unto them.

The person refusing to pray did so because they reasoned that the Bible says, "God gives to every man...as he wills." Therefore, one would be violating, or preempting God's will to ask for the manifestation of any gift of the Holy Ghost, since God sovereignly gives "as he wills."

We must take care not to be the victim of unscriptural, restrictive limitations. This certainly falls into that category. We are instructed to ask.

- *JAM 4:2 ...yet ye have not, because ye ask not.*

If it is wrong to ask for a gift of the Spirit because we would not be trusting the sovereign will of God *"who divides severally to every man as he wills,"* then James spoke in error when he said the following concerning wisdom--a gift of the Spirit:

- *JAM 1:5 If any of you lack wisdom, let him ask of God, that giveth to all men liberally, and upbraideth not; and it shall be given him.*

If it would be a violation of the sovereign will of God to ask for the manifestation of a gift of the Spirit, then why did Paul instruct the church to pray that they may interpret whenever they spoke in tongues.

- *1CO 14:13 Wherefore let him that speaketh in an unknown tongue pray that he may interpret.*

No, it is not wrong to ask God for the gifts and their full manifestation. Jesus had this to say:

- *LUK 11:13 If ye then, being evil, know how to give good gifts unto your children: how much more shall your heavenly Father give the Holy Spirit to them <u>that ask him</u>?*

For one to pray to receive any of the manifestations of the gifts of the Spirit is certainly not out of order, neither is it out of order for a brother to pray for another to experience the full manifestation of the gifts, as God wills and divides severally (which means individually and separately) among the members of his body.

The word of wisdom and knowledge are both named as gifts of the Spirit. We find Paul praying for his brethren in the church at Ephesus saying:

- *EPH 1:17 That the God of our Lord Jesus Christ, the Father of glory, may give unto you the spirit of wisdom and revelation in the knowledge of him:*

There are many who are uncomfortable concerning the manifestation of the gifts of the Spirit and their uneasiness and caution produce fear and apprehension. This usually results in a hands-off policy, which is tragic when it comes to the wonderful gifts of the Spirit.

The gifts of the Spirit are exactly what they are called – "GIFTS." And they are from the Heavenly Father through his Son, Jesus Christ, himself. They are marvelous and to be desired. Paul said, *"desire spiritual gifts (1 CO 14:1)."*

There is never anything wrong with asking God for something that may not be present, or manifest in one's life, even though it is a free gift. I would say to anyone, if you have not received the manifestation of a gift that has been promised to you, ask for it... boldly. Go to the throne of grace and find out why you do not have it, and get it by faith. Ask others to pray with you...*"earnestly contend for the faith once delivered to the saints"* (JUD 1:3)...*"resist the devil"* (JAM 4:7), who does not want you to enjoy the gifts and blessings of God.

## Jesus foretold about speaking in tongues

The last words which Jesus spoke before he ascended back to heaven had to do with the supernatural gifts of the spirit that would be manifested through his disciples as they continued to minister in his name. This is important because they are the parting words of Jesus. In my Bible the following words are printed in red and stand out on the page:

- *MAR 16:17 And these signs shall follow them that believe; In my name shall they cast out devils; they shall speak with new tongues;*
  *18 They shall take up serpents; and if they drink any deadly thing, it shall not hurt them; they shall lay hands on the sick, and they shall recover.*

The next verses continue as follows:

*19 So then after the Lord had spoken unto them, he was received up into heaven, and sat on the right hand of God.*
*20 And they went forth, and preached every where, the*

*Lord working with them, and <u>confirming the word with signs following</u>.*

Although it was not a complete list in verse 17 and 18, Jesus listed some of the supernatural things that would occur as confirmation of the word of the Lord.

Chapters fourteen through seventeen of the Gospel of John give detailed information and instructions concerning the Holy Ghost. These were also last minute instructions and teachings directly from Christ and must be accepted word-for-word. The thing that matters most is not what *we* believe about the Holy Ghost and speaking in other tongues, but what *Jesus* believes. Jesus believes in speaking with other tongues (languages) as the Holy Spirit gives the utterance.

Speaking in other tongues simply means, "speaking in other languages," or a language *"other"* than the language of the speaker. Most commonly used is the phrase, *"speaking with tongues,"* appearing eight times. The words *"other tongues"* is used twice. It is understood that the speaker is making verbal utterances in a language which is completely unknown to the speaker, and is usually unknown to the audience. The exception is that on the day of Pentecost devout Jews were present from fifteen different nations who heard the Galilean disciples speaking in the native languages of the foreigners who understood what they were speaking. They knew these simple Galileans could not naturally speak in the language of this diverse assemblage of foreign Jews who were amazed.

- *ACT 2:7 And they were all amazed and marvelled, saying one to another, Behold, are not all these which speak Galilaeans?*
  *8 And how hear we every man in our own tongue, wherein we were born?*
  *9 Parthians, and Medes, and Elamites, and the dwellers in Mesopotamia, and in Judaea, and Cappadocia, in Pontus, and Asia,*
  *10 Phrygia, and Pamphylia, in Egypt, and in the parts of Libya about Cyrene, and strangers of Rome, Jews and proselytes,*

*11 Cretes and Arabians, we do hear them speak in our tongues the wonderful works of God.*

## Speaking with tongues is a miracle

Paul made it clear that when one speaks with tongues valid languages are being spoken. Paul used the word *"voices,"* and said they all were significant, or had a meaning somewhere in the world.

- *1CO 14:10 There are, it may be, so many kinds of voices in the world, and none of them is without signification. 11 Therefore if I know not the meaning of the voice, I shall be unto him that speaketh a barbarian, and he that speaketh shall be a barbarian unto me.*

It is important to realize that when one speaks with tongues by the utterance of the Holy Ghost it is a miracle because a literal human language is being spoken which could be understood somewhere in the world.

It is of equal importance to know that one cannot speak in tongues except through utterance given by the Holy Ghost. It is not necessary to help, prime, or assist the Holy Ghost, for he is well able to give utterance without fleshly aid.

## Speaking in tongues at will

The idea of "speaking in tongues at will" has practically become a doctrine with some, and has been a source of confusion. It must be clearly understood that speaking in tongues is truly supernatural, and is not done under the control of the mind or will of the person doing the speaking. They are speaking as they are given utterance by the Holy Ghost. To deviate from this rule opens the door to carnality and fleshly manipulation of what is supposed to be a totally spiritual manifestation. Anyone who is practicing this teaching should stop immediately, and search the word of God.

This belief has been based on an incomplete statement taken from a very important verse. I once heard a minister encouraging people to speak in tongues at will. He coached them into going into some form of non-intelligible gibberish, actually just jabbering on their own. He kept repeating the phrase, "they spake with other tongues," emphasizing, "they spake...they spake." His audience did not know he was misquoting the passage. Not one time did the minister quote the complete verse for had he done so, it would have contradicted what he was saying. Furthermore, the text does not say "they spake." Read it for yourself to see who the source of the speaking was:

- *ACT 2:4 And they were all filled with the Holy Ghost, and began to speak with other tongues, as the Spirit gave them utterance.*

It does not say, they spoke, but it says *"they were filled ... and began to speak as the Spirit gave them utterance."* When Jesus told his disciples that supernatural signs would follow, or accompany believers, he listed speaking with new tongues along with some other amazing supernatural gifts. Not one of these supernatural manifestations of the Spirit can be manipulated or controlled by the human mind, and this includes speaking with new tongues.

The people on the day of Pentecost were not speaking from the source of their own mind, but were speaking from a supernatural source of utterance. All who were speaking in other tongues were Galileans (Jews who lived in Galilee). These Galileans knew only their native language and yet a phenomenal miracle was occurring. There was no manipulation of the manifestation because it was totally unpremeditated by all of them. The one receiving the Holy Ghost did not have the slightest notion, or preconceived idea that this phenomenon would occur. This supernatural sign was strictly from God, and not from their minds. The foreigners who were present in Jerusalem knew these simple people would not be able to do this, except by a miracle.

No effort should be made to reduce what happened on the day of Pentecost to nothing more than what these simple Galileans could do in the natural. I heard another person misquoting the Bible and he honestly was not aware of it.

They kept quoting these words, "they spake in their own tongue wherein they were born." He was so positive the Bible said this, it was impossible to convince him, even by showing, that the Bible did not say such. He finally settled on Acts 2:6 as his proof that the Gentiles were speaking in their own language. This verse is as follows:

- *ACT 2:6 Now when this was noised abroad, the multitude came together, and were confounded, because that every man heard them speak in his own language.*

He contended that "his" referred to the one doing the speaking. Of course it was the multitude which heard their own language. Common sense shows there would be nothing so exciting about a Galilean speaking in his own language that great crowds would come together to hear him. There were Galileans all over town speaking in the language of the Galileans and it brought no crowds together.

But when a man from Cappadocia, or Asia, or Mesopotamia, in passing by, happened to hear someone speaking his language, it certainly caught his attention--to hear his own language being spoken in Jerusalem by a Galilean who was a non-scholar.

One can be sure that he would turn aside to find what was going on. The first startling thing was to hear the Galilean glorifying and praising Jesus Christ as the only begotten of the Father, crucified, risen, ascended, and now at the right hand of the Father as head of his kingdom.

After fifty days of almost total silence from the followers of Jesus, Most all religious Jews were certain that this "Jesus business" had been silenced forever. But now, these simple Galileans are speaking of him, and to him, powerfully, and of all things, in the languages of the foreigners?

One can imagine how this amazed the foreign Jew, half-believing...half-disbelieving ... as he rushed out to tell others what he had just witnessed. It did not take long, in those days of news by word-of-mouth for a massive crowd to gather. These religious Jews crowded around because they knew they were hearing and witnessing a miracle.

- *ACT 2:7 And they were all amazed and marvelled, saying one to another, Behold, are not all these which speak Galilaeans?*
  *8 And how hear we every man in our own tongue, wherein we were born?*

Verse eight settles the matter. Make no mistake, speaking in other languages by the utterance of the Holy Ghost is a miracle, and this truth must be upheld if the integrity of speaking in tongues is to remain intact.

Some who suppress the idea of speaking in other tongues suggest that after the Holy Ghost fell on the one hundred and twenty believers, they went out into the streets and began to witness to these religious Jewish men who were in Jerusalem to celebrate the feast of Pentecost.

There is no indication that the disciples went out into the street at all. They did not go to the multitudes, the multitudes came to them. They certainly were not witnessing in the common sense of the term. Most assuredly, they were witnessing to the greatness of God and magnifying Christ, but they were doing it in other tongues. They had no idea what they were saying, because it was not in their own language.

- *1CO 14:14 For if I pray in an unknown tongue, my spirit prayeth, but my understanding is unfruitful.*

Paul clearly taught that when one is speaking or praying in other tongues by the utterance of the Holy Ghost, it is the Holy Spirit praying through their submitted human spirit…during which their understanding is unfruitful. It is not them speaking, but the Holy Ghost. This fact has already been established from the scripture:

- *ACT 2:4 And they were all filled with the Holy Ghost, and began to speak with other tongues, <u>as the Spirit gave them utterance</u>.*

**"AS THE SPIRIT GAVE THEM UTTERANCE"** should be kept as a cardinal watchword, and speaking in tongues never be reduced to something that can be done by the will, or discretion of a person.

## The Comforter

The giving of the Holy Ghost has important significance to God the Father, and to Jesus, his Son, or else it would not have happened. The Holy Ghost was sent to the church ten days after Christ ascended back to the Father.

Jesus had told his disciples he was not going to leave them alone after his departure, but would comfort their loneliness by requesting the Father to send the Holy Ghost to dwell with them. The comfort of having the physical presence of Christ would be replaced by the indwelling presence of the Holy Ghost as their comforter. Those who have received him to this extent of personal reality testify to the comforting presence of the Holy Ghost.

- *JOH 14:16 And I will pray the Father, and he shall give you another **Comforter**, that he may abide with you for ever;*
- *JOH 16:7 Nevertheless I tell you the truth; It is expedient for you that I go away: for if I go not away, the **Comforter** will not come unto you; but if I depart, I will send him unto you.*

Jesus told his disciples that the Holy Ghost would not depart, or go back to the Father, but would remain with them until the end of the world. This gives clear indication that the Holy Ghost was not given to the early disciples only, because they certainly would not live until the end of the world. Peter quoted that the Holy Ghost was given to *"them who are afar off, even as many as the Lord our God shall call."* We today are included--we are afar off from them--and are called by the Lord unto salvation.

People who truly understand the importance of the indwelling of the Holy Spirit openly welcome him into their hearts and lives. They are extremely appreciative of his comfort in times of need and are grateful for his intercession before God on their behalf. They relish those times when the Spirit assists them in praise and worship before God and his Christ. They soon become aware of situations where he gives them wisdom and knowledge in dealing with their daily problems of life when the right decision is critical. The Holy Spirit becomes to them exactly what Jesus said he would be ... a Comforter and Guide. And, of great importance is how he reveals truth from the word of God.

- *JOH 14:26 But the Comforter, which is the Holy Ghost, whom the Father will send in my name, he shall teach you all things, and bring all things to your remembrance, whatsoever I have said unto you.*
- *JOH 16:13 Howbeit when he, the Spirit of truth, is come, he will guide you into all truth: for he shall not speak of himself; but whatsoever he shall hear, that shall he speak: and he will shew you things to come.*
  *14 He shall glorify me: for he shall receive of mine, and shall shew it unto you.*
  *15 All things that the Father hath are mine: therefore said I, that he shall take of mine, and shall shew it unto you.*

# CHAPTER 8

# PROPHESY ABOUT SPEAKING IN OTHER TONGUES

The earliest mention of speaking in other tongues is found in a prophesy by Isaiah.

- *ISA 28:9 Whom shall he teach knowledge? and whom shall he make to understand doctrine? them that are weaned from the milk, and drawn from the breasts.*
  *10 For precept must be upon precept, precept upon precept; line upon line, line upon line; here a little, and there a little:*
  *11 **For with stammering lips and another tongue will he speak to this people.***
  *12 To whom he said, This is the rest wherewith ye may cause the weary to rest; and this is the refreshing: yet they would not hear.*

This is an amazing prophesy. It is clearly the responsibility of the Holy Ghost to teach knowledge and to give the understanding of doctrine (v. 9). Those who do not want to leave the milk of the word have a hard time dealing with the doctrines concerning the Holy Ghost, and like an infant, they want to stay with the breast. The *"strong meat"* of the word is more than they can digest (HEB 5:14).

## The teacher

Isaiah asks *"whom shall he teach knowledge? and to whom shall he make to understand doctrine?"* The Biblical answer is "only those who are in a correct spiritual relationship with Christ can be taught by the Holy Spirit." No other teacher is qualified to place *"precept upon precept"* and *"line upon line"*...to take a truth from the word of God in one place *("here a little")*, and then from another place *("there a little")*, and *"rightly divide"* the word of God to reveal the truth of the Bible.

It is like taking the pieces of a puzzle and placing them in their right place so the full picture can be revealed.

* *2TI 2:15 Study to shew thyself approved unto God, a workman that needeth not to be ashamed, rightly dividing the word of truth.*

Isaiah was given a prophetic view of New Testament believers, those *"to whom he would teach knowledge...and make to understand doctrine."* He identified them as those who speak *"with stammering lips and another tongue."* It is evident Isaiah prophetically saw New Testament Christians who were baptized in the Holy Spirit and who spoke in other tongues. This is clearly the way he identified them as the one to whom God would teach knowledge and make to understand doctrine.

This does not exclude any believer, because all who are born again have received the Holy Ghost. If they have not spoken in tongues, that is not the fault of God, or of Jesus, or of the Holy Ghost. And, it may not be their fault alone. Many Christians are functioning in environments that hide those truths from them. Therefore, ignorance of the truth concerning this matter can be the problem. Of course there are those who have outright rejected this truth and have willfully chosen to refuse the knowledge or the experience.

---

## All truth

Jesus said concerning the Holy Ghost:

- *JOH 16:13 Howbeit when he, the Spirit of truth, is come, he will guide you into <u>all truth</u>: for he shall not speak of himself; but whatsoever he shall hear, that shall he speak: and he will shew you things to come.*
*14 He shall glorify me: for he shall receive of mine, and shall shew it unto you.*
*15 <u>All things</u> that the Father hath are mine: therefore said I, that he shall take of mine, and shall shew it unto you.*

The Holy Ghost has full access to *"all"* the knowledge of Christ who has access to the full knowledge of his heavenly Father. Jesus explained this in the above statement. The limitless knowledge of truth to which we have access through the Holy Ghost...is *"<u>all truth</u>."*

Therefore, The Holy Ghost, as the designated divine teacher of the word of God--since he wrote the book--is qualified to put it *"precept upon precept, line upon line,"* and to rightly divide it *"here a little and there a little."* A key passage is as follows:

- *2PE 1:21 For the prophecy came not in old time by the will of man: but holy men of God spake as <u>they were moved by the Holy Ghost</u>.*

Paul placed much emphasis on the direct inspiration of the word of God.

- *2TI 3:16 All scripture is given by inspiration of God, and is profitable for doctrine, for reproof, for correction, for instruction in righteousness:*
*17 That the man of God may be perfect, throughly furnished unto all good works.*

Any knowledge about Christ, truth, or the gifts of the spirit comes only through the Holy Ghost. Whatever one learns should be cherished and carefully guarded. It must first be gained, and then kept.

- *2TI 1:14 That good thing which was committed unto thee
  keep by the Holy Ghost which dwelleth in us.*

Surely Paul had this in mind when he told Timothy to *"study to
show thyself approved unto God, a workman that needeth not to be
ashamed, rightly dividing the word of truth"* (2 TIM 2:15).

When the truth is spoken, then that truth must be revealed by
the Holy Spirit before the hearers can receive it into their hearts.
Truth is first received into the mind, and there it is considered, then
accepted or rejected. When a person does not allow the Holy Spirit to
control or teach, truth can be rejected by the carnal, fleshly, logical,
reasoning mind.

## Some will not believe

God gave the Old Testament prophet, Isaiah, a truly supernatural
revelation of how things would be in the church age concerning the
Holy Spirit. God chose to show him a glimpse of speaking in other
tongues, and that it would be a spiritually restful and refreshing
experience for believers to possess the Holy Ghost as an indwelling
Spirit. God also showed him that even after giving all this, yet some
would not hear.

- *ISA 28:11 For with stammering lips and another tongue
  will he speak to this people.
  12 To whom he said, This is the rest wherewith ye may
  cause the weary to rest; and this is the refreshing: yet
  they would not hear.*

Many people become uneasy at the mention of the Holy Ghost,
and have difficulty accepting speaking in other tongues. Some
cannot deny the Biblical authenticity of the Holy Ghost and the
accompanying gifts, but they place the demonstration and operation
of spiritual gifts under such stringent regulations that the chance of
the manifestation of tongues or any other gift ever happening in their
life is practically nil...and they strongly influence others around
them to also suppress the reality of the Holy Spirit.

God had spoken through the Prophet Isaiah, *"with another*

*tongue will I speak unto this people."* He then said, *"and this is the refreshing wherewith I will cause the weary to be refreshed."*

What better confirmation could there be than to quote God himself? What more could we ask today as scriptural proof for believing in the miracle of speaking in other tongues as the Spirit gives the utterance? How could anyone reject such a thrilling experience?

If God called it a *"refreshing,"* it certainly merits special attention. Yet, God sadly injected, *"in spite of this, some will not hear."*

## Early and latter rain

Joel prophesied concerning the outpouring of the Holy Spirit and compared it to the early and latter rain. He was referring to spring rain that comes during the time of planting that is necessary for germination of seed (early rain), and then to the summer rain (latter rain) that is needed to cause the final development of plants and the production of fruit and seed in the pod, making ready for harvest.

- *JOE 2:23 Be glad then, ye children of Zion, and rejoice in the LORD your God: for he hath given you the former rain moderately, and he will cause to come down for you the rain, the former rain, and the latter rain ...*

The *"former rain moderately"* found its significance on the day of Pentecost. The main thrust of Joel's prophesy had to do with the latter rain, the big rain which finishes off the crop. Joel's prophesy indicated that the first rain was a moderate rain...evidently in comparison to the latter rain...an outpouring of the Holy Spirit which would occur in the last days just prior to the second coming of Christ.

## Pentecost not the last day outpouring

On the day of Pentecost, Peter did not say that which was occurring right then was the fulfillment of the prophesy of Joel, but he said, *"this is that which was spoken by the prophet Joel."* Then Peter quotes about the great outpouring which would occur in the last days

Correlating this with other scriptures concerning the end time establishes that there shall be a definite *"last days"* just prior to the second coming of Christ that shall be characterized by a mighty outpouring of the Holy Ghost. God has plans for a huge harvest in the end time and the outpouring of the Holy Ghost plays a big part in it. The Holy Ghost was poured out on the day of Pentecost, but that was not the last days outpouring. That was *"the former rain moderately"* (JOE 2:25).

## Before the great and notable day

This outpouring will, without doubt, occur *"before the great and notable day of the Lord come."* Now here is the point: Joel prophesied--over eight hundred years before Christ--concerning a great outpouring of the Holy Spirit that would come from God in the last days. An initial outpouring was given to the church on the day of Pentecost, with the explanation, *"this is that"* (the same experience of being filled with the Holy Spirit) which will be poured out during the last days.

## Upon all flesh

The final outpouring shall be of such proportions that it is said, *"I will pour out my Spirit upon **all flesh**."* This gives reason to pay special attention to the matter of being filled with the Holy Spirit.

A close study of the word of God reveals that the last days has a broad application, and then it also pinpoints a time just prior to the second coming of Christ. The great last-day outpouring of the Spirit will come to pass just as it was prophesied:

- *ACT 2:17 And it shall come to pass in the last days, saith God, I will pour out of my Spirit upon all flesh: and your sons and your daughters shall prophesy, and your young men shall see visions, and your old men shall dream dreams:*
*18 And on my servants and on my handmaidens I will pour out in those days of my Spirit; and they shall prophesy:*
*19 And I will shew wonders in heaven above, and signs*

*in the earth beneath; blood, and fire, and vapour of
smoke:
20 The sun shall be turned into darkness, and the moon
into blood, before the great and notable day of the Lord
come:
21 And it shall come to pass, that whosoever shall call
on the name of the Lord shall be saved.*

It is *"sound doctrine"* to state that, since the day of Pentecost, every one who repents and is placed into Christ *(baptized into Christ)* receives the outpouring of the Holy Spirit and should walk in the fullness of the experience.

- *ACT 2:38 Then Peter said unto them, Repent, and be
  baptized every one of you in the name of Jesus Christ
  for the remission of sins, <u>and ye shall receive the gift of
  the Holy Ghost</u>.
  39 For the promise is unto you, and to your children,
  and to all that are afar off, even as many as the Lord
  our God shall call.*

Peter said *"ye <u>shall</u> receive the gift."* One should not allow their natural inhibitions to prevent the supernatural manifestations from freely occurring. Jesus said the Holy Ghost would abide with his followers *"for ever."*

- *JOH 14:16 And I will pray the Father, and he shall give
  you another Comforter, <u>that he may abide with you for
  ever</u>;
  17 Even the Spirit of truth; whom the world cannot
  receive, because it seeth him not, neither knoweth him:
  but ye know him; for he dwelleth with you, and shall be
  in you.*

No Christian is exempt from this indwelling of the Spirit. He is given to all.

When one buys an automobile they can pick the equipment they want--air conditioner, electric door locks, power antenna, power windows, etc. The Holy Ghost is not an embellishment like fancy hubcaps..."*take it or leave it.*" The infilling of the Holy Ghost is not optional equipment. He comes with the package just like a steering wheel comes with an automobile, and is just as necessary.

Today, if you get Jesus, you get the Holy Ghost which he said he would send from the Father immediately upon arriving back into heaven.

- *JOH 16:7 Nevertheless I tell you the truth; It is expedient for you that I go away: for if I go not away, the Comforter will not come unto you; but if I depart, I will send him unto you.*

The following verse should establish forever that the Holy Ghost is given to <u>everyone</u> who calls upon Christ in obedience.

- *ACT 5:32 And we are his witnesses of these things; and so is also the Holy Ghost, whom God hath given to them that obey him.*

# CHAPTER 9

# THE TURN OF THE 20ᵀᴴ CENTURY

Historically truth regarding the baptism with the Holy Spirit was smothered and lost by the church as grievous wolves entered the flock beginning with the end of the first century. This was predicted by the apostle Paul.

- *ACT 20:29 For I know this, that after my departing shall grievous wolves enter in among you, not sparing the flock.*
  *30 Also of your own selves shall men arise, speaking perverse things, to draw away disciples after them.*
  *31 Therefore watch, and remember, that by the space of three years I ceased not to warn every one night and day with tears.*

The resultant decline of truth in the church brought on by these wolves led to the loss of most cardinal truths. Justification by faith totally disappeared from the scene as these false teachers replaced grace with their pagan works. The eventual takeover of the church by Constantine in the fourth century led to various religious teachers throughout the centuries who are revered by some as renowned scholars. Opponents of speaking in tongues point out that these great scholars never mentioned the baptism in the Holy Spirit in a Pentecostal sense, therefore, to them this is proof that God intended for tongues to cease from the church soon after the original apostles died off.

The fact is, through these apostate church fathers almost all truth was lost as the church faded into dismal darkness for centuries. This caused the entire world to sink into the dark ages which is a historical fact.

Not until Martin Luther rediscovered the truth regarding justification by faith as opposed to the Catholic works for righteousness, such as penance that had been imposed on Christian religion, did the light of truth begin to shine again.

Added to this was the revelation given to John Wesley that God expects followers of Christ to live in holiness and sanctification as an inseparable result of the new birth. And then more emergence of truth occurred when the light of the baptism with the Holy Spirit began to shine again. This enlightenment was accompanied by fresh understanding of the fruit of the Spirit and the reality of the gifts of the Spirit.

## Resistance to Speaking in Tongues

Why is speaking in tongues not allowed today by many denominations, ministers, and leaders who claim to have been baptized in the Spirit? The answer is basically a historical one. Just prior to the turn of the twentieth century a sovereign work of God occurred wherein the manifestation of the gift of tongues was poured out on churches and groups of believers within a short period of time at different points around the world.

By this time the church had evolved into many divergent denominational groups that passed legislations which set the boundaries of beliefs allowed for their constituents. As could be expected, these traditional religious groups began to experience spontaneous Holy Spirit fires blazing up within their ranks and most resisted it because it did not fit into their prescribed orthodox doctrine.

This original outpouring which spread around the globe seems to have started in a church on Azuza Street in Los Angeles. Visitors to the three-year long revival took the message with them to various separate locations, mostly remote and isolated from each other. The spreading fire was not the result of promotions by men because there was little or no contact or communication between the various groups which could have enabled them to coordinate the timing of this outstanding event. It was not until a considerable time later that the close proximity of timing was discovered. Each group which had experienced the outpouring believed it to be a repeat and continuation of Pentecost. The near-simultaneous global outpouring gives evidence that it was a sovereign work of God.

The recipients of the outpouring searched the word of God to confirm its Biblical soundness. Much to their delight they confirmed the exact experience in the Bible and believed they had rediscovered a serious void and oversight in their contemporary theology concerning the baptism in the Holy Ghost. They concluded that the baptism in the Holy Ghost had been given to the early church in like fashion on the day of Pentecost. There was no reason that it should not continue as a normal practice of the church until Jesus comes. There was no Biblical reason to condemn these outpourings which were occurring in their day.

This spiritual phenomenon spread like a prairie fire as many Spirit-filled evangelists spanned the globe sharing the word of God regarding the rediscovery of this wonderful truth that had always been in the Bible, and especially in the New Testament revelation which introduced Christ as the Baptizer in the Holy Ghost. John the Baptist said:

- *MAT 3:11 I indeed baptize you with water unto repentance: but he that cometh after me is mightier than I, whose shoes I am not worthy to bear: he shall baptize you with the Holy Ghost, and with fire:*

**Jesus said:**

- *LUK 24:49 And, behold, I send the promise of my Father upon you: but tarry ye in the city of Jerusalem, until ye be endued with power from on high.*

## Unpremeditated--Unmanipulated

While the early church waited in Jerusalem for the coming of the Holy Ghost, as promised by Jesus, they did not have the slightest ideas what form this experience would take. Speaking in other tongues was a totally involuntary surprise, and there was no pre-programming coming from Jesus. Human effort, knowledge, or ingenuity had nothing to do with the manifestation of tongues...it was a sovereign operation of God confirming the arrival of the Holy Spirit who had taken up his abode within them. The outpouring at the turn of the twentieth century saw the same thing happen--totally involuntary and unpremeditated. The flame of enthusiasm spread rapidly.

## Division developed

Earlier in this book I brought attention to the great divide that separates Christians today. Sad to say, it was not long before lines of division were deeply drawn while two separate theological camps developed early in the twentieth century. A serious chasm divided Christianity into new religious orders identified as "Pentecostals" and "Non-Pentecostals." These remain today as the most dominant point of division within Christianity, comparable to the Catholic/ Protestant separation.

The Non-Pentecostals consisted of all the major old-line denominations which took a firm stand against the Pentecostal persuasion. Several new denominations developed over Pentecostalism and the rift became set in doctrinal concrete. Today all churches are classified as either Pentecostal or Non-Pentecostal.

## Cause for division--Two separate works

By hindsight the reasons for the rift are easy to see. The Pentecostals developed the doctrine that, since they were already saved, and had later been baptized in the Holy Ghost, that, being born again and being baptized in the Holy Ghost must be two separate works of grace. The doctrine naturally followed that the baptism in the Holy Ghost was an experience subsequent to the new birth. Biblical support for this position was taken from Paul's question, *"have ye received the Holy Ghost since ye believed"?*

*"Since ye believed"* became the doctrinal basis for teaching that the experience of being baptized with the Holy Ghost occurs "after" (or "since) one becomes a believer. Pentecostals began to teach other Christians that every saved person must move on into receiving the baptism in the Holy Ghost. Most saved people resented this and outright rejected the idea as an insult to their spiritual integrity. They were not willing to admit there was something missing from their spiritual experience.

Non-Pentecostals contended they had received the Holy Spirit when they were saved. Pentecostals strongly denounced this based on their personal experience, claiming that receiving the Holy Spirit was a separate experience. Furthermore, Pentecostals rigidly taught that speaking in other tongues was the initial evidence of having received the Holy Ghost. Therefore tongues became mandatory before one could claim the baptism in the Spirit. Pentecostals were in the minority and were easily rejected or even expelled from churches.

## Second work of grace--Sanctification

Prior to this outpouring of the Holy Ghost the followers of the Wesleyan revival had, in previous decades, developed the doctrine of sanctification as a second definite work of grace and had been exhorting saved people to go beyond the initial work of salvation unto an experience of entire sanctification. This experience of sanctification demanded renouncing habits and sins which most did not relish giving up, therefore most rejected deeper spirituality, wanting to hold to their tobacco (especially snuff), their corn squeezin, and their Saturday night barn dancing.

The sanctification adherents were known as part of the Holiness Movement. History records great sweeping revivals as preachers of sanctification spanned the globe with this additional light. Meetings, lasting for weeks and months, saw phenomenal changes in lives of rogues and villains as the cleansing power of the blood confirmed messages on holiness which were preached from stumps, brush arbor podiums, vacant lots, store buildings, and school houses. Most traditional pulpits were closed to them.

The scriptural fact is that holiness should "not" have been taught as a second work of grace, but should have been proclaimed as an integral and inseparable part of the new birth. This cleansing sanctification had been left out of the salvation equation, but was now being rediscovered as an important truth, but was mistakenly taught as a second definite work of grace.

Since the time of the Cross of Christ and his resurrection, sanctification had always been an initial part of the salvation process but had been lost theologically during the decline which resulted in the dark ages. Sanctification is not a "second work" but is a part of the process of being washed spiritually when one is born again.

- *1CO 6:9 Know ye not that the unrighteous shall not inherit the kingdom of God? Be not deceived: neither fornicators, nor idolaters, nor adulterers, nor effeminate, nor abusers of themselves with mankind,*
  *10 Nor thieves, nor covetous, nor drunkards, nor revilers, nor extortioners, shall inherit the kingdom of God.*
  *11 And such were some of you: but ye are washed, but ye are sanctified, but ye are justified in the name of the Lord Jesus, and by the Spirit of our God.*

## Sanctification by the Spirit

Sanctification is a work of the Holy Spirit in the body, soul, spirit, and mind of anyone who is converted to Christ. Verse 11 given above should be reviewed with special attention given to the last phrase, *"by the Spirit of our God."* Also carefully notice that this sanctification by the Spirit is associated with justification.

Another important passage on this subject which employs the Holy Ghost in the cleansing process is the following:

- *TIT 3:5 Not by works of righteousness which we have*

*done, but according to his mercy he saved us, by <u>the washing of regeneration, and renewing of the Holy Ghost;</u>*

Those who rediscovered the truth concerning sanctification did not want to offend their peers by telling them they were not saved, which was probably the actual truth, since the fruit of the born-again life was not evident. But, instead of preaching holiness as a truth that had been omitted, or dropped, from the doctrine of salvation, sanctification was re-added as a second experience, or work of grace. It was presented as a newly discovered experience that all believers should seek.

The sad truth is that the doctrine of sanctification as a second work of grace came about because those seeing this truth did not have the strength to stand up in the face of professing Christianity and preach the galling truth that many were probably not even saved because they showed no signs of sanctification and cleansing which should be descriptive of a born-again child of God, and indicative of the new birth.

It was easier to say, sure, you are saved, but you now need to be sanctified. This became doctrinal confusion because it is not exactly what the Bible says. The word of God clearly teaches that being born again requires cleansing from sin. Sanctification accompanies conversion. One becomes a new creature at the time of conversion. Just a few of the many scriptures which clearly indicate that cleansing accompanies the original, or initial, washing of the blood are as follows:

- *2CO 5:17 Therefore if any man be in Christ, he is a new creature: old things are passed away; behold, all things are become new.*
- *ROM 6:11 Likewise reckon ye also yourselves to be dead indeed unto sin, but alive unto God through Jesus Christ our Lord.*
*12 Let not sin therefore reign in your mortal body, that ye should obey it in the lusts thereof.*

- *ROM 8:2 For the law of the Spirit of life in Christ Jesus hath made me free from the law of sin and death.*
- *ROM 8:10 And if Christ be in you, the body is dead because of sin; but the Spirit is life because of righteousness.*
- *2TI 2:19 Nevertheless the foundation of God standeth sure, having this seal, The Lord knoweth them that are his. And, Let every one that nameth the name of Christ depart from iniquity.*
- *REV 1:5 And from Jesus Christ, who is the faithful witness, and the first begotten of the dead, and the prince of the kings of the earth. Unto him that loved us, and washed us from our sins in his own blood,*

It cannot be denied that the holiness movement did rediscover the truth of sanctification, and we can thank God for that. These were people who were willing to give up anything and everything for the sake of the gospel of Christ. They were going back and picking up a link that had been missing. The church had become extremely carnal, worldly, and morally depraved. How great it would have been if the preachers of sanctification had shot straight from the hip and told it like it was…that the religionists needed to get saved in a cleansing, washing, renewing, regenerating, and sanctifying way.

## Third work of grace

The holiness movement was a ripe field for the Pentecostal message, and many accepted the baptism in the Spirit. Many from the traditional churches also accepted the message and received the truth concerning the baptism in the Holy Ghost. Those who became Pentecostals from the Wesleyan background declared the baptism in the Holy Ghost to be the "third" work of grace…teaching the necessity of being progressively (1) saved, then (2) sanctified, and then (3) filled with the Holy Ghost.

This gave rise to a rift between Pentecostals because those who were not from the Wesleyan background did not accept sanctification as a "second definite work of grace." Therefore when they accepted the baptism in the Holy Ghost, they did so as the second work of grace, and not the third. These consisted mainly of Calvinists who looked at sanctification as an attempt to be saved by works...by trying to be "holier-than-thou."

Further division developed because some taught sanctification as a "progressive" gradual cleansing extension of the salvation experience rather than an "instantaneous" definite experience. Therefore the two largest Pentecostal denominations (the Church of God of Cleveland, Tennessee, and the Assembly of God of Springfield, Missouri) developed out of the turn of the century outpouring. They differed on whether the baptism in the Holy Ghost was a second or third experience ... and whether sanctification was an instantaneous or progressive work of grace.

To further complicate the doctrine, the United Pentecost denomination came into existence preaching that baptism in the Holy Ghost was the first work of grace, and that one could not claim to be saved until after they had spoken in tongues as the initial evidence that the Holy Ghost had taken up residence in their body temple.

They also taught that there was only one God who was manifested through three separate personalities which were first the Father, who then became manifested as the Son, and later was manifested in the person of the Holy Ghost. This group became known as *"Oneness."*

## Denominational rejection

All old-line major denominational groups eventually rejected the Pentecostal approach to the baptism in the Holy Ghost. Not one denomination was converted. Pentecostalism by this time had taken on a stigma within formal religious circles and was considered to find its roots among the poor, low class and uneducated. Also, their worship services were less structured, and more spontaneous and evangelistic.

Anything which smacked of a spiritual nature, especially the gifts of the spirit such as healing, discerning of spirits, casting out devils, speaking in tongues, interpretation of tongues, word of wisdom, word of knowledge, faith, working of miracles, etc., prompted a verdict of rejection by formal organized religion…who declared that all such manifestations was given only to the early church and was not supposed to be a part of today's doctrinal system. Isn't it amazing that all the above-mentioned gifts are listed in the Bible, and yet they are rejected at will by those who choose to do so?

Actually, the rejection by all denominations was not a rejection of the Holy Ghost, but was a rejection of the manifestation of the gifts of the Spirit. In fact, the denominational backlash was the following: they began to declare they had received the Holy Ghost at the time of being saved and resented being told that they had not received him. But, these groups rejected any literal function of the gifts of the spirit, especially speaking in tongues.

The conflict over speaking in tongues became rigidly set, with Pentecostals declaring that speaking in other tongues was the initial evidence that the Holy Spirit baptism had occurred; the other side declared that according to First Corinthians Chapter 13, tongues had ceased.

## Dark ages Reviewed

The dark ages are of such importance that it is fitting to further review its impact. How, in its early history, did the church ever get away from speaking in tongues and exercising other gifts of the spirit? The apostle Paul prophesied that soon after his death the church would begin to go into apostasy, or veer gradually away from the truth. We know from Paul's instructions that speaking in tongues was commonly practiced in the early church, but somewhere it ceased to function as a common occurrence.

History reveals that within three hundred years after Christ the church had gone into almost total apostasy and remained so for a thousand or more years. This resulted in the "dark ages" which students of history know well.

Religious leaders which gained control of the church substituted everything scriptural, spiritual and supernatural with their own creeds, dogmas and traditions. The pope replaced Christ as the head of the church. State government and political powers appointed the ministry. The administration and office work of the Holy Spirit was replaced by the judgment and decision-making authority of these councils, and members of the body of Christ became slaves and pawns of an evil and corrupt religious tyranny that has taken centuries from which to recover and break away.

The 1984 edition of the Encyclopedia Britannica, Volume 5, page 401, gives this account:

> **Saint Cyprian, bishop of Carthage in the mid-3rd century, led the Christians in North Africa through the crises of the persecutions under the Roman emperors Decius (249-251) and Valerian (253-260). His teaching on the nature of the church and its sacraments and on the office of a bishop molded Christian thought...**

Saint Cyprian lost his position of leadership and went into hiding for a period because of his doctrines, but was able to overcome his opposition and came back into leadership. The above text continues:

> **Cyprian returned to Carthage (early 251) and at a council of bishops in May 251 was able to regain his authority...Three important principles of church discipline were thus established. First, the right and power to remit deadly sins, even that of apostasy, lay in the hands of the church; secondly, the final authority in disciplinary matters rested with the bishops in council as repositories of the Holy Spirit; and, thirdly, unworthy members among the laity must be accepted in the New Israel of Christianity just as in the Old Israel of Judaism.**

It is obvious that the headship of Christ--the forgiver of sins--was taken over by men who claimed the right to remit deadly sins? It is equally clear that the office work of the Holy Spirit's authority and discipline was preempted by councils of men who claimed to be the repositories of the Holy Spirit.

From this point the church went into a horrible darkness and falling away, and remained in this condition for centuries. It has been a long, hard, and slow struggle to regain the truth which was covered and smothered by these evil men and seducers of which Paul sadly wrote.

To resist these religious powers meant banishment, imprisonment, or most likely death. Let's read a little more in the encyclopedia:

> **Cyprian held three councils between the autumn of 255 and September 256. The last, at which 87 bishops were present, decided unanimously that there could be no Baptism outside the church, just as there could be neither faith, hope, nor salvation for those outside it. A minister could not dispense what he himself did not possess, namely, the Holy Spirit.**

Here is a definite point when the Holy Spirit was suppressed practically into oblivion. The "bishops in council" were declared to be the repository of the Holy Spirit, and an ordinary "minister could not dispense what he himself did not possess, namely, the Holy Spirit."

If the "bishops in council" were the only ones who could claim the power and authority of the Holy Spirit, and no other ministers except these 87 bishops could do so, that left everyone else out. It is no wonder that the truth concerning the Holy Spirit was unknown to the church for centuries following that decree. This is where the truth regarding the Holy Spirit fell through the cracks of legislated religious dogma.

It is hard to comprehend that decisions made so many centuries back could have so much influence on religious thinking hundreds of years later. It is a fact, though, that denominations that developed centuries later carried forward much of the preconceived doctrines of these councils. The hard lines of denominational authority cannot be denied. If one changed from one denomination to another, their water baptism was not accepted as valid, but they were required to be re-baptized in the new denomination according to their authority.

The list is endless and overwhelmingly contains restraints placed on the Holy Spirit, not by God, but by men in their councils. The atrocity is that the average church member was totally deprived of the Holy Spirit since He (the Holy Spirit) was restricted by church authority to a select religious council. This brought a total vacuum and ignorance regarding the Holy Spirit for centuries.

## A fresh outpouring

It was in this kind of vacuum that a fresh outpouring came in the late eighteen-hundreds and early nineteen-hundreds among people who knew absolutely nothing about the Holy Spirit. In spite of this outpouring, the repression of the Holy Spirit's manifestation and supernatural gifts has continued to this day in many church circles by decrees from their ruling councils.

Beginning primarily with Martin Luther, there began a reformation that has progressed through many stages, ministries, outpourings and restorations. This reformation has seen distinct leaders, men of God who were able to break with tradition and bring back into existence truth that had been completely smothered and covered by man-made doctrines and practices...John Wesley, Finney, Spurgeon, to name a few.

Then, after centuries of absence, as mentioned above, there came a sovereign restoration of the operation of the Holy Spirit directly in the lives, ministries, and worship-assemblies of the church. This was a radical break with the traditions that had been in vogue for centuries within the organized church institutions, but it was not a radical break with the word of God--it was a "radical return" to the traditions of the word of God and to the church such as described in the fourteenth chapter of First Corinthians.

## Doctrine based on human experience

Several major mistakes were made at the turn of the century when the Holy Ghost was poured out. Pentecostals based their doctrine of a second or third experience on what had happened to them personally rather than going strictly by the Bible. Doctrine is not established by human or personal experience, but by the word of God.

## The author's walk of faith

I was raised in The Church of God, a Pentecostal denomination, with headquarters in Cleveland, Tennessee. My teen years were spent living in Cleveland. We lived about five blocks from the General Offices of the denomination. The denominational High School Academy, Junior College and Bible College were about three blocks from our home.

I graduated from the Academy and completed my freshman year at the Junior College. I participated in almost every extracurricular activity offered which included singing in the Lee College Quartet, president of the college choir, president of the high school senior class, president of the Beta Club Honor Society, captain of the College Freshmen volleyball team, played basketball and football, both in high school and college, and was elected to "Who's Who in American Colleges and Universities.

My mother became a college professor, and retired after twenty-seven years at Lee College. My Father graduated from the Bible College several years previously, which was what brought us to Tennessee and the school originally.

Needless to say, I was born and bred Church of God and cut my teeth on Church of God benches as mom and dad were in church faithfully every time the door opened. My father was an ordained minister of the Church of God denomination.

I was deeply ingrained in all the Church of God doctrines, and especially believed, along with my peers, that one had not received the Holy Ghost until they had spoken in other tongues. Hardly a church service occurred in those days without the opportunity being given for one to testify. Almost every testimony would include the following: "I am glad I am saved, sanctified, filled with the Holy Ghost with the initial evidence of speaking in other tongues, and have seen the light on the great Church of God."

## David and Goliath

I became the pastor of the Childress, Texas, Church of God denomination at age nineteen in the year of nineteen hundred and fifty three. I thought I knew our doctrines well and one of my first encounters was with the pastor of the largest church in town, the Church of Christ. I met him by chance at a local automobile repair shop. He had pastored that church for thirty years and could spot a stranger in town a mile away.

I am sure I looked like a prospective church member, and he began to make my acquaintance only to learn I was the new pastor at the little Pentecostal church. He began to subtly antagonize this new kid on the block in front of several people who knew him well. He was making sport of me when he asked, "Well son, what do you preach down there at that little church?"

My zeal knew no limits and I was ready to take him on, if that is what it took to defend our gospel which I felt was being challenged. I stated that I preached that one must be saved, sanctified, filled with the Holy Ghost with the initial evidence of speaking in other tongues as the Spirit gives the utterance, and then join the Church of God.

He quizzed, "so you preach that speaking in other tongues is the 'initial evidence' of being baptized in the Holy Ghost." I proudly responded, "I sure do." He then asked, "Where is the term 'initial evidence' found in the Bible?"

I said, "I don't know the exact location, but I will find it for you and let you know." He then said, "son, don't waste your time because it is not in there." I put up a little hedging argument because he seemed so dominantly positive, but I thought, "it has to be in there because I've heard it all my life. I'll find it"!

He then said, "Preacher, I'll tell you what I will do. If you can show me where that is located in the Bible, I will come join your church and let you baptize me in water; in fact, I will stand before your congregation and eat my Bible page by page."

Of course, everyone around laughed and haw-hawed real big. I knew right then I was going to really study so I could prove what we believed. This was just my first encounter with the rude awakening that I, too, could possibly be caught up in doctrines and traditions of men simply because I was born into it.

This preacher was on a roll and the crowd around increased as mechanics, office personnel, and other customers began to gather around for the kill! I tried to think of some excuse to walk away but he would not let me. He kept firing loaded questions at me, with each one bringing a response of laughter from the crowd.

Each question took on a deeper tone of sarcasm as he quizzed, "what goes on down there...do you heal the sick? What percentage gets healed? Do you pray for the sick in every service? Are there any local people that we know who have been healed? I would like to visit them and check it out. When was the last time someone got healed? Was it healings like the Bible--blind eyes, deaf ears, crippled limbs"?

He continued, "you know, I have a responsibility as a local pastor to check these claims out, for the protection of my flock that I pastor."

My nineteen-year old head was swimming and under my breath I was praying, "God help me; get me out of here; stop this harassment! He has the advantage because he is an older man with a lot more experience...Lord, he's probably in his sixties...gray headed, and distinguished looking." I was not aware that Church of Christ ministers are usually well schooled in the art of debate...having studied it in their seminaries.

But, the ordeal went on. He asked, "do you all shout and jerk and jump when the Holy Ghost comes upon you? I have heard that some jump benches and others roll all over the floor screaming and shouting to the top of their voices. They call them 'Holy Rollers.' Is that right? Doesn't it get a little scary with that invisible Ghost floating around in the church and taking hold of the people, shaking and moving them around? It seems to me it would be like a giant invisible mosquito flying around, grabbing an arm and throwing it in the air, then a leg...jerking it into a kick. What does it feel like to have the Holy Ghost take you over"?

I knew he was exaggerating normal Pentecostal worship, and

I had not experienced the emotional excesses he described, but it would be futile to deny that such had doubtless occurred somewhere, sometime.

He then began to rail on the emotional nature of Pentecostal worship characterized by crying and laughter, worship and praising, joy and shouting. He then changed the tempo, looked me in the eye soberly like he was going to force a confession out of me, and said, "Do you shout?" Before I could answer he asked demandingly, "tell me, what makes you shout? Isn't it all just emotionalism?"

By this time I was desperately praying on the inside, "God help me! Give me something to say." I felt like I was in the lion's den. All I had done was come in this place of business to get my car worked on and had run into this.

I did not know it, but his tactic was to keep me off balance by not allowing time to answer anything before he would fire another intimidating question that was loaded to the extent that it favored his point by the way it was asked. He had the skill to answer his own questions by his own questions, or at least to make it appear there was no answer on my part. The laughter of the crowd that had become several bodies deep was roaring in my brain.

He had set me back on my heels by his first question about the *"initial evidence."* When I stepped into his trap through ignorance he had me going his way and was successful in keeping me off balance and defensive, while he was definitely on the offense.

## Answer with a question

But, when he asked the question, "what makes you shout," I felt a little surge of the Holy Ghost in my nineteen-year-old spirit. I was totally dependent upon his help at that point, and I quickly asked, "God, what shall I say? How shall I answer"?

The Holy Ghost communicated with me, Spirit to spirit, just as real as if it had been an audible conversation, and said, "Do as Jesus did--answer him with a question. Ask him what makes him laugh."

I had not the slightest idea where I was headed, but I said by faith, "I'll make a deal with you. If you will answer my question, then I will answer yours." He responded, "fair enough, what is your question"?

I knew at that point I had absolutely no answer to his question, and did not know what I would say after he answered my question. I then asked him the question the Holy Ghost had given me, "what makes you laugh?"

He cleared his throat, changed the tone of his voice like a professor about to give a profound lecture, looked down his nose at me, and said, "well that ought to be easy enough to answer." I sensed tenseness in the crowd. His face began to show signs of unexpected pressure, and I fully believe an obvious anointing had come upon me that he had never encountered. It was almost like David and Goliath. I sensed a little taste of what David must have felt as he was forced into total dependence upon God.

The preacher began an eloquent discourse on laughter, changing the tone and sound of his voice to that of an orator. In a deeper, Shakespearian voice he said, "you see, when God created man, he gave him an intellect, and an almost spiritual perception to comprehend words, ideas, situations, and experiences in communication with others that are ironic, coincidental, unique, or contains special factors of witticism and humor."

He continued, "God also gave man the intelligent ability to communicate in words, or spoken language. And, besides this he gave us another form of communication known as crying and laughter. Each serves a useful purpose of expressing sorrow or joy, or the conveying to another that we have caught the witticism of their pun, or joke, or ironic situation that is so coincidental that it is funny. When these things occur, laughter is a normal, human, emotional response to a natural impulse through intellectual perception."

Just as he was finishing his speech, it was obvious that he was becoming aware that he was setting himself up for an indefensible rebuttal.

I responded, "Exactly! And, when God created me he placed in me a spiritual ability to respond to the divine impulse of his presence and anointing through praise, worship, adoration, exuberant joy, and even sometimes shouting and cheering similar to rejoicing at a ball game over a touchdown by the hometown team."

I continued, using almost his exact words, "shouting is a normal, human, emotional response to a divine impulse through spiritual perception. I do not deny that it is emotionalism in its best and most Biblical form. Just as a person can overdo even laughter, so have Pentecostals sometimes gone beyond the Spirit's expression and worship, and I cannot defend that, but there is such a thing as a purely Spiritual emotionalism expressed in genuine laughter, praise, joy, exuberance, worship, thanksgiving, hallelujahs and excitement and genuine pleasure in these ways that believers can respond to God's presence, and their awareness of his divine word, and gratitude for his grace, goodness, kindness, mercy, forgiveness, and saving power...that is better than making a touchdown...and should be equally enjoyed and celebrated in a purely human and emotional way...but definitely as a response to a divine impulse not feigned or worked up by the one rejoicing in and by the Spirit."

There was a loud silence. He was taken aback by my answer and before he could recover, the crowd began to heckle him; "he's got you preacher; you let that little boy put you down; what have you got to say preacher"?

Clapping and cheering began, and got louder. The crowd began to disperse, slapping one another on the back and laughing at the preacher who had lost. Some came and shook my hand expressing their amazement at my ability to hang in there. Some said they were going to come hear me preach sometime. It was obvious that some were of a different denomination than the Church of Christ and were delighted to see Goliath fall. While some were not yet ready for "Pentecost," they knew they had heard a truth.

One thing is for sure, they did not know how my head was whirling and how my heart was beating out of my chest. I had been involved in real spiritual warfare far beyond anything I had ever experienced. The crowd had obviously forgotten about his first question concerning "tongues as the initial evidence" where I had lost, and lost big. But, I did not forget it. There was a little more to this encounter.

It seemed obvious that the Holy Ghost had completely discomfited the Church of Christ preacher and he was unable to regain his composure. In fact, he became visibly upset at the jeering of the crowd, and when he did try to talk, they prevented him by their jesting and poking fun at him.

## I'll believe it my way

He finally turned to me and said, "I have got to go, but come see me at my office sometime, and maybe I can help you get things straight. As he turned to walk away I said, "Well, you believe it your way and I'll believe it mine, and we'll both hope to make it to heaven." He agreed with a nod.

I did not realize that I was parroting something else that I had heard all my life and it even seemed to make sense. But, the Holy Ghost stopped me in my tracks and said, "Wait a minute! No you don't! You have no right to believe it your way, and that man believe it his way." He then brought the following scripture to my mind:

- *2PE 1:20 Knowing this first, that no prophecy of the scripture is of any private interpretation.*
  *For the prophecy came not in old time by the will of man: but holy men of God spake as they were moved by the Holy Ghost.*

## No private interpretation

The Holy Ghost continued, "You have no right to your private interpretation, and that man to his. You both had better believe it God's way. Don't ever say that again to anybody, because it is not truth."

I left that place with an intense desire to study to show myself approved unto God, a workman that needeth not to be ashamed, rightly dividing the word of truth (2TI 2:15).

# CHAPTER 10

# WHAT ABOUT THE INITIAL EVIDENCE?

Now, what about this matter of speaking in other tongues as the initial evidence of the in-filling of the Holy Ghost? Is it the initial evidence, or is it not?

The traditional Pentecostal belief has been that one can be saved without being baptized in the Holy Ghost. Also, before one can claim to be filled with the Holy Ghost they must first experience speaking in other tongues as the initial evidence that he has come into the believer. In all Pentecostal churches there are those who experience difficulty in being able to speak in other tongues. They are considered not to be filled, but only saved.

Pentecostals consider most Christians outside Pentecostal denominations to be saved, but not filled with the Holy Ghost because they have not spoken in other tongues. Even though some Non-Pentecostals claim to have received the Holy Ghost, this is rejected by the Pentecostals because they have not received the initial evidence of tongues. This has become one of the most drastic dividing lines in the body of Christ and is a major source of division. In fact this is the first level of division between traditional denominational classifications--Pentecostal and Non-Pentecostal, which simply means that one speaks in tongues and the other does not.

It seems reasonable that we should all take another look at the Bible to see what it actually does say. If speaking in other tongues is truly the initial evidence, then this must be scripturally defined. If not, then this should be equally established Biblically. It should not be necessary to read between the lines to prove such an important issue.

What if...just suppose...that in our search we discovered something so Biblically sound that it would be welcomed by both sides...and could serve to heal the breach that has existed for many years between churches, preachers, teachers, kinfolk and friends. All communities are split right down the middle over the issue of speaking in tongues; therefore it is incumbent on the entire church to find the truth, and the whole truth on the matter. This is a reasonable endeavor.

- *EPH 4:1 I therefore, the prisoner of the Lord, beseech you that ye walk worthy of the vocation wherewith ye are called,*
  *2 With all lowliness and meekness, with longsuffering, forbearing one another in love;*
  *3 Endeavouring to keep the unity of the Spirit in the bond of peace.*
  *4 There is one body, and one Spirit, even as ye are called in one hope of your calling;*
  *5 One Lord, one faith, one baptism,*
  *6 One God and Father of all, who is above all, and through all, and in you all.*

Give special notice to verse five..."*one faith.*" There is only one faith, therefore this means there is one truth, regarding the matter of speaking in tongues, and its function in the life of the church. The Holy Ghost will not teach two different things because there is only "*one faith.*" It behooves all of us to come to the knowledge of that one faith, which is "*the knowledge of the Son of God.*" Paul continued in the above passage:

*13 Till we all come in the unity of the faith, <u>and of the</u> <u>knowledge of the Son of God</u>, unto a perfect man, unto the measure of the stature of the fulness of Christ:*

The *cause and effect* has been that Pentecostalism today evolved out of the ranks of traditional Christianity. The new Pentecostals sought to scripturally justify their reasons for breaking away from the old church system and dogma, which they believed had rejected a newly re-discovered truth.

By the same token, traditional Non-Pentecostal Christianity sought to enforce separatism by their firm rejection of anything as radical as speaking in unknown tongues. In fact, not only tongues, but the manifestation of all other gifts of the Spirit were equally rejected or modified within traditional Christianity.

On the other hand, Pentecostalism opened the doors wide to embrace all gifts of the Spirit: healing, prophesy, interpretation of tongues, miracles, faith, casting out devils, etc., believing that the truth does not take anything away, but gives something better.

## An even higher truth

Without doubt, the Pentecostals had unearthed a buried truth, but in the process they added a doctrine which says that receiving the Holy Spirit does not occur when one is born again. The truth is that baptism with the Holy Ghost--meaning receiving the indwelling of the Holy Spirit--is an integral part of the new birth experience.

That is why I am writing this book. I believe the higher truth was overlooked that **"one does receive the Holy Spirit at the time of the new birth, and they have the full potential for manifestation of all the *'fruit'* of the Spirit, and all the *'gifts'* of the Spirit, including speaking in other tongues by the utterance of the Holy Ghost."** In fact, the gift of the Holy Spirit is a sign from God, himself, that he has redeemed a person, and the blood of Jesus has covered their sins.

## First things first--When does one receive the Holy Ghost?

Before we attempt to answer the question concerning tongues

as the initial evidence of the baptism in the Holy Ghost, let's take first things first. A more pressing question at this point is, "does one receive the Holy Ghost at the time of the new birth?" If so, is it incorrect to place the baptism in the Holy Ghost as a second or third experience?

Let's begin looking into this by making some observations on which we can probably agree.

**First:** The entire salvation experience is accomplished through the administration and operation of the Holy Spirit from the very beginning--reproof of sin, conviction, and drawing to Christ.

- *JOH 16:8 And when he is come, he will reprove the world of sin, and of righteousness, and of judgment:*

**Second:** It is the Holy Spirit that guides one into truth and into understanding the knowledge of Christ.

- *JOH 16:13 Howbeit when he, the Spirit of truth, is come, he will guide you into all truth: for he shall not speak of himself; but whatsoever he shall hear, that shall he speak: and he will shew you things to come.*
  *14 He shall glorify me: for he shall receive of mine, and shall shew it unto you.*

**Third:** Salvation is a process that comes about through acknowledging the truth about the Father, the Son, and the Holy Ghost.

- *2TI 2:25 In meekness instructing those that oppose themselves; if God peradventure will give them repentance to the <u>acknowledging of the truth</u>;*

**Fourth:** Believing is required, but believing alone is not enough to meet God's requirements for salvation. Believing must be accompanied by obedience.

- *1PE 1:2 Elect according to the foreknowledge of God the Father, through sanctification of the Spirit, <u>unto obedience</u> and sprinkling of the blood of Jesus Christ: Grace unto you, and peace, be multiplied.*

**Fifth:** Salvation, or the process resulting in being born again, is a multi-faceted experience that includes believing in God the Father and God the Son, confession, repentance, justification, regeneration, resurrection, baptism into Christ (not referring to water baptism), and baptism with the Holy Spirit.

- *ROM 10:10 For with the heart man believeth unto righteousness; and with the mouth confession is made unto salvation.*
  *11 For the scripture saith, Whosoever believeth on him shall not be ashamed.*
- *ACT 2:38 Then Peter said unto them, Repent, and be baptized every one of you in the name of Jesus Christ for the remission of sins, and ye shall receive the gift of the Holy Ghost.*
- *TIT 3:5 Not by works of righteousness which we have done, but according to his mercy he saved us, by the washing of regeneration, and renewing of the Holy Ghost;*
  *6 Which he shed on us abundantly through Jesus Christ our Saviour;*
  *7 That being justified by his grace, we should be made heirs according to the hope of eternal life.*

## Salvation is a process

It is unlikely that the process of salvation happens instantly, or all in one day. The Holy Spirit works on a person usually for periods differing in length, depending upon the individual and their circumstances. The time between the initial encounter with the Holy Spirit over conviction for sins and when one finally surrenders in repentance and confession can be very short, or very long. Some do not repent until on their death-bed. Others move quickly, all in one day, or night.

I have personally witnessed to individuals for as much as twenty-five years before the Holy Spirit was able to move them on into salvation. On the other hand I have seen people who were basically ignorant of the Bible and the plan of salvation, but they knew there was a God in Heaven, and a hell to shun. In one session of prayer, confession, believing and receiving, they were born again and filled with the Holy Spirit...and some even spoke in tongues immediately as the Spirit gave the utterance.

When the believers began speaking in other tongues on the day of Pentecost it was a total surprise to them. They had not been preconditioned in any way to expect the things that happened; neither could they have spontaneously initiated such a thing. It was a sovereign work of God.

## The temple of the Holy Ghost

This is something that must be believed, based strictly upon the word of God which says that, when a person is saved, their body becomes the temple of the Holy Ghost. Paul emphatically reminded the Christians at Corinth that the Holy Ghost dwelled within them:

- *1CO 3:16 Know ye not that ye are the temple of God, and that the Spirit of God dwelleth in you?*

He asked the same question again:

- *1CO 6:19 What? know ye not that your body is the temple of the Holy Ghost which is in you, which ye have of God, and ye are not your own?*
  *20 For ye are bought with a price: therefore glorify God in your body, and in your spirit, which are God's.*

What is the basis for stating that one's body is the temple, or dwelling place, of the Holy Ghost? This is given in verse 20: *"For (because) ye are bought with a price."* This means that everyone who has been purchased by the blood should know and believe that their body has become the temple of the Holy Ghost...no ifs, ands, or buts...or maybe so. There is no waiting period, or tarrying until.

Once a person studies this matter, it becomes quite obvious that the Holy Ghost is an automatic gift from the Father to his newly born sons and daughters. The following passage says that the manifestation of the Spirit is given to *"every man,"* which means everyone who is saved, or responds to the call to salvation.

- *1CO 12:7 But the manifestation of the Spirit is given to every man to profit withal.*

## The called

*"The called"* is an important phrase in the writings of the apostle Paul. By studying the context where the phrase is used by Paul, it becomes clear that God is <u>not</u> selective when he calls men to salvation, but the call goes out to everyone. Nevertheless, only those that respond are referred to as *"the called."* Peter said the promise of the Holy Spirit is given to those who respond to God's call to salvation.

- *ACT 2:39 For the promise is unto you, and to your children, and to all that are afar off, even as many as the Lord our God shall call.*

Paul taught that the Holy Spirit works together with the Father and the Son to help those who are *"the called."* The Spirit is said to help their infirmity (human weakness), and to make intercession to the Father for them when they do not know how to pray.

- *ROM 8:26 Likewise the Spirit also helpeth our infirmities: for we know not what we should pray for as we ought: but the Spirit itself maketh intercession for us with groanings which cannot be uttered.*
  *27 And he that searcheth the hearts knoweth what is the mind of the Spirit, because he maketh intercession for the saints according to the will of God.*
  *28 And we know that all things work together for good to them that love God, to them **who are the called** according to his purpose.*

## All things work together

Verse 28 has usually been explained as meaning that when disappointments, difficulties, reversals, and hardships come, they will eventually work out to our good. But if we stick strictly to the context, we can easily see that *"all things"* was speaking specifically of actions of the Father, the Son and the Holy Spirit who are working together on behalf of the believer *"for good to them that love God... who are the called."*

Just prior to this statement Paul had spoken of the Spirit praying for us...and said *"he that searches the heart,"* meaning God the Father, knows what the mind of the Spirit is. Jesus is at the right hand of the Father also making intercession for us. Therefore, the cooperative divine intercession by the Father, the Son, and the Holy Spirit, must have been meant as the *"all things"* (all three) that are working together for our good. Paul's summary of what he has just said is immediately apparent:

- *ROM 8:31 What shall we then say to these things? **If God be for us, who can be against us?***

## The Holy Spirit--Our Intercessor

The Holy Spirit is in the middle of this process on our behalf--as our intercessor--and He does not ask amiss, but makes intercession for the saints *"according to the will of God."*

This intercessory work is for those who have been baptized into Christ at salvation, and enjoy a special benefit associated with speaking in other tongues. Two times in this passage Paul uses terms that lets us know he considered that *all who are saved* are beneficiaries of the intercession of the Spirit. He said, *"he maketh intercession for the saints,"* and then, *"to them who are the called."*

As we go farther into the writings of Paul it will become evident that if a person is saved, they do have the Holy Ghost dwelling within them. This letter to the Romans was not addressed to the "Spirit Baptized," but to the "called," and to the "saints."

- *ROM 1:6 Among whom are ye also the called of Jesus Christ:*
  *7 To all that be in Rome, beloved of God, called to be saints: Grace to you and peace from God our Father, and the Lord Jesus Christ.*

## Ye "shall" receive

On the day of Pentecost when Peter gave the invitation to receive Christ, it was a foregone conclusion that they would receive the gift of the Holy Ghost...not maybe, but *"shall."*

- *ACT 2:38 Then Peter said unto them, Repent, and be baptized every one of you in the name of Jesus Christ for the remission of sins, and ye **shall** receive the gift of the Holy Ghost.*
  *39 For the promise is unto you, and to your children, and to all that are afar off, even as many as the Lord our God shall call.*

To those whose sins have been remitted the statement is made, *"and ye shall receive the gift of the Holy Ghost."* This is a *"promise"* from God *"unto you, and to your children, and to all that are afar off, even as many as the Lord our God shall call."* This includes all who have responded in obedience to the call to repentance--everyone who is saved.

## "Hath" given

Soon after the day of Pentecost when the council of Jerusalem was demanding that they not speak any more in the name of Jesus, Peter made the following statement:

- *ACT 5:32 And we are his witnesses of these things; and so is also the Holy Ghost, <u>whom God hath given to them that obey him</u>.*

Peter did not say that God *"will give,"* but *"hath given."* There was no doubt in Peter's mind that the Holy Ghost was given to everyone without a moments delay upon their repentance and obedience to the call of God. Once they had received the remission of sin, they received the gift of the Holy Ghost. This is stated quite clearly.

- *EPH 1:13 In whom ye also trusted, after that ye heard the word of truth, the gospel of your salvation: in whom* *also **after that ye believed**, ye were **sealed** with that holy Spirit of promise,*

*14 Which is the earnest of our inheritance until the redemption of the purchased possession, unto the praise of his glory.*

## The moment of receiving – *"After that ye believed"*

No waiting period, or time lapse is indicated here: *"after that ye believed, ye were sealed with that holy Spirit of promise."* Not after you are saved, or after you speak in tongues, or as a second or third work of grace after being saved.

Paul said *"after that ye believed."* **Believing** is the first positive step which triggers the outpouring of God's promises. God's salvation promise certainly involves the Holy Spirit as the concluding and confirming seal as the proof of salvation. This is why Paul said, *"ye were sealed with that Holy Spirit of promise"* (EPH 1:23 above). Believing in God's only begotten Son is absolutely required before one can obtain everlasting life.

- *JOH 3:16 For God so loved the world, that he gave his only begotten Son, **that whosoever believeth in him should not perish, but have everlasting life.***

The gift of the Holy Ghost is God's response to repentance which occurs **because one believes in Jesus.**

Peter said this on the day of Pentecost:

ACT 2:38 Then Peter said unto them, **Repent**, and be baptized every one of you in the name of Jesus Christ for the remission of sins, and ye **shall** receive the gift of the Holy Ghost.

Peter also stated that the Holy Ghost was given to Cornelius and his household because they *"believed on the Lord Jesus Christ":*

- *ACT 11:17 Forasmuch then as God gave them the like gift as he did unto us, who **believed** on the Lord Jesus Christ; what was I, that I could withstand God?*

Jesus confirmed this by the following statement:

- *JOH 7:39 But this spake he of the Spirit, **which they that believe on him should receive**:*

Receiving the Holy Spirit cannot be separated from the new birth. It is not a second work or a separate work of grace, but is given at the time of the new birth as a seal of confirmation that one has been born again.

## Immediately after Believing

These scriptures confirm that one is sealed with the Holy Spirit as the fulfillment of God's promise to those who believe in Jesus. Let me say it again. The gift of the Holy Spirit is God's response to those who believe..."after" they believe. Believing in the Son is the first step. The Holy Spirit is given because of this believing.

One should accept this truth by faith and desire and expect the manifestations of spiritual gifts and fruit without delay. Speaking in other tongues was a spectacular miracle because the Holy Ghost was speaking through them in a language which was not their own, and which the speaker did not understand, but the language was a valid foreign language which could be understood if a person familiar with the language were there to hear it. All languages spoken by the Holy Ghost has a meaning somewhere.

- *1CO 14:10 (NIV) Undoubtedly there are all sorts of languages in the world, yet **none of them is without meaning.***

# CHAPTER 11

# BAPTIZED, FILLED, FELL UPON, POURED OUT, RECEIVED, FALLEN, GIVEN, SHED ABROAD

Various Biblical terms are used to describe when the Holy Ghost manifests his gifts through believers. Some of the various terms are listed in the title of this chapter. When an outpouring of the Holy Spirit was given it was described in various ways, such as *"they were all 'filled' with the Holy Ghost"* (Acts 2:4).

When Peter went to Cornelius' house and taught them about Jesus, the Holy Ghost *"fell"* on them:

- *ACT 10:44 While Peter yet spake these words, the Holy Ghost fell on all them which heard the word.*
  *45 And they of the circumcision which believed were astonished, as many as came with Peter, because that on the Gentiles also was poured out the gift of the Holy Ghost.*

*46 For they heard them speak with tongues, and magnify God.*

The Jews which came with Peter were astonished *"because that on the Gentiles was 'poured out' the gift of the Holy Ghost."* It sounds like what happens when a bucket of water is poured upon someone. They are baptized, or engulfed by the Holy Ghost. They are drenched through-and-through; filled; saturated; soaked. *"Fell"* and *"poured out"* indicates that the Holy Ghost comes from above. This is because Jesus is the Baptizer.

Taking all scripture, especially statements made by Jesus Christ, it appears like giving a person a drink of water, not with a cup of water but a well of water. And even more, just imagine placing that well inside of them so they would never thirst again...since that well would flow within them continually for the rest of their life.

Jesus talked with the woman of Samaria at Jacob's well about this very thing. Asking for a drink of water was a means of opening the truth about spiritual water.

- *JOH 4:13 Jesus answered and said unto her, Whosoever drinketh of this water shall thirst again:*
  *But whosoever drinketh of the water that I shall give him shall never thirst; but the water that I shall give him shall be in him a well of water __springing up into everlasting life__.*

## Springing up into everlasting life

One should never diminish the importance of being filled with the Holy Spirit. Especially, after all Jesus said about the expediency of his Father sending the Spirit to dwell within those who believe in him. Jesus and other writers described the Holy Spirit as a comforter, guide, teacher, revealer of truth, reprover, conscience activator, giver of power, anointer, source of wisdom and knowledge, faith, discernment, intercessor, communicator with God, advocate, and much more.

The entire salvation process begins with the ministry of the

Spirit and leads to eternal life, *"springing up into everlasting life."* Jesus told the woman at the well the following:

- *JOH 4:23 But the hour cometh, and now is, when the true worshippers __shall__ worship the Father in spirit and in truth: <u>for the Father seeketh such to worship him.</u>*
  *24 God is a Spirit: and they that worship him __must__ worship him in spirit and in truth.*

On another occasion Jesus even went beyond the analogy of a *well* of water, and likened the outpouring of the Spirit to a *river* of water.

- *JOH 7:37 In the last day, that great day of the feast, Jesus stood and cried, saying, If any man thirst, let him come unto me, and drink.*
  *38 He that believeth on me, as the scripture hath said, out of his belly shall flow __rivers of living water.__*
  *39 (But this spake he of the Spirit, which they that believe on him should receive: for the Holy Ghost was not yet given; because that <u>Jesus was not yet glorified.</u>)*

## Glorified

The great outpouring of the Holy Spirit came on the day of Pentecost which occurred after Jesus was *"glorified,"* meaning after he was raised from the dead and had ascended to the Father. Jesus explained that *"glorified"* meant that he would again be with the Father.

- *JOH 17:5 And now, O Father, glorify thou me with thine own self with the glory which I had with thee before the world was.*

Jesus' glorification brought us into the era of the Holy Spirit, the living water Jesus gives to everyone who believes in him. Ezekiel spoke of a time when a *"new Spirit"* would be given to dwell within *"new hearts."*

- *EZE 36:26 A new heart also will I give you, and a new spirit will I put within you: and I will take away the stony*

*heart out of your flesh, and I will give you an heart of*
*flesh.*
*27 And I will put my spirit within you, and cause you*
*to walk in my statutes, and ye shall keep my judgments,*
*and do them.*

It can be said without contradiction, God desires that every believer might worship him in the power and anointing of the Holy Spirit (JOH 4:24 above). Jesus told the woman at the well, *"for the Father seeketh such to worship him."*

It is not unusual for a person who receives the Holy Spirit at the time of their conversion, or new birth, to experience a baptismal outpouring, an overflowing well of spiritual water that springs forth with praises like an artesian fountain that spontaneously flows. The Holy Spirit falls upon them as Jesus, the Baptizer from heaven, completely submerges them, soaking their innermost being with himself through the power of the Spirit, while their body becomes the temple of the Holy Ghost.

## Not yet fallen at Samaria

When Philip preach at Samaria many believed the word of God and rejoiced in the miracles that they saw and experienced.

- *ACT 8:5 Then Philip went down to the city of Samaria,*
  *and preached Christ unto them.*
  *6 And the people with one accord gave heed unto those*
  *things which Philip spake, hearing and seeing the*
  *miracles which he did.*
  *7 For unclean spirits, crying with loud voice, came out*
  *of many that were possessed with them: and many taken*
  *with palsies, and that were lame, were healed.*
  *8 And there was great joy in that city.*

There was definitely a good reception of the gospel of Jesus Christ…so much that they were baptized in water.

- *ACT 8:12 But when they believed Philip preaching the*
  *things concerning the kingdom of God, and the name*

*of Jesus Christ, they were baptized, both men and women.*

But, what about this situation in Samaria where it is said regarding the Holy Ghost, *"For as yet he was fallen upon none of them?"* **Pentecostals have used this to say they were saved, but had not yet been given the Holy Ghost**. If this is true, then it can be solidly argued that the baptism in the Holy Ghost is a second, or subsequent experience. But, let's not jump to conclusions just yet.

Only after some apostles came from Jerusalem and laid their hands on the Samaritans did the Holy Ghost fall upon them.

- *ACT 8:14 Now when the apostles which were at Jerusalem heard that Samaria had received the word of God, they sent unto them Peter and John:*
  *15 Who, when they were come down, prayed for them, that they might receive the Holy Ghost:*
  *16 (For as yet he was fallen upon none of them: only they were baptized in the name of the Lord Jesus.)*
  *17 Then laid they their hands on them, and they received the Holy Ghost.*

During all this revival fervor the Holy Ghost had not *"fallen"* on one single person. In spite of all that had happened--the miracles, devils cast out, baptism in water--we do not actually know how many of them were truly born again at that point. Getting excited over seeing miracles take place does not guarantee that one is born again. This might sound like a radical statement, but being delivered from unclean spirits does not guarantee that one has been born again. If this is all that happens, it just means that the old sinner has been delivered from the possession of evil spirits which had taken up their abode in the individual.

If deliverance from evil spirits is not soon followed by a new occupancy the subsequent condition of the person delivered can be worse. Cleaning out the devils is only part of what must happen to one who has been so possessed. Jesus himself taught that an empty house which remains unoccupied--even if it has been swept and shined--is still empty and open prey for unclean spirits to return. The indwelling of the Holy Spirit should replace that of evil spirits and is God's plan for new occupancy. Keep in mind that the following is Jesus speaking:

- *MAT 12:43 When the unclean spirit is gone out of a man, he walketh through dry places, seeking rest, and findeth none.*
  *44 Then he saith, I will return into my house from whence I came out; and when he is come, he findeth it empty, swept, and garnished.*
  *45 Then goeth he, and taketh with himself seven other spirits more wicked than himself, and they enter in and dwell there: and the last state of that man is worse than the first.*

Unusual circumstances existed at Samaria. Witchcraft and sorcery were deeply entrenched. A sorcerer named Simon had bewitched them for years and Satan had a powerful stronghold there. Remember that it was here Jesus had talked to the woman at the well. She had been married to five different men and was living with the sixth to which she was not married. The moral climate must have been quite low.

The New Bible Dictionary says, (Page 1061) **"Samaria itself was long considered by the prophets a center of idolatry (Is. 8:4; 9:9; Je. 23:13; Ezk. 23:4; Ho. 7:1; Mi. 1:6)."**

There was a major problem with Simon, the sorcerer.

- *ACT 8:9 But there was a certain man, called Simon, which beforetime in the same city used sorcery, and bewitched the people of Samaria, giving out that himself was some great one:*
  *10 To whom they all gave heed, from the least to the greatest, saying, This man is the great power of God.*
  *11 And to him they had regard, because that of long time he had bewitched them with sorceries.*

It was on these ears that the gospel was falling, and it was this kind of people out of which evil spirits were cast. They were baptized in water, but we have no guarantee that they had been converted. Even today many who are baptized go down a dry sinner and come up a wet sinner. Jesus had told Nicodemus:

- *JOH 3:3 ...Verily, verily, I say unto thee, Except a man be born again, he cannot see the kingdom of God.*

If this were the case in Samaria, then this would explain why the Holy Ghost had not yet fallen upon any of them.

Let's now look more specifically at Simon the sorcerer.

- *ACT 8:13 Then Simon himself believed also: and when he was baptized, he continued with Philip, and wondered, beholding the miracles and signs which were done.*

Just because Simon believed what he saw, and was even baptized in water does not mean that he was born again. James warned against believing, while failing to bring forth the fruit (*works*) of conversion as evidence of the new birth.

- *JAM 2:19 Thou believest that there is one God; thou doest well: the devils also believe, and tremble. 20 But wilt thou know, O vain man, that faith without works is dead?*

That which followed indicates that Simon was not truly converted. He saw his profession going down the drain and quickly attempted to seize the opportunity to continue his religious dominance over the people...if he could duplicate what these Christians were doing.

- *ACT 8:18 And when Simon saw that through laying on of the apostles' hands the Holy Ghost was given, he offered them money, 19 Saying, Give me also this power, that on whomsoever I lay hands, he may receive the Holy Ghost. 20 But Peter said unto him, Thy money perish with thee, because thou hast thought that the gift of God may be purchased with money.*

*21 Thou hast neither part nor lot in this matter: for thy heart is not right in the sight of God.*

*22 Repent therefore of this thy wickedness, and pray God, if perhaps the thought of thine heart may be forgiven thee.*

*23 For I perceive that thou art in the gall of bitterness, and in the bond of iniquity.*

## Thy heart is not right

A plausible key to the delay in the whole Samaritan situation can be found in verse 21: *"Thy heart is not right in the sight of God."* This could well apply to all people in Samaria who were being drawn to the miraculous ministry manifested through Philip, and yet the Holy Ghost did not fall on the people until God searched their hearts and found them justified in his sight.

These extenuating circumstances could well be the reason that the Holy Ghost had fallen upon none of them. Simon was actually lagging behind the rest of the people in his spiritual progress. In summary, the text says that Simon believed and was baptized, and yet his heart was not right in the sight of God. Jesus, who is the baptizer, knew all hidden factors, and could well have withheld his stamp of approval (the Holy Ghost) until he could see the fruit of repentance meeting his requirements as he judged their hearts.

John the Baptist who announced Jesus as the Baptizer with the Holy Ghost made this appropriate statement:

- *MAT 3:8 Bring forth therefore fruits meet for repentance:*

Just three verses later John said the following:

*11 I indeed baptize you with water unto repentance: but he that cometh after me is mightier than I, whose shoes I am not worthy to bear: he shall baptize you with the Holy Ghost, and with fire:*

This was a refining, cleansing, and purging fire that accompanies the ministry of Christ when he baptizes with the Holy Ghost.

> *12 Whose fan is in his hand, and he will throughly purge*
> *his floor, and gather his wheat into the garner; but he*
> *will burn up the chaff with unquenchable fire.*

In those days after wheat was harvested it was placed on a threshing floor where the grain was separated from the chaff which was the husk around the grain. Using large scoops the wheat and chaff were thrown into the air while the wind was blowing briskly. The wind plus waving huge fans were used to blow the chaff away from the heavier grain, and the chaff was then burned to dispose of it.

Here again we see a close correlation between repentance and conversion and the baptism with the Holy Ghost. Jesus, who judges the heart knows when *"fruit meet for repentance"* has been brought forth (meaning fruit sufficient for repentance). God alone can judge when his requirements for repentance have been met. This had not happened with Simon, and probably not with his religious followers whom he had deceived for so many years. We can rest assured that the Holy Ghost fell upon them when the time was right...when God judged them acceptable for his stamp of approval...and not as a second work of grace--subsequent to the new birth-- but as an indispensable, inseparable part of their conversion experience.

After the true condition of Simon's heart had been revealed he appealed to the apostles to pray for him:

- *ACT 8:24 Then answered Simon, and said, Pray ye to the Lord for me, that none of these things which ye have spoken come upon me*

From this repentance we can hope that, even though it is not related in the text, Simon the Sorcerer's full conversion was accompanied by the same ministry that had effectively laid hands on the others, and he too was baptized in the Holy Spirit, but at best we do not know. I am inclined to not sell God's grace short.

## Another consideration

In the above explanation I have considered the possibility that the process of redemption was at work in the Samaritans, and Christ knew when to confirm their conversion with the gift of the Holy Ghost. But, now let's look at this from another Biblical perspective. I am not attempting to draw a hard, fast line, but to honestly attempt to rightly divide the word of God on the matter of being baptized in the Holy Ghost…especially when the actual baptism occurs.

Let's assume that they were truly born again and had been given the Holy Ghost at the time of their conversion, but for some reason, the Holy Ghost had not yet manifested any of his gifts through them…especially, speaking in tongues.

## Fallen

The question is, "why, then, had the Holy Ghost not fallen upon any of them?" It will help if we look more closely into the term *"fallen."* Along with this we will consider other related terms such as *filled, poured out, fell, given, baptized, etc.* In some instances these terms apply to the original receiving of the Holy Ghost, and they sometimes apply to subsequent times when special verbal and spiritual manifestations of gifts of the Spirit are experienced by those who had been previously baptized.

The point I am making is that one can be "filled" with the Holy Ghost after having once received him. I have given many scriptures which state that God gives the Holy Ghost to everyone who is truly born again…when they are born again. With this in mind let's give additional consideration to why the Holy Ghost had not fallen on the people at Samaria.

I propose that some were truly born again, while others were not, but they were all being brought in by the same gospel net. If they were born again they had been given the Holy Ghost, but as yet, he had *"fallen upon none of them."* If they were not yet born again, naturally there had been no manifestation of the Spirit because they were not yet baptized. But when the apostles came from Jerusalem they had the ministry and power of God to break through the barriers that were holding back the full falling of the Holy Ghost.

I further propose that this is what is needed throughout Christianity today. There are millions of people upon whom the Holy Ghost has not *"fallen"* because of doctrinal entanglements which have prevented a full revelation of the gifts of the Spirit in their lives.

In the case of Samaria, and in all similar cases, for those who were newly born again babes in Christ, it is true that the Holy Ghost is given to all who are saved. It must be accepted that they received the gift of the Holy Ghost, but the manifestations of the Spirit were not forthcoming. It is not out of the question to think that, due to their occult circumstances, and perhaps even waiting to see what their revered spiritual leader, Simon the Sorcerer's reaction might be, they held back and quenched the Spirit.

Based on the many scriptures I have given, there can be no Biblical reason to believe they had not been given the Holy Spirit if they were truly born again. It does seem reasonable to speculate on how they had been given the Holy Ghost as a gift of the Father, but had not experienced the overwhelming filling, or falling, or pouring out, which is accompanied with manifestations of the spoken or verbal gifts. This is what happened when the apostles came from Jerusalem. Philip knew that something was incomplete, and this is expressed by the statement, *"only they were baptized in the name of the Lord Jesus."* Let's review the passage:

- *ACT 8:14 Now when the apostles which were at Jerusalem heard that Samaria had received the word of God, they sent unto them Peter and John:*
  *15 Who, when they were come down, prayed for them, that they might <u>receive</u> the Holy Ghost:*
  *16 (For as yet he was <u>fallen</u> upon none of them: only they were baptized in the name of the Lord Jesus.)*
  *17 Then laid they their hands on them, and <u>they received</u> the Holy Ghost.*

## Received

One might protest, they received after hands were laid upon them. Let's consider this word "receive." It is possible that the Holy Ghost had been given to the Samaritans, but they had not received him immediately. This appears to be a case of "delayed receiving."

The truth is, God has given many the Holy Ghost in this present day, but they have not "received" him in the sense they have not understood, or accepted him. An example of this could be as follows:

A person could see that their widowed mother is becoming frail, and in need of someone to help her with the housework, lawn care, grocery buying, and other daily tasks. She is in need of companionship, friendship, protection and comfort. To help the mother in her infirmities the concerned child arranges for someone to provide this needed assistance and sends them to their mother.

There could be a variety of responses on the part of the mother. She could be hard of hearing and fail to hear the knock on the door, or the doorbell. The one sent as a companion could remain on the front porch for a long time waiting to be received. Or, the mother could answer the door and refuse to let them come in. Or, she could receive them into the house but fail to communicate with them, sitting them in a corner and having no more to do with them. She could see no need for their help and fail to take advantage of the benefits available to her. Or, she could even resent their help.

The truth is, the helper (comforter) has been given to her, but she has not "received" them. In this sense the question is quite appropriate, *"have ye **received** the Holy Ghost since ye believed?"* It is not a matter of whether the Holy Ghost has been *given*, but has he been *received*...or accepted?

Does not a similar circumstance exist all around us today? There are many saved people who have because of peer pressure suppressed or denied the manifestations of the Holy Spirit. Is not the church world today full of Christians who have been born again and who have been given the Holy Ghost, and yet he has not *"fallen"* upon them?

Why did ministers come from Jerusalem? These ministers had become quite experienced in the operation of the gifts of the Spirit. This was a spiritual battle with the devil and a host of evil spirits that had long controlled the people of Samaria. The apostles had the ministry and power to lead the people to victory. The church today needs strong ministers who can help Christians who are bound by tradition to break loose from those bonds and experience the *falling, filling,* and *outpouring* of the Spirit which they have already been given, but who lies dormant within them.

According to Greek scholars *receiving* has two important Biblical applications. One means to *receive in the mind.* The other has to do with *receiving in the heart.* One must go beyond receiving factual information about the Holy Spirit in their mind, and receive him into their heart. This means accepting him and his indwelling presence by faith...and accepting the *"sign"* as a Biblical fact.

- *1CO 14:22 Wherefore tongues are for a sign ...*
- *1CO 12:7 But the manifestation of the Spirit is given to every man to profit withal.*

One must not be afraid to desire the fullness of spiritual gifts which accompany the indwelling of the Holy Spirit.

- *1CO 12:1 Now concerning spiritual gifts, brethren, I would not have you ignorant.*
- *1CO 14:1 Follow after charity, and desire spiritual gifts ...*

## Why no involuntary falling

There is one final question that must be discussed. Why did the falling, receiving, pouring out, etc., of the Holy Spirit on the day of Pentecost occur without any hindrance or premeditation on the part of those who were baptized? Why was it an involuntary manifestation, and yet at Samaria the Holy Ghost did not immediately fall on everyone?

The answer lies in the fact that in all other recorded situations in the New Testament where the Holy Ghost baptism fell with spontaneous manifestations, the spiritual circumstances were entirely different. In these situations their hearts were right before God.

At Cornelius' house God had seen the heart of Cornelius who was devout before God and had influenced his whole household accordingly.

- *ACT 10:1 There was a certain man in Caesarea called Cornelius, a centurion of the band called the Italian band,*
  *2 A devout man, and one that feared God with all his house, which gave much alms to the people, and prayed to God alway.*

The pagan and idolatrous witchcraft that saturated the hearts in Samaria was not present in Cornelius' house.

In Ephesus, the twelve disciples had been baptized by John the Baptist, and were following in the teaching of his ministry to prepare for the Messiah, even though they were very limited in knowledge and truth. They were believers. Their heart was not contaminated with evil that must be overcome before their heart could be considered right in the sight of God. They were ready and received quickly.

- *ACT 19:1 And it came to pass, that, while Apollos was at Corinth, Paul having passed through the upper coasts came to Ephesus: and finding certain disciples,*
  *2. He said unto them, Have ye received the Holy Ghost since ye believed? And they said unto him, We have not so much as heard whether there be any Holy Ghost.*
  *6 ...And when Paul had laid his hands upon them, the Holy Ghost came on them; and they spake with tongues, and prophesied.*
  On the day of Pentecost, the same was true regarding those who waited patiently according to the command of Jesus, and were marvelously and miraculously baptized in the Holy Ghost and began to speak with other tongues as the Spirit gave them utterance.
- *ACT 1:14 These all continued with one accord in prayer and supplication, with the women, and Mary the mother of Jesus, and with his brethren.*
  *15 And in those days Peter stood up in the midst of the disciples, and said, (the number of names together were about an hundred and twenty,)*

*2:1 ... And when the day of Pentecost was fully come, they were all with one accord in one place.*

*2 And suddenly there came a sound from heaven as of a rushing mighty wind, and it filled all the house where they were sitting.*

*3 And there appeared unto them cloven tongues like as of fire, and it sat upon each of them.*

*4 And they were all filled with the Holy Ghost, and began to speak with other tongues, as the Spirit gave them utterance.*

Today, I believe there are millions of people who believe in Christ, but they are so entangled in doctrines and traditions of men that render their hearts not right in the sight of God. They have been under ministries and church dogmas which have filled them with disbelief regarding the truth about the Holy Spirit. They are so confused that they do not know what to believe. They are also under such peer pressure that they have no liberty to believe the truth, even when they read it for themselves in their own Bible. They are so prejudiced against anything that sounds like Pentecostalism that they even ignore all that pertains to that subject, and discredit anyone who might believe differently from them, their preacher, their church, and their denomination. They are entangled much like the people in Samaria.

With such people, even though many are saved, short of a great deliverance it is quite unlikely that they would ever experience the Holy Ghost *"falling"* upon them, just like happened in the New Testament. Regardless of what Jesus said on the subject, they may go to their grave having missed the reality of one of the greatest gifts and blessings which Jesus said so much about. To Jesus it was extremely urgent and expedient for them to receive, and yet because of so many things that are contrary to the truth in their heart, the Holy Spirit which was given to them when they were born again may never be able to demonstrate to them his fullness.

Hopefully they are not in the same situation as Simon the Sorcerer where his heart was not right toward God. Anyone who feels this shoe fits them must pray similar to how Simon prayed:

- *ACT 8:24 Then answered Simon, and said, Pray ye to the Lord for me, that none of these things which ye have spoken come upon me.*

Believers must pray for these millions that they will be able to come in contact with ministries much like the early apostles who came from Jerusalem, who will have the power, anointing, and spiritual authority to ferret out the misinformation that fills their hearts, thus keeping them not right in the sight of God.

It is no coincidence that just today, as I am writing on this book, my wife showed me a card which she received almost four years ago from a dear, dear friend in the Lord. I have copied the following from that card:

> "Thank you so much … especially, Margaret, about your helping me learn about God's Spirit. I still have those teachings on the difference between the gift of tongues as used in the service, and the devotional tongues. As you know, that experience of the baptism changed my life, and I'll always be thankful for your experience and your willingness to teach me about the deeper things of God.
>
> "Thank you for your many words of encouragement over the past few years. They have meant so much.
>
> "Love,
> "Carmen"

Carmen is a University Professor and a highly degreed Psychological Counselor. Her background was far removed from anything that had to do with being filled with the Holy Spirit. Even though she was heavily involved in church activities, and was a Pianist, Organist, and Choir Director of the highest level of Classical and refined performance, she had no knowledge of the Biblical truths regarding the indwelling of the Holy Spirit and the manifestation of the gifts of the Spirit as outlined in the Bible. Today she carries on her varied professional pursuits, and deeply enjoys the indwelling of the Holy Spirit.

# CHAPTER 12

# IT SHALL COME TO PASS IN THE LAST DAYS

- *ACT 2:17 And it shall come to pass in the last days, saith God, I will pour out of my Spirit upon all flesh:*

By far a majority of Christians today are in churches, and under the teaching of ministers who forbid speaking in tongues. This is in spite of the admonition in the Bible which says, *"forbid not to speak in tongues"* (1CO 14:39). The pastor of the largest church in my city, while preaching before his congregation of several thousand, said in a televised message, "we do not speak in tongues in this church." One of his reasons for saying that was because many in his church were already speaking in tongues, and he was trying to head it off. It is most likely that anyone under his ministry who is born again and given the Holy Ghost in response to their faith in Christ will not experience the *falling,* or *filling* of the Holy Ghost, so long as they are under the influence or bondage of such a ministry. Someone must come along who can tell them the truth about the baptism in the Holy Ghost which they have been given--but not yet accepted.

As Christ perfects his church prior to his second coming, things are going to change drastically. Such religious leaders are not going to be able to hold people in bondage for long because there is a gigantic groundswell of the Holy Ghost with speaking in other tongues taking place right now.

## Confirming news articles

The following was copied from a news release by BBC News in Great Britain;

### Pentecostal Church 'sees growth'

WEDNESDAY, 9, JANUARY 2008

**Manchester University's Dr David Voas, who studied English Church Census data, said Pentecostals were "the fastest growing group within Christianity."**

**He predicted they were third largest, behind Catholics and Anglicans.**

**The forecasts were based on figures from the English Church Census, conducted by the independent charity Christian Research and sponsored by the Economic and Social Research Council.**

**Jonathan Kerry, coordinating secretary for worship and learning for the Methodist Church in Great Britain, said: "Methodism was born out of revival movements in the 18th Century and further renewal in the 19th.**

**"However, like many historic denominations, the Methodist Church now struggles to respond to new movements of God's spirit without feeling that it is betraying the past."**

http://samandsaira.blogspot.com/2008/01/pentecostal-church-sees-growth-co-bbc.html

++++++++

# A Pentecostal Growth Explosion – Over A-Fourth of Christendom

May 24, 2012

The Pentecostal movement itself continues to grow at a rapid rate. It is arguably the fastest-growing component of Christendom today. Johnson, Director of the Center for the Study of Global Christianity (located at Gordon-Conwell Theological Seminary) gave a new report on the status of Spirit-Empowered churches. The Center has recently adopted the term "Renewalists" to represent the three key sectors of this movement, including Classical Pentecostals, Mainline Denominational Charismatics and Independent Charismatics. At present, it is estimated that these groups combined make up 584 million worldwide, or 26 percent of all Christians.

http://www.patheos.com/blogs/robertcrosby/2012/05/a-pentecostal-growth-explosion-over-a-fourth-of-christendom/

+++++++++

## A Quick Question

### Is Pentecostalism Christianity's next reformation?

**The quick answer:** It is, if one looks globally at the entire Christian world.

**The longer answer:** Christianity's "next wave" may come in Pentecostal form. With an estimated 500 million followers, Pentecostalism now comprises the second largest communion of Christians in the world, more than Protestants and Anglicans combined. With its continued growth and its unique understanding of Christian experience, Pentecostalism promises to reshape Christianity in the 21st century. http://hirr.hartsem.edu/research/quick_question32.html

Year: 2011 (Used by permission of Hartford Institute for Religious Research, Hartford Seminary )

++++++++

The following is an excerpt from the magazine
*"Christianity Today" 24 years ago:*

**World Growth at 19 Million a Year**
November 16, 1998

**About 25 percent of the world's Christians are Pentecostal or charismatic, historian Vinson Synan, dean of the Regent University School of Divinity in Virginia Beach, VA, told the triennial Pentecostal World Conference (PWC) in Seoul in September. An estimated 450 million are charismatic or Pentecostal.**

**"The continuing explosive growth of Pentecostalism indicates that the renewal will continue with increasing strength into the next millennium," Synan declared. "Not only is growth occurring in eye-catching megachurches, but in tens of thousands of small local churches that are planted each year in big cities and remote villages."**

http://www.ctlibrary.com/ct/1998/november16/8td28a.html
Used by permission of Christianity Today, Carol Stream, IL 60188

## Opening the gift

The Holy Spirit himself was called a *"Gift"* from God.

- *ACT 2:38 Then Peter said unto them, Repent, and be baptized every one of you in the name of Jesus Christ for the remission of sins, and ye shall receive the **gift** of the Holy Ghost.*
- *ACT 11:17 Forasmuch then as God gave them the like **gift** as he did unto us, who believed on the Lord Jesus Christ; what was I, that I could withstand God?*

It is like receiving a large Christmas gift box which contains many other gifts that must be opened to see everything that is included within the package. When God sent the Holy Spirit to the church to dwell within believers he came with his bags packed with fruits and gifts – the fruit of the Spirit and the gifts of the Spirit.

People are discovering what they received through the Holy Ghost when they were born again and are developing an intense desire to walk in the fullness of his power and manifestations...of the *fruit* and of the *gifts* of the Spirit. Tradition could not hold the Samaritans back for long, especially when the right kind of anointed ministry came along. This is why Paul said:

- *1CO 2:4 And my speech and my preaching was not with enticing words of man's wisdom, but in <u>demonstration of the Spirit</u> and of power:*
  *5 That your faith should not stand in the wisdom of men, but in the power of God.*

The entire church needs to be exposed to the demonstration of the Spirit and of his power. Paul's heart ached for those to whom he ministered that they might experience the fullness of the Holy Spirit.

- *EPH 3:14 For this cause I bow my knees unto the Father of our Lord Jesus Christ,*
  *15 Of whom the whole family in heaven and earth is named,*
  *16 That he would grant you, according to the riches of his glory, to be strengthened with might **by his Spirit in the inner man;***
  *17 **That Christ may dwell in your hearts** by faith; that ye, being rooted and grounded in love,*
  *18 May be able to comprehend with all saints what is the breadth, and length, and depth, and height;*
  *19 And to know the love of Christ, which passeth knowledge, that ye might be filled with all the fulness of God.*

Notice the correlation Paul draws between having the *"Spirit in the inner man"* and *"Christ dwelling in your hearts."* Biblically, these two are inseparable...one goes with the other. It makes no difference in which order one tries to place them. If you get Jesus, you get the Holy Spirit. If you get the Holy Spirit, you get Jesus. This is an integral part of the salvation process.

Also, if you get the Holy Spirit, you get the gifts. How you demonstrate them depends on you to a great extent. You can quench their manifestation. You can forbid speaking in tongues, not only for yourself, but for others...and you may exert a strong influence on others that will silence the Holy Spirit for them as well as you. But, this does not negate what the word of God has to say about the Holy Ghost's ministries, gifts, and fruits. They are present and available regardless of whether or not one acknowledges them.

Paul encouraged Timothy against being intimidated by fear, thus allowing the gift of the Holy Ghost to lie dormant within him.

- *2TI 1:6 Wherefore I put thee in remembrance that thou stir up the gift of God, which is in thee by the putting on of my hands.*
  *7 For God hath not given us the spirit of fear; but of power, and of love, and of a sound mind.*

There is little doubt that Paul was speaking about the Holy Ghost. He is the gift which is *"in"* the believers, and there are Biblical examples where the Holy Ghost came with the laying on of hands. Sometimes he just *"fell"* on believers, other times they were *"filled"* when hands were laid on, such as at Ephesus.

- *ACT 19:6 And when Paul had laid his hands upon them, the Holy Ghost came on them; and they spake with tongues, and prophesied.*

Paul also told Timothy not *to neglect* the gift.

- *1TI 4:14 Neglect not the gift that is in thee, which was given thee by prophecy, with the laying on of the hands of the presbytery.*
  *15 Meditate upon these things; give thyself wholly to them; that thy profiting may appear to all.*

## Neglect not the gift

From the above passage we can know the gift can be *"neglected."* If every believer in Christ would begin to meditate upon the things of the Spirit, and give themselves wholly to them, it would not be long before a powerful impact would be made throughout the entire church.

Laying on of hands by anointed ministers of Christ can help struggling believers to stir up and release the gift which is in them. I predict there will be a mighty wave of this very thing in the last days.

I encourage everyone who has been saved to accept by faith that they have been given the Holy Ghost as the *"earnest of their inheritance"* (EPH 1:14), and as proof they are a child of God (ROM 8:16).

- *EPH 1:13 In whom ye also trusted, after that ye heard the word of truth, the gospel of your salvation: in whom also after that ye believed, ye were sealed with that holy Spirit of promise,*
  *14 **Which is the earnest of our inheritance** until the redemption of the purchased possession, unto the praise of his glory.*
- *ROM 8:16 The Spirit itself beareth witness with our spirit, **that we are the children of God**:*

Therefore, one must stir up this gift which is within them, meditate upon all aspects of being filled with the Spirit, and give themselves wholly to them. Paul said *"desire spiritual gifts"* (1CO 14:1).

Once this issue is settled in a person's mind their spiritual strength, power, and authority in the word, and in the presence of God is awesome. The witness of the Spirit has a forceful effect, especially when it is fortified by a host of scriptures that assures one that they have been given the Spirit as a gift. One should not rest until this issue has been settled with them personally. Jesus said, *"Blessed are they which do hunger and thirst after righteousness: for they shall be filled"*(MAT 5:6).

Jesus told his disciples that they would receive power to *"be witnesses"* after the Holy Ghost had come upon them. He did not say "power to witness," but power to "be" witnesses. The infilling of the Holy Ghost is a *living experience.*

- *ACT 1:8 But ye shall receive power, after that the Holy Ghost is come upon you: and ye shall **be** witnesses unto me...*

This was beautifully demonstrated when Peter preached to the household of Cornelius.

## The tragedy of uninformed leaders

It is regrettable that so many Christians have been raised in situations where they have been deprived of information about the Holy Spirit.

It makes no difference how long one has been under bondage to uninformed spiritual leaders; they must experience the liberty of the sons of God. Following are some scriptures having to do with *liberty* that should encourage those who are in bondage to obtain their liberty in the Spirit.

- *LUK 4:18 The Spirit of the Lord is upon me, because he hath anointed me to preach the gospel to the poor; he hath sent me to heal the brokenhearted, to preach deliverance to the captives, and recovering of sight to the blind, <u>to set at liberty them that are bruised,</u>*
- *2CO 3:17 Now the Lord is that Spirit: and where the Spirit of the Lord is, there is <u>liberty</u>.*
- *GAL 5:1 Stand fast therefore in the <u>liberty</u> wherewith Christ hath made us free, and be not entangled again with the yoke of bondage.*

It is evident that the church is entering the *"last days"* and every believer should expect a great outpouring of the Holy Spirit upon all flesh. Jesus is again breathing upon the church and saying, *"receive ye the Holy Ghost."*

Each individual must honestly and nobly break into the liberty of truth regarding the Holy Spirit.

# CHAPTER 13

# WALKING IN THE SPIRIT

We now have the Bible wherein written records and detailed accounts are given for our information and guidance. We know that it is God's will that all followers of Christ acknowledge the reality of being filled with the Holy Spirit and learn to live and walk in the power and authority of the Spirit. This gives one power over the flesh, the world, and the devil. Take a look at the following verses that have to do with walking, or living in the Spirit.

- *GAL 5:16 This I say then, Walk in the Spirit, and ye shall not fulfil the lust of the flesh.*
- *ROM 8:1 There is therefore now no condemnation to them which are in Christ Jesus, who walk not after the flesh, but after the Spirit.*
  *6 ... For to be carnally minded is death; but to be spiritually minded is life and peace.*
  *10 ... And if Christ be in you, the body is dead because of sin; but the Spirit is life because of righteousness.*
  *13 ... For if ye live after the flesh, ye shall die: but if ye through the Spirit do mortify the deeds of the body, ye shall live.*

*14 For as many as are led by the Spirit of God, they are the sons of God.*

One must not down-play the infilling of the Holy Spirit, nor overlook the presence and activity of the Holy Spirit in the life and ministry of Jesus. After Jesus was baptized in water by John the Baptist, the Holy Spirit descended from heaven in the form of a dove and the Holy Spirit *"remained"* upon Jesus.

- *JOH 1:33 And I knew him not: but he that sent me to baptize with water, the same said unto me, Upon whom thou shalt see the Spirit descending, and <u>remaining on him</u>, the same is he which baptizeth with the Holy Ghost.*

Without this baptism with the Holy Spirit, Jesus would have been powerless. He carried out his entire ministry by the power of the Spirit. It was even the Holy Spirit that raised him from the dead.

- *ROM 8:11 But if the Spirit of him that raised up Jesus from the dead dwell in you, he that raised up Christ from the dead shall also quicken your mortal bodies by his Spirit that dwelleth in you.*

Jesus came to be our example in all things, and just as we must be empowered by the Holy Ghost in order to live the Christian life, even so it was necessary for Jesus, because he became as a man when he took upon himself human flesh.

- *ROM 8:3 ... God sending his own Son in the likeness of sinful flesh, and for sin, condemned sin in the flesh:*

Jesus gave up his first estate and became as an ordinary man with all human, fleshly limitations and infirmities.

- *HEB 4:15 For we have not an high priest which cannot be touched with the feeling of our infirmities; but was in all points tempted like as we are, yet without sin.*

Without the Holy Ghost to anoint, empower, and lead him, he would have been just another human being.

Immediately after receiving the Holy Spirit, Jesus was led into combat training against his prime an*tagonist...the devil.*

*MAT 4:1 Then was Jesus led up of the spirit into the wilderness to be tempted of the devil.*

After the Holy Spirit came upon Jesus he was immediately, and thereafter, *"led of the Spirit."* One of the first things Jesus did after his temptation and victory in the wilderness was to go into the synagogue at Nazareth and read about himself from Isaiah the prophet:

- *LUK 4:18 <u>The Spirit of the Lord is upon me</u>, because he hath anointed me to preach the gospel to the poor; he hath sent me to heal the brokenhearted, to preach deliverance to the captives, and recovering of sight to the blind, to set at liberty them that are bruised,*
  *19 To preach the acceptable year of the Lord.*
  *20 And he closed the book, and he gave it again to the minister, and sat down. And the eyes of all them that were in the synagogue were fastened on him.*
  *21 And he began to say unto them, This day is this scripture fulfilled in your ears.*

This was a profound statement by Jesus...that his ministry would be accomplished through the power and anointing of the Holy Spirit which was *"upon"* him. Notice how Jesus introduced this passage (v. 18), *"The Spirit of the Lord is <u>upon</u> me."* Peter confirmed this at Cornelius' house:

- *ACT 10:38 How <u>God anointed Jesus of Nazareth with the Holy Ghost</u> and with power: who went about doing good, and healing all that were oppressed of the devil; for God was with him.*

This is a clear mandate to all who desire to follow Jesus as the example for their life. The baptism in the Spirit is just as essential for us as it was for Jesus. It is no wonder that the devil has fought this truth so hard. He knows that Jesus' disciples will be able to overcome him by the same Holy Spirit that dwelled in Jesus. Satan also knows that the ministry of Christ will continue in his followers by the power of the same Spirit that anointed Jesus.

Jesus became our example in all things, even to the extent of being baptized with the Holy Ghost. Jesus knew that it would be just as necessary for men to receive a baptism in the Spirit as it was for him to receive. When Jesus anticipated his return to heaven, he promised that he would ask the Father to send the Holy Ghost to dwell in all Christians. Jesus knew that the Holy Ghost would give them power to continue his ministry on earth.

- *JOH 14:12 Verily, verily, I say unto you, He that believeth on me, the works that I do shall he do also; and greater works than these shall he do; because I go unto my Father.*

Speaking concerning this, Jesus used the word *"expedient,"* which means *extremely urgent.*

- *JOH 16:7 Nevertheless I tell you the truth; It is expedient for you that I go away: for if I go not away, the Comforter will not come unto you; but if I depart, I will send him unto you.*

Jesus is our example for living and walking in the Spirit. One must be aware of the many New Testament truths pertaining to the necessity of being filled with the Spirit, walking in the Spirit, living in the Spirit, and satisfying one's thirst for spiritual things. *"This is the refreshing wherewith ye shall cause the weary to be refreshed."* This is also the way to prevent walking in the flesh (carnal living).

- *ROM 8:10 And if Christ be in you, the body is dead because of sin; but the Spirit is life because of righteousness.*
  *11 But if the Spirit of him that raised up Jesus from the dead dwell in you, he that raised up Christ from the dead shall also quicken your mortal bodies by his Spirit that dwelleth in you.*
  *12 Therefore, brethren, we are debtors, not to the flesh, to live after the flesh.*

*13 For if ye live after the flesh, ye shall die: but if ye through the Spirit do mortify the deeds of the body, ye shall live.*

Jesus attended the great Jewish festival, the feast of Tabernacles. As he watched the milling throngs eating and drinking to their fill, he knew they were still hungry and thirsty spiritually, and this religious festival had been nothing more than a feast of empty religion. He knew their inner hunger and thirst could be satisfied only by the infilling of the Holy Spirit. He finally could stand it no longer and he cried out with a loud voice:

- *JOH 7:37 In the last day, that great day of the feast, Jesus stood and cried, saying, If any man thirst, let him come unto me, and drink.*
  *38 He that believeth on me, as the scripture hath said, out of his belly shall flow rivers of living water.*
  *39 (But this spake he of the Spirit, which they that believe on him should receive: for the Holy Ghost was not yet given; because that Jesus was not yet glorified.)*

As mentioned above, Jesus had promised his disciples that when he returned to heaven he would ask the Father to send the Holy Spirit to dwell in them.

- *JOH 14:16 And I will pray the Father, and he shall give you another Comforter, that he may abide with you for ever;*
  *17 Even the Spirit of truth; whom the world cannot receive, because it seeth him not, neither knoweth him: but ye know him; for he dwelleth with you, and shall be in you.*

This is an important passage because it lets us know that the Holy Ghost would soon dwell within the believers. Prior to this time the Holy Spirit was in heaven along with the heavenly Father. (Jesus had also been in heaven before he came to earth). The three are individual spiritual beings, each a heavenly personage, with their distinct individuality. While heaven was their base of operation, they participated in the lives and affairs of men in omnipresent form. Throughout the Old Testament the Spirit was *with* men on many occasions. But he did not actually dwell *within* like he would after the day of Pentecost. This is why Jesus said, *"he dwelleth with you, and shall be in you."*

Jesus knew that being filled with the Holy Spirit would be so spiritually satisfying that it compared to a long thirst-quenching drink of water (JOH 7:37-39). Carefully notice the explanation in parenthesis; *"(But this spake he of the Spirit, which they that believe on him should receive)."* Jesus here establishes that the Spirit is given to those who believe on him. He said, *"out of his belly shall flow."*

All Christians should believe, and *"should receive"* the Holy Ghost. This should remove all doubt that Jesus expected everyone who believed on him to receive the Holy Ghost.

When someone departs on an extended trip, their last-minute instruction is the most important thing on their mind. Jesus' last instructions--spoken just before he ascended up into heaven--were as follows:

- *LUK 24:49 And, behold, I send the promise of my Father upon you: but tarry ye in the city of Jerusalem, until ye be endued with power from on high.*

Jesus stressed the importance of what he had said about receiving the Holy Ghost, and was concerned that his disciples should realize the urgency of obeying his words which he had spoken concerning receiving the Holy Ghost. Jesus felt so strongly about this matter that he told his disciples if they loved him, they would keep his words concerning the Holy Ghost. Notice this unbroken connection beginning with verse 26 in the following passage:

- *JOH 14:23 Jesus answered and said unto him, If a man love me, he will keep my words: and my Father will love him, and we will come unto him, and make our abode with him.*
  *24 He that loveth me not keepeth not my sayings: and*

*the word which ye hear is not mine, but the Father's which sent me.*

*25 These things have I spoken unto you, being yet present with you.*

*26 But the Comforter, which is the Holy Ghost, whom the Father will send in my name, he shall teach you all things, and bring all things to your remembrance, whatsoever I have said unto you.*

*27 Peace I leave with you, my peace I give unto you: not as the world giveth, give I unto you. Let not your heart be troubled, neither let it be afraid.*

Jesus continues making statements about the "Comforter":

- *JOH 15:26 But when the Comforter is come, whom I will send unto you from the Father, even the Spirit of truth, which proceedeth from the Father, he shall testify of me:*
  *27 And ye also shall bear witness, because ye have been with me from the beginning.*

The main ministry of the Holy Ghost is to witness concerning Jesus. He cannot do this except by the use of human instrumentality. Jesus was saying here that the Holy Ghost is going to testify of me, and you shall be the means by which he is able to bear witness of me. This was so important to Jesus that his main topic just prior to his ascension had to do with the soon coming of the Holy Ghost.

- *ACT 1:8 But ye shall receive power, after that the Holy Ghost is come upon you: and ye shall be witnesses unto me both in Jerusalem, and in all Judaea, and in Samaria, and unto the uttermost part of the earth.*

## Why stress speaking in tongues

One might ask, "why place so much emphasis on speaking in tongues? Should not more emphasis be placed on the other gifts of the Spirit? There is such a need for the true gift of spiritual wisdom and knowledge. What about the need for healing? There are many people who need to be healed. The need for healing will surely become more acute as political problems with healthcare, medical insurance, and the availability of medical facilities and doctors continue to deteriorate."

The answer: The reason for emphasis on speaking in other tongues is that there must be a universal awareness and acknowledgment regarding the serious need for the baptism in the Holy Ghost to be a literal reality in the lives of all Christians throughout the world.

The Bible says *"tongues are for a sign"* (1CO 14:22). It does not say healing, or wisdom, or discerning, etc., are for a sign that the Holy Ghost dwells within a believer. When a person truly experiences speaking in tongues by the miraculous utterance of the Holy Ghost, they are convinced overwhelmingly that the Holy Spirit permanently dwells within their body. They become a firm believer who will be inclined to desire all the Spiritual gifts, and will glorify God in their bodies as they experience the manifestations and operations of the Spirit through them.

Speaking in other tongues as the Spirit gives the utterance is a personal experience that confirms to a believer as a supernatural sign that their body, has become a dwelling place of the Holy Spirit.

- *1CO 6:19 What? know ye not that your body is the temple of the Holy Ghost which is in you, which ye have of God, and ye are not your own?*

The manifestations of all the gifts of the Spirit are extremely important, and must be exercised diligently as needed, but one must know for sure that the Author of the gifts abides within them. Speaking in tongues is a starting point regarding all of the gifts. In the early church they knew that the Holy Ghost dwelled within believers because they heard them speak with tongues and magnify God.

- *ACT 10:45 And they of the circumcision which believed were astonished, as many as came with Peter, because that on the Gentiles also was poured out the gift of the Holy Ghost.*

> *46 For they heard them speak with tongues, and magnify God.*

Peter summarized the matter by asking, *"What was I that I could withstand God."* I believe as we go further into the end time, we will see more believers manifesting genuine, confirmable operations of all the gifts of the Holy Spirit.

The words of Jesus give encouragement to trust him for more as he says, *"Blessed are they which do hunger and thirst after righteousness: for they shall be filled"* (MAT 5:6). Paul's prayer adds to one's confidence in believing that the fulness of the Spirit is available and attainable to those who believe; *"That he would grant you, according to the riches of his glory, to be strengthened with might by his Spirit in the inner man"* (EPH 3:16).

- *GAL 5:16 This I say then, **Walk in the Spirit**...*
  *25 ...If we live in the Spirit, let us also **walk in the Spirit**.*

# CHAPTER 14

# UNDERSTANDING
# SUPERNATURAL
# VERBAL GIFTS

The gift of prophesy is fully explained in the New Testament and consists of speaking in one's own language in a way that is understandable by the person or audience hearing that which is spoken. Prophesy is miraculous because it is spoken by supernatural utterance as the Holy Spirit is speaking verbally and audibly through a person's vocal instrument.

The scripture also gives information about similar supernatural utterances, except they are not spoken in the natural language of the speaker, and usually not in the language of the hearer. The verbal or oral gifts are listed among nine gifts of the Spirit given by Paul. I have them in bold type in the following passage:

- *1CO 12:8 For to one is given by the Spirit the word of wisdom; to another the word of knowledge by the same Spirit;*
  *9 To another faith by the same Spirit; to another the gifts of healing by the same Spirit;*

*10 To another the working of miracles; to another* **prophecy***; to another discerning of spirits; to another* **divers kinds of tongues***; to another* **the interpretation** **of tongues***:*

## A STUDY OF THE GIFT OF OTHER TONGUES

The term "tongues" in the context of the gifts of the Spirit refers to supernatural utterances by the Holy Spirit that are spoken in a language that is not the language of the person speaking.

What is the usefulness or purpose for speaking in other tongues? This particular manifestation must be of some value because Paul wanted the church to understand the verbal and oral gifts of the Spirit and their proper function and operation.

God's word says, *"forbid not to speak with tongues"* (1CO 14:39). A straightforward statement like that should make one take notice regarding the importance of the gift. God said "don't forbid it," therefore we must know what the Bible says concerning the correct usage of the gift.

### The proper use for tongues

There are at least three correct uses for speaking in tongues, and they are all edifying. When Paul was teaching concerning the proper use of tongues he said, *"Let all things be done unto edifying"* (1CO 14:26).

The three main functions are as follows:

1. **To allow the Holy Spirit to praise, worship, and magnify God the Father and Jesus Christ his Son.**

2. **To allow the Holy Spirit to pray intercessory prayers for us when we do not know what to pray for ourselves or others.**

3. **To bring a message or a word from God to the church within an assembled worship meeting. In order for this kind of speaking in tongues to be scripturally correct, If the manifestation of**

**tongues is occupying the attention of the entire congregation, it should be accompanied by the operation of the gift of "interpretation of tongues."**

## Diverse kinds of tongues

Among the nine gifts of the Spirit given in First Corinthians chapter twelve, it does not just say tongues (singular), but *"divers kinds of tongues." "Divers"* is an interesting word. It means "several; various;" therefore the meaning is "various" kinds of tongues, or different kinds. Quite simply, there are tongues of praise, tongues of intercession, and tongues for interpretation. *"Diverse"* can also mean "spoken in various different languages," such as occurred on the day of Pentecost.

## 1. Tongues of Praise and worship of God

Jesus wants us to understand that the Holy Ghost is real, genuine, valid, and comes from God the Father, and is of such truth that the Holy Ghost is even called *"the Spirit of truth."* Jesus gave insight into the ministry of the Holy Spirit by saying he would *"testify"* of Christ.

- *JOH 15:26 But when the Comforter is come, whom I will send unto you from the Father, even the Spirit of truth, which proceedeth from the Father, he shall testify of me:*
- *JOH 16:13 Howbeit when he, the Spirit of truth, is come, he will guide you into all truth: for he shall not speak of himself; but whatsoever he shall hear, <u>that shall he speak</u>: and he will shew you things to come.*
  *14 He shall glorify me: for he shall receive of mine, and shall shew it unto you.*

Jesus said *"that shall he speak,"* meaning he shall speak in human languages. Jesus said concerning the Holy Ghost, *"he shall testify of me,"* and *"he shall glorify me."* This is exactly what happened on the day of Pentecost when those who were filled with the Holy Ghost spoke in other tongues. The religious Jews, who were foreigners, were able to understand the Galileans when they supernaturally spoke in tongues--the various languages of the foreigners – and these foreigners testified that these simple Galileans were glorifying God:

- *ACT 2:11 ...<u>we do hear them speak</u> in our tongues <u>the wonderful works of God</u>.*

At Cornelius' house when they were all filled with the Holy Ghost it says:

- *ACT 10:45 And they of the circumcision which believed were astonished, as many as came with Peter, because that on the Gentiles also was poured out the gift of the Holy Ghost.*
  *46 For <u>they heard them speak with tongues</u>, **and magnify God**.*

## 2. Tongues of intercession

Besides praising God, the second important function of tongues by the Holy Ghost is to give Christians the power to pray in the Spirit. Frequently we all come to situations where we do not know what to pray for as we should. The infirmity, or weakness of our flesh, and the limitation of our own mind to reason out or think through the problem is augmented and helped by the Holy Ghost who dwells within us continually, twenty-four hours a day. He is with us through every problem and he knows exactly what we need. Furthermore, he knows what the Father's will is and can pray accordingly. Seldom do we know this by ourselves.

Here is the picture of what is going on in the Spirit world. God the Father is on his throne in heaven and Jesus is sitting at his right hand. Jesus is there to make intercession for us before the Father. His help to us is like an attorney before a judge.

- *ROM 8:34 Who is he that condemneth? It is Christ that died, yea rather, that is risen again, who is even at the right hand of God, who also maketh intercession for us.*

Jesus also functions as our High Priest.

- *HEB 4:14 Seeing then that we have a great high priest, that is passed into the heavens, Jesus the Son of God, let us hold fast our profession.*
  *15 For we have not an high priest which cannot be touched with the feeling of our infirmities; but was in all points tempted like as we are, yet without sin.*
  *16 Let us therefore come boldly unto the throne of grace, that we may obtain mercy, and find grace to help in time of need.*

In addition to the intercessor in Heaven, Christians also have an intercessor on earth, dwelling within them in the person of the Holy Spirit. He is always aware of our needs every moment of our lives. And, he is in constant communication with our intercessor in Heaven. Jesus is continually looking into our heart because, as a good shepherd, he is concerned about the care of his sheep. Jesus always knows what is going on with us because the Holy Ghost keeps him informed.

I can picture many three-way discussions on our behalf between the Father, the Son, and the Holy Ghost. When we are praying in our own language, and the prayer changes to where another language is spoken by the Spirit, it can be prayers of praise, but very likely may be prayers of intercession wherein the Holy Ghost is praying on our behalf, asking for the things we need, even when we do not know what to pray for. The Holy Ghost always asks for the right thing, and never asks amiss, because he prays according to the will of God.

- *ROM 8:26 Likewise the Spirit also helpeth our infirmities: for we know not what we should pray for as we ought: but the Spirit itself maketh intercession for us with groanings which cannot be uttered.*
  *27 And he that searcheth the hearts knoweth what is the mind of the Spirit, because he maketh intercession for the saints according to the will of God.*

Jesus knows the mind of the Spirit. Paul became so excited over this wonderful gift that he exclaimed,

- *ROM 8:31 ...What shall we then say to these things? If God be for us, who can be against us?*

Those who are opposed to audible, verbalized speaking in tongues usually suggest that the above intercession of the Spirit is silent – unspoken or under the breath intercession--because of the statement *"with groanings which cannot be uttered."* But this statement must be taken in context. This is taking place when *"the Spirit itself maketh intercession"* which, according to viable scriptural references, meant the Spirit was speaking audibly in tongues. This was occurring during a situation where one did not know what to pray for, and was unable to think of, or utter, any request to God that would be a solution to their problem. There was nothing they could utter that would seem to suggest an answer to their need.

In this situation the Holy Spirit would begin to pray, uttering prayers on one's behalf that they could not utter themselves. In previous instances in the New Testament, the utterance of the Holy Ghost was audible and verbal. On the day of Pentecost the believers *"began to speak with other tongues as the Spirit gave them utterance"* (ACT 2:4). The Holy Spirit simply uttered for them in tongues what they could not utter on their own. He makes intercession, always asking for the right thing...*"because he maketh intercession for the saints according to the will of God"* (v. 27). This is why verse 26 says, *"but the Spirit itself maketh intercession for us with groanings which cannot be uttered."*

Any doctrine that would deprive a child of God from enjoying this benefit of the Holy Spirit is not truth. Those who embrace the intercession of the Holy Spirit can experience it frequently, as the need arises...even daily. And, all speaking in tongues, even intercession, can be – and should be--verbalized audibly by the utterance of the Holy Spirit. The terms *"intercession"* and *"groanings"* suggests verbalized audible prayers. It would not be reasonable to think that as one is praying the Holy Spirit begins to pray in tongues as he makes intercession, and he goes silent with no verbal utterance.

## 3. Tongues for interpretation

A third function of praying in tongues is for the edification of the church when they are assembled in orderly worship. The fourteenth chapter of First Corinthians is filled with information about the operation of the Holy Ghost in an assembled meeting. The main purpose for the instructions in this chapter is to help the church know about the proper and orderly manifestation of tongues, although many other pieces of vital information are given throughout the chapter.

## Interpretation of tongues

Interpretation of tongues is a valuable supernatural gift by the Holy Spirit because without it the congregation would not know the meaning of that which was spoken in other tongues.

- *1CO 14:13 Wherefore let him that speaketh in an unknown tongue pray that he may interpret.*

Paul explained that, in a worship service where Christians were gathered together, it was not good to take a lot of time speaking in other tongues which no one could understand. Therefore he instructed that if one should feel the impetus to speak in tongues, and should do so, they should pray that God would use them to give the interpretation of the message which had just been spoken in tongues. *"Interpretation of tongues"* is as supernatural as speaking in other tongues. It is spoken in one's own native language that is also the language of others in the meeting. Such interpretation of tongues is as miraculous and supernatural as speaking in other tongues. Just as the Holy Ghost gives the utterance in *"other tongues"* (other languages), even so he gives the utterance for *"interpretation of tongues"* in an understandable language. If one could do it on their own it would not be necessary for one to *"pray that he may interpret."*

Interpretation of tongues is not limited to the person speaking in tongues, for the interpretation can also come through another person. Paul instructs that one, or two, or at the most three may speak in tongues before an interpretation is given. He then advises that *one* interpret.

- *1CO 14:27 If any man speak in an unknown tongue, let it be by two, or at the most by three, and that by course; and let one interpret.*
  *28 But if there be no interpreter, let him keep silence in the church; and let him speak to himself, and to God.*

Paul's advice was that if an interpretation was not soon forthcoming, those who have spoken in tongues should not keep on, but if they felt the anointing to continue speaking, to do so quietly in their mind or under their breath.

Speaking in tongues for the purpose of interpretation gives the church a powerful means for hearing from the Holy Spirit in a current and supernatural way. One important guideline must be that, anything that is claimed to be interpretation must be in total agreement with the word of God...and limited to truth as revealed in the word...no new doctrinal revelations. It can include prophetic foretelling and warnings of future events. It can also be revelatory regarding sin and iniquity that may be concealed and hidden in the hearts and lives of unclean persons. It can also apply to the proper interpretation of doctrinal matters in Scripture.

## Valid languages

Some things need to be established as a basis for understanding these instructions of Paul. It is important to reiterate that when Paul spoke of *"tongues,"* he was speaking of known foreign languages.

The Expositor's Bible Commentary, volume ten, page 278, makes this observation:

> **"...On the basis of the phenomenon of foreign languages spoken of in Acts 2:5-12, we have argued that the tongues referred to in 1 Corinthians 14:13-15, 20-25 were also foreign-language tongues--not ecstatic utterances, gibberish, or non-understandable erratic variations of consonants and vowels with indiscriminate modulation of pitch, speed, and volume."**

This commentary says they were speaking valid foreign languages, or tongues which had meaning somewhere in the world.

## Tongues of angels

An idea prevails with some people that tongues is a "heavenly language," or the "tongues of angels," or a "prayer language" not known in the world, and is therefore unknown to the devil. This is not scripturally sound because it is not based on solid scriptural interpretation, but again, "reading between the lines."

In the first place, the devil is of such supernatural intelligence that he knows every language. He was originally a prince among angels and it is not consistent that he would not know his own original language--the language of angels.

The idea of a heavenly language has been taken from the following statement:

- *1CO 13:1 Though I speak with the tongues of men and of angels, and have not charity, I am become as sounding brass, or a tinkling cymbal.*

Paul was speaking in a hypothetical sense, with the word *"though"* meaning "if" I could. This is not to be taken as though he is inferring that he actually could perform these supernatural gifts such as tongues and prophesy without possessing charity. His point is, any demonstration or semblance of a gift of the Spirit without the presence of charity is a farce. It is a counterfeit, and not the real thing.

We are told that it takes love in order for faith to work. Love is the motor which makes the vehicle go.

- *GAL 5:6 For in Jesus Christ neither circumcision availeth any thing, nor uncircumcision; but faith which worketh by love.*

Fleshly religious works without charity do not avail anything. Paul was merely saying, "though I should speak with the gift of tongues, and even speak in the language of angels, if I do not have charity, I am become a sounding brass, or a tinkling cymbal."

He was exposing the futility of any religious charitable act or operation of a supernatural gift without having the genuine motive of charity.

There is no indication that he is suggesting that when one speaks in tongues they might be using the language of angels. This is the only scripture that mentions the tongues of angels, and to suddenly base such an important doctrine on this one verse seems extremely hasty. It is reasonable that something of that magnitude should have several supportive scriptures so that one would be able to rightly divide the word of truth to substantiate the doctrine.

## Languages in the world

When Paul gave instructions concerning speaking in tongues, he did not allude to a heavenly language, but only to languages ("*voices*") in the world, or languages spoken by men in the world.

- *1CO 14:10 There are, it may be, so many kinds of voices in the world, and none of them is without signification.*
  *11 Therefore if I know not the meaning of the voice, I shall be unto him that speaketh a barbarian, and he that speaketh shall be a barbarian unto me.*

Truly, speaking in tongues is a valid human language spoken somewhere in the world. The NIV translation of the above passage makes this quite clear:

- *1CO 14:10 (NIV) Undoubtedly there are all sorts of languages in the world, yet none of them is without meaning.*
  *11 If then I do not grasp the meaning of what someone is saying, I am a foreigner to the speaker, and he is a foreigner to me .*

## Actual foreign words

It is obvious that Paul considered utterances in unknown tongues to be actual intelligible "words" of a legitimate foreign language, although unknown to him or the hearers in his presence, yet valid and known somewhere. He called them *"words."*

- *ICO 14:18 I thank my God, I speak with tongues more than ye all:*
  *19 Yet in the church I had rather speak five **words** with my understanding, that by my voice I might teach others also, than ten thousand **words** in an unknown tongue.*

Paul's use of the term _"words"_ gives unquestionable credibility to speaking in other tongues as being literal human languages.

## Biblical soundness a necessity

It is important that we remain Biblically sound. Chapter and verse must be given for everything we believe and teach. It disturbs me to hear someone excitedly tell another--who is inquisitive about the gift of tongues--"Oh, I love to pray in my heavenly language because the devil does not know what I am saying. Therefore he can not run ahead of me and intercept the things for which I have been praying."

It disturbs me even more to watch the inquirer take on a puzzled look, wondering where the Bible says that. Or, to see one that accepts anything and everything--without question or Biblical proof – as they exclaim, "wow! I didn't know that. Do you mean that we can pray to God and the devil doesn't know what we are saying?"

When I hear such, it behooves me to question, does the devil not really know what we are saying when we pray in tongues, especially if we supposedly pray in the _"tongues of angels?"_ If this is not true, we have a false security in thinking the devil is in the dark concerning what we are doing spiritually. Therefore, we may really be vulnerable to Satan's devices if we think he is unaware. Make no mistake, he is informed and is planning his strategy. The Bible speaks of his wiles and cunning craftiness.

It is inconceivable that there is a language in the world that he does not know. Furthermore, it is inconceivable that he cannot understand heavenly languages. He carries on conversations with God and with the angels. He was at one time the prince of angels. No, it simply will not hold water that Satan cannot understand what is being said when one speaks in tongues.

When one is speaking in tongues they are speaking in languages *"that are in the world."* The Expositor's Bible Commentary, Volume 10, Page 273 has this to say:

> **"Paul's speaking of the languages of the world along with his reference to the "foreigner" (barbaros, "barbarian"...) substantiates the conclusion that in his discussion of tongues he has in mind known foreign languages. Phonai ("languages") can at times mean "voices," "sounds" (cf. v.7; Rev. 5:2), but here in connection with aphonos ("without meaning"), it indicates languages that can convey meaning by their systematic distinction of sounds. The "meaning" (dynamin, literally "power") of the language refers to its "power" to convey meaning."**

When we go beyond what a verse actually says, it then becomes necessary to distort other passages of scripture to try and make it say what we want. Such is the case of the following verse taken entirely out of context.

- *EPH 3:10 To the intent that now unto the principalities and powers in heavenly places might be known by the church the manifold wisdom of God,*

This verse has been erroneously used, to teach that when one is speaking in the tongues of angels they are actually speaking to the angels, who are the principalities and powers in heavenly places. It is mistakenly said that when one speaks in the tongues of angels, instructions and commands are being given to the angels concerning how they are to carry out the work of God in the earth. This theory says that, by the medium of speaking in tongues in the language of angels, (so they can understand), the church makes angels aware of what God's will and wisdom desires to be done as they, the angels watch over his word to perform it.

## Avoid the term "heavenly language"

Everyone must avoid using any term or phrase that is not in the

Bible. While there is no scriptural support for the idea of a "heavenly language" there are many who use the term and claim to speak in a heavenly language when they are speaking in other tongues. This contributes to the confusion that exists concerning speaking in tongues, especially when this is coupled with the claim that the devil cannot understand what is said since he is not privy to this language. I put the *heavenly language* in the same classification with the *language of angels*, and refrain from using the terms in relation to speaking in tongues simply because they are not Biblically sound. *"Sound"* means solid, without flaws. Remember that the word of God says,

- *TIT 2:1 But speak thou the things which become **sound doctrine**:*
- *1TI 4:16 Take heed unto thyself, and unto the doctrine; continue in them: for in doing this thou shalt both save thyself, and them that hear thee.*

## Prayer Language

Another confusing matter concerns the use of the term "prayer language." The idea that each person is given a certain specific prayer language, supernaturally created just for them as their exclusive and unique language, which will always be used by the Holy Ghost, is not Biblically provable. Confusion will be caused by any idea that is not scripturally sound.

I have heard people discuss their "prayer language" in such a way that it turns many people off who know enough about the Bible to know their strange ideas are not sound. In the first place, the Holy Ghost is not limited to using only the same language over and over with any individual. He has access to all languages in existence.

Some people become practically possessive over their "prayer language," and discuss it as they would a diamond ring. I overheard two women discussing their prayer language and it went something like this: "Oh honey, has God given you your prayer language"? "Oh yes dear, and it is so beautiful. It sounds like poetic French, or maybe

Italian--one of those romantic languages." "Oh, I would love to hear it. Could you speak a little for me?"

Whereupon the first lady obliged the second by speaking a few phrases in her lovely language. "Oh isn't that heavenly…it must be a heavenly language. Here is what mine sounds like," and the second lady gave a little demonstration of her prayer language.

"How beautiful!" responded the first. "That just has to be the language of angels. And you know what is so thrilling? The devil doesn't know what we are saying, so he can't intercept our prayer and figure out a way to sabotage our answer from God."

It may have been exciting to these women, but it is sheer fantasy Biblically. It is important that speaking in tongues be kept on the level that is a miracle due to the fact that literal languages known somewhere in the earth are being spoken. Also, It must be maintained that one does not speak in tongues on their own initiative, but only by the utterance of the Holy Ghost.

- *ACT 2:4 And they were all filled with the Holy Ghost, and began to speak with other tongues, <u>as the Spirit gave them utterance</u>.*

### "<u>They</u>" spake with tongues

Never forget that speaking in other tongues is a miracle because Acts 2:4 says they spoke with tongues *"as the Spirit gave them utterance."*

While I was pastoring in the Church of God denomination, I was invited to a home prayer meeting where a number of people from various Non-Pentecostal backgrounds were coming together because of their interest in speaking in other tongues. I knew only one person present, the one that invited me, and he was a former pastor of a Christian Church denomination in Oklahoma.

There was a guest speaker from another city in Texas, and he kept stressing the phrase, "they spake with tongues"…with the emphasis on "they." I could not draw from memory a scripture that said exactly those words, and I could quote verbatim most scriptures on the subject. He later enlarged his statement to say, "the Bible says they were all filled with the Holy Ghost and they spake with tongues." I knew this was not an exact quote, but I kept listening.

He then quoted a portion of a verse where foreigners who were visiting Jerusalem, and heard the Galileans speaking in their languages which said:

- *ACT 2:11 ...we do hear them speak in our tongues the wonderful works of God.*

The guest speaker began to stress heavily, we do hear "them" speak, claiming that "they" were doing the speaking. He repeated over-and-over "them speak...them speak...we do hear 'them' speak."

He then asked everyone to come forward who wanted to speak in tongues. I saw the weakness of the invitation, but said nothing. But, I did observe in my own spirit that he should have asked for those who wanted to be filled with the Spirit to come forward. One should never seek for tongues, but seek for the Holy Spirit ... accompanied by scriptural manifestations.

About ten people came forward and sat in a row of chairs. He began to instruct them something like this: "Now you must remember that you will be doing the speaking, so get your tongue and vocal cords ready. Everybody say 'Ah.' Now that wasn't hard, was it?

"Now, you are going to have to not be afraid to be silly for Jesus. It will sound strange and childish to you, and even a little foolish, but don't be afraid to be a fool for Jesus. How many of you, when you were infants beginning to speak said 'mother,' or 'father' distinctly? None of you, but you said ma-ma, or da-da.

"Just begin to jabber something...anything...disengage your intelligence...don't worry about how you sound...you will sound better with practice. Your language will improve."

A few were trying to follow his instructions, but most felt so silly they could not accommodate him very much. They were looking around desperately looking for someone to help them out, and I mean, "Out the door."

Finally, in desperation he stopped and realized he must give a little more instruction concerning how to speak with tongues. He asked, "how many of you were raised on the farm"? A few hands went up. "Did you have a well pump? Most of you know what an old well pump is. Do you remember how that you had to save a little water in the bucket so when the leather gasket dried out and would not pump, you could prime the pump by pouring water down the top of the pump? This is the way it is with speaking in tongues. You have to prime the pump by starting out yourself. Remember, it says "they spake with tongues.

"Now, start saying anything. Say Ba Ba black sheep--say something! Now get started. Go ahead now"! A few reluctantly followed his instructions, but they were the most befuddled group I had ever seen. I thought, "how utterly ridiculous."

Suddenly the Holy Ghost said inside my spirit, "say something."

I responded silently, "I am not going to say anything. These are not my members, therefore not my responsibility. Beside, I do not know any of them."

The response of the Spirit was so emphatic ... it shocked me. He said, "you do not decide the sheep over which you are shepherd. The Lord decides that. The idea that you are limited to just the denominational members under your pastorate is false. You look out for 'my sheep' where ever you may find one!"

I spoke up saying, "might I say something?" The man in charge gave me a cold stare and said, "I know I am not going to like what you have to say, but go ahead." He then went over to a corner of the room and stuck his nose as far into the corner as possible and began to pout.

I said, "I have been listening and would like to make some observations. Allow me to quote the Bible accurately and completely:

- *"ACT 2:1 And when the day of Pentecost was fully come, they were all with one accord in one place.*
  *2 And suddenly there came a sound from heaven as of a rushing mighty wind, and it filled all the house where they were sitting.*

> *3 And there appeared unto them cloven tongues like as*
> *of fire, and it sat upon each of them."*

I pointed out that this was an experience that came from "heaven," and not from their mind or intellect. I stated that on the day of Pentecost they had not the slightest idea of what was about to happen and the speaking in tongues fell on them totally unexpectedly, and was just as miraculous as the supernatural sound of a rushing mighty wind, and as phenomenal as the cloven tongues of fire that sat on each of them. I then proposed that speaking in tongues is a miracle in the strictest sense.

I continued to quote:

- *ACT 2:4 And they were all filled with the Holy Ghost, and began to speak with other tongues, **as the Spirit gave them utterance**.*

I stressed, as the *"**Spirit**"* gave them utterance. It does not say, "they" spake with tongues. I said, "the Holy Ghost does not need any help. He is well able to give the miracle of tongues on his own."

All who were sitting in the chairs began to respond in praises to God, and various ones made statements such as, "That is the way I want to receive it." "That sounds like the Bible to me." "I don't want it to be me. If I speak in tongues, I want it to be the Holy Ghost."

I reminded them that John the Baptist had said Jesus was the baptizer in the Holy Ghost; therefore one must look in faith to Jesus as the Baptizer. John said:

- *MAT 3:11 I indeed baptize you with water unto repentance: but he that cometh after me is mightier than I, whose shoes I am not worthy to bear: he shall baptize you with the Holy Ghost, and with fire:*

I encouraged them to begin worshipping and magnifying God in their own language, because this is what the disciples did while they were waiting for the promise of the Holy Ghost.

- *LUK 24:49 And, behold, I send the promise of my Father*

*upon you: but tarry ye in the city of Jerusalem, until ye*
*be endued with power from on high.*
*50 And he led them out as far as to Bethany, and he lifted*
*up his hands, and blessed them.*
*51 And it came to pass, while he blessed them, he was*
*parted from them, and carried up into heaven.*
*52 And they worshipped him, and returned to Jerusalem*
*with great joy:*
*53 And were continually in the temple, praising and*
*blessing God.*

As the group began gently praising and blessing God, I reminded them that Jesus said, *"He, the Comforter, shall glorify me,"* and that it was very scriptural that the Holy Ghost would begin to give miraculous utterance, using their voice and tongue to praise God in another language, which would not be gibberish, but a valid language.

Tears began to flow, spontaneous rejoicing sprang forth in almost irresistible artesian flowing, and one by one the Holy Ghost began to speak through them all in other tongues. This went on for probably thirty minutes, interspersed with expressions of joy and delight, as worshipful conversation flowed between all in the house...except for the brother in the corner. He remained there throughout the rest of the meeting, even after it had been dismissed by the hostess.

I tried to shake hands with him and he refused. I gave him a pat on the shoulder anyway, and asked him to consider what I had said. I really felt sorry for him, but I felt that divine order and government by the Holy Ghost had been demonstrated. One of the functions of the Holy Ghost is to *"set government in the church"*...a very needed phase of his ministry to the church, and one of which we will be seeing more as the church is more perfected and draws nearer to the second coming of Christ.

## Cease not to warn

One might caution that information such as the above should not be included in this book for fear it might scare someone away from seeking for knowledge about deeper truth regarding being filled with the Holy Spirit. I am aware of this possibility, but I trust in God to help me warn every person regarding how Satan will attempt to turn them from the truth. I believe by faith that those who hunger and thirst after righteousness will recognize the truth when they hear it, and they will not allow themselves to be diverted from their pursuit of truth when they are warned regarding negative and false issues they may encounter.

Throughout the writings of Paul he constantly warned regarding false brethren and erroneous teachings that could throw one off track. Some of these include the following:

- *ACT 20:26 Wherefore I take you to record this day, that I am pure from the blood of all men.*
*27 For I have not shunned to declare unto you all the counsel of God.*
*28 Take heed therefore unto yourselves, and to all the flock, over the which the Holy Ghost hath made you overseers, to feed the church of God, which he hath purchased with his own blood.*
*29 For I know this, that after my departing shall grievous wolves enter in among you, not sparing the flock.*
*30 Also of your own selves shall men arise, speaking perverse things, to draw away disciples after them.*
*31 Therefore watch, and remember, that by the space of three years **I ceased not to warn every one night and day with tears.***
*32 And now, brethren, I commend you to God, and to the word of his grace, which is able to build you up, and to give you an inheritance among all them which are sanctified.*
- *MAT 7:15 Beware of false prophets, which come to you in sheep's clothing, but inwardly they are ravening wolves.*
*16 Ye shall know them by their fruits. Do men gather grapes of thorns, or figs of thistles?*

*17 Even so every good tree bringeth forth good fruit; but a corrupt tree bringeth forth evil fruit.*

*18 A good tree cannot bring forth evil fruit, neither can a corrupt tree bring forth good fruit.*

*19 Every tree that bringeth not forth good fruit is hewn down, and cast into the fire.*

*20 Wherefore by their fruits ye shall know them.*

*21 Not every one that saith unto me, Lord, Lord, shall enter into the kingdom of heaven; but he that doeth the will of my Father which is in heaven.*

- *PHI 3:1 Finally, my brethren, rejoice in the Lord. To write the same things to you, to me indeed is not grievous, but for you it is safe.*

  *2 Beware of dogs, beware of evil workers, beware of the concision.*

  *3 For we are the circumcision, which worship God in the spirit, and rejoice in Christ Jesus, and have no confidence in the flesh.*

- *COL 2:6 As ye have therefore received Christ Jesus the Lord, so walk ye in him:*

  *7 Rooted and built up in him, and stablished in the faith, as ye have been taught, abounding therein with thanksgiving.*

  *8 Beware lest any man spoil you through philosophy and vain deceit, after the tradition of men, after the rudiments of the world, and not after Christ.*

  *9 For in him dwelleth all the fulness of the Godhead bodily.*

  *10 And ye are complete in him, which is the head of all principality and power:*

**Peter gave a similar warning:**

- *2PE 3:17 Ye therefore, beloved, seeing ye know these things before, beware lest ye also, being led away with the error of the wicked, fall from your own stedfastness.*

  *18 But grow in grace, and in the knowledge of our Lord*

*and Saviour Jesus Christ. To him be glory both now and*
*for ever. Amen.*

## Pentecostal concepts and misconceptions

I was raised in Pentecostal circles where it was taught that a person would get saved and then receive the Holy Ghost thereafter. Converts usually went into a long session of days, weeks, months, and even years tarrying until they were endued with power from on high. Tarrying was considered normal since this is what happened with the disciples who tarried in Jerusalem for ten days prior to Pentecost, waiting to receive the Holy Ghost.

In our churches tarrying was usually prolonged because it was also taught that the Holy Ghost would not dwell in an unclean temple, therefore it would be necessary to receive the second definite work of grace known as sanctification before one could expect the Holy Ghost to come in. This meant that one could be saved without being cleansed, therefore must experience sanctification afterwards. Many people struggled desperately with this, having a hard time being set free, or sanctified from addictive habits such as tobacco, and from worldly relationships in which they had been involved.

While the definite experience of sanctification was often elusive, those who received an experience of joy were encouraged to acknowledge receiving the experience of sanctification based on that joy. This meant they were now candidates for receiving the Holy Ghost, whereupon they began the often long and arduous process of "tarrying" and "seeking" until they were filled with the Holy Ghost.

In this doctrinal environment, failing to realize that one does, in fact, receive the Holy Ghost when they are born again has been a major obstacle to many seeking to be baptized in the Holy Ghost. It has also been a barrier between Pentecostals and Non-Pentecostals who have been told that they have been born again, but are not yet filled with the Holy Ghost because they have not spoken in other tongues.

This has produced a backlash against Pentecostals and their doctrines concerning being filled with the Spirit. Difficulty in receiving their baptism in the Spirit by faith, due to the practice of tarrying, has caused many to never experience the fullness of the Spirit. Frustration has caused many to completely reject the idea of being filled with the Spirit...and sometimes resolve the matter by saying, "it's just not for me ... and they sometimes become opponents to the message concerning the baptism in the Spirit. Also, some settle for the persuasion that they are filled with the Spirit, but tongues is not given today.

## Chronic seekers

For many years I was of the persuasion which was traditional in Pentecostal circles, and expected as the norm, that tarrying might entail a long period of time, maybe weeks, or months, and sometimes years.

I once preached a revival meeting for a fairly large church where there were twenty-five people which had been seeking, or "tarrying," for the baptism in the Holy Ghost for several years...ranging from two to twenty-five years.

At the time, I did not know Biblically to tell them they had already received the Holy Ghost...when they were born again. Today I would tell them to accept their baptism as a Biblical fact, and to expect to experience any, and all, of the gifts (demonstrations) of the Spirit--including speaking in other tongues. I have learned that it is much easier to experience speaking in other tongues after one believes by faith they have received the Holy Ghost into their body-temple ... and it is 100% scripturally sound.

I became heavily burdened for these people because I knew something had to be wrong. I knew that the early church tarried for ten days, but they were waiting, as Jesus had instructed, until the Holy Spirit came for the first time. It is not logical that this should set a precedent today that tarrying should be an expected prolonged prelude to being filled with the Holy Ghost.

When the invitation was given at the end of the sermon, this group of chronic seekers responded immediately because they desperately wanted to receive the Holy Spirit. They kneeled at various places around the front of the church, and became the focus of attention as others came forward to give prayerful assistance and encouragement as they "tarried" for the infilling of the Holy Ghost. They were seeking for the manifestation of the gift of tongues as the initial evidence which would confirm that they had been baptized with the Holy Ghost. After a while, they all gave up--convinced that tonight was not the night--but were reassured in their own minds that their fervency had been demonstrated, and that God would someday reward their diligence.

Before someone thinks I am being too critical, let me say that I am thankful for this much. Many have received the fullness of the Holy Ghost under such circumstances because God is merciful in spite of our lack of Biblical knowledge and wisdom. God has done the best he could under the circumstances. I received the Holy Ghost under such circumstances, and it was a valid experience, but I remember the unnecessary difficulty in receiving the gift of tongues because I believed that the Holy Ghost would come in only as I began to speak in tongues. I believed I must experience speaking in tongues as evidence that the Holy Ghost had come in. My peers would not allow me to believe the Holy Ghost dwelled in me prior to when I spoke in other tongues.

The next day the pastor of the church where I was leading the revival hesitantly and cautiously approached me, warning me that these people were "chronic seekers," and had about exhausted everybody in the church, as well as every evangelist that had come along. He advised me against letting them occupy too much of my time, which would prevent me from ministering to others--especially new people who also had needs.

I became heavily burdened for these precious people who were having such a struggle with allowing the Holy Spirit to manifest his gifts through them. I began to fast and pray while seeking God's anointing to empower me to help these people. They had become a problem to the church and the pastor. They were in total frustration and desperation...wondering why they could not receive the Holy Ghost just like many others around them who had received. They could see it in the Bible, but were completely perplexed in their attempt to experience it.

After three days of fasting and seeking God, I asked him, "What can I do or say that will help them?" The answer came clearly, "teach them that Jesus is the Baptizer." This was opened to me in a dimension that I had not seen before. That evening I preached on "Jesus - The Baptizer."

I explained how it was not necessary, nor Biblical that they should tarry for days, or weeks, months, or years. I suggested that they all had their own mental or psychological barriers that had been built up that prevented their believing and receiving. Some of them felt that sooner-or-later the right preacher would come along to lay hands on them and the Holy Ghost would fall on them. Some had thought I might be the right one, and so they rushed forward the first night of the meeting.

Some expected to be so overpowered by a mighty rush, and surge of spiritual power that they would be practically slain in the Spirit. Others expected a quiet, soft, gentle breeze of the Spirit to blow through their soul, relaxing all their tensions while they sweetly and quietly began to speak in other tongues...finally victorious after a long, hard battle for submission. Others even expected to be baptized in the quietness of their own home.

I had concluded that they were all seeking for the evidence of tongues more than for the person of the Holy Spirit. They were more conscious of the utterances coming out of their mouth, than the praise that was coming from their heart. They were not aware of the presence of the Holy Spirit in their heart...and of his dwelling in their bodies as his temple.

With strong emphasis, I explained why they should seek for the indwelling of the Holy Spirit because of who he is, and because of the fruit of the Spirit--love, joy, peace, longsuffering, gentleness, goodness, faith, meekness, temperance--and for the gifts of the Spirit--the word of wisdom, the word of knowledge, faith, the gifts of healing, the working of miracles, prophecy, discerning of spirits, divers kinds of tongues, the interpretation of tongues--which he gives to those who receive him...in whom he takes up his abode.

They were then encouraged to focus their attention on the

scriptures which magnify Christ as the one who baptizes in the Holy Ghost, realizing that when men laid hands on others, it was only symbolic of Christ's hands. One must look to Jesus only, as the author and finisher of their faith. One must not pre-conceive how they will be baptized, or how they will begin speaking in other tongues. One must rest in praises of Jesus while appreciating all the reasons for which the Holy Ghost was given to the church. One must not praise, just for the sake of praising, but must praise "for something."

They were encouraged to practice the reality of Jesus, believing and conceiving of him as very present...and being there to help them yield and submit their whole being--their body--to him as vessels to contain the precious oil...the gift of the Spirit.

- *1CO 6:19 What? know ye not that your body is the temple of the Holy Ghost which is in you, which ye have of God, and ye are not your own?*
  *20 For ye are bought with a price: therefore glorify God in your body, and in your spirit, which are God's.*
- *2CO 4:7 But we have this treasure in earthen vessels, that the excellency of the power may be of God, and not of us.*

With this teaching fresh in their spirits, all "chronic seekers" came forward, along with several who were newly converted, but had followed in the old tradition of first getting saved, then at a later time receiving the Spirit. I reminded them that the Bible says at the time the Holy Ghost was poured out, the disciples were in one accord with each other. They were encouraged to embrace a spirit of unity and love toward their brethren.

- *ACT 2:1 And when the day of Pentecost was fully come, they were all with one accord in one place.*

Also, it was shown how the disciples were praising and magnifying God when the Holy Ghost fell upon them.

- *LUK 24:51 And it came to pass, while he blessed them, he was parted from them, and carried up into heaven.*

*52 And they worshipped him, and returned to Jerusalem with great joy:*
*53 And were continually in the temple, <u>praising and blessing God.</u>*

What happened that night, and for the next two nights was phenomenal. As these "chronic seekers" forgot about everything but Jesus, it began to be easy for them to believe in Jesus as the Baptizer...that he would help them walk in the power of the Holy Spirit. One-by-one they began to receive the manifestation of the gift of tongues, by which glorified and magnified the Lord. In addition, most began to speak boldly in English as well--interspersed with speaking in other languages--telling the church of the greatness of God. It was truly a dual manifestation of prophetic utterance by the Holy Ghost...part in their own language and part in tongues (languages) unknown to them. The supernatural anointing upon them was very obvious...without doubt, as obvious as what Simon the sorcerer saw when the Holy Ghost was poured out at Samaria, or as obvious as when the Holy Ghost fell on the men at Ephesus.

- *ACT 19:6 And when Paul had laid his hands upon them, the Holy Ghost came on them; and they spake with tongues, and prophesied.*
  *7 And all the men were about twelve.*

In helping these people, I had drawn from some of my own struggles which I had experienced while seeking to be baptized in the Holy Ghost. I warned them against allowing the devil to take advantage of their sincerity, making it difficult for their intellectual mind to release the control of their speech in order to allow the Holy Spirit to speak through them.

They committed their fears and reservations to Christ and their mind was not even on their speaking, or vocalization. Rather, their spirit was in tune with the Holy Spirit as he elevated their praises--in their own language--to a glorious, flowing river of worship...lavishing praises upon the Father and his Son. The transition to praises in other tongues was spontaneous, taking no self effort at all.

They knew for themselves, without any doubt, that they had spoken as the Spirit had given them utterance. Some soon became quiet...some were exuberant...some praised and rejoiced for a long while...others fell into pensive thought while basking in the presence of God--and the fellowship of such loving saints--because the entire church seemed to be re-baptized along with them. Joyous worship and praise flowed late into the night...but no one cared about the late hour...they were caught up in praise and worship.

But, the lady who had been "tarrying" for twenty-five years was still seeking. I asked God if there was anything I could say or do to help her. I asked her a few questions, as I felt led of the Lord. Her spirit seemed so dry, and her level of faith was at the bottom. She was aware that all the others were rejoicing in victory, and she alone was unfulfilled.

I asked her if, during the past twenty-five years she had ever experienced any spontaneous praise filled with joy and worship that seemed to flow out of her like an artesian well. I gave here the words of Christ:

- *JOH 7:38 He that believeth on me, as the scripture hath said, out of his belly shall flow rivers of living water. 39 (But this spake he of the Spirit, which they that believe on him should receive:*

She said this had happened numerous times, but not in a long time. It was obvious that disappointment had overpowered her courage to even expect an answer. She could not even muster up any excitement or hope that she might be filled.

The congregation became quiet as they listened carefully to my instructions, because they were aware of her situation. I began to quietly seek for a word of wisdom from God who soon spoke into my spirit these words: "ask her if she has ever groaned or agonized in the Spirit." I did so, and she replied that years ago this had happened to her. I was then prompted to ask her how long it had been since tears of joy and praise had come forth. She wondered why she could no longer cry...which she had previously done...in a deep and spiritually satisfying way.

I explained to her that those tears and groans were expressions of the Holy Spirit which he had demonstrated as normal human emotions quickened by the Spirit, but she had not recognized it, and had held back through timidity. I explained that God had given her a spoonful, but she had not received it by faith because it was not a shovelful, or a bucketful.

I encouraged her to submit to the Spirit, and if she ever again experienced groaning, crying, or even stammering lips, to accept it by faith, and to give the Holy Ghost credit for whatever he was giving…and, most of all, to not let the devil talk her out of accepting the beginnings of more to come.

She confessed that every time something happened that might have been the beginning of a manifestation of the Spirit, the devil was right there cautioning her to "be careful that you do not get in the flesh…make sure it is the Holy Ghost, and not you." I quoted to her the following scriptures:

- *ROM 8:26 Likewise the Spirit also helpeth our infirmities: for we know not what we should pray for as we ought: but the Spirit itself maketh intercession for us with groanings which cannot be uttered.*
- *ISA 28:11 For with stammering lips and another tongue will he speak to this people.*
  *12 To whom he said, This is the rest wherewith ye may cause the weary to rest; and this is the refreshing…*

I told her that sometimes these groanings and stammering lips often precede fluent speaking in other tongues, and these must be accepted as by the Holy Spirit, and not from her mind or will.

I explained that Paul said, the spirit of the Prophet is subject unto the prophet, and one can suppress speaking in tongues when there is no interpreter present. It is evident, that by the same token we can suppress, or limit the Holy Spirit's ability to speak through us--as she must have been doing…for other reasons.

I laid hands on her by faith, and eyes that had been dry for years began to swell with tears. I felt certain God was about to rain on her desert. I encouraged her to accept those tears as a manifestation of the indwelling presence of the Holy Ghost. I was beginning to realize how close to the truth I actually was when I assured her the Holy Ghost had come into her a long time ago, but she had not been able to allow him to manifest his presence because she was trying to make sure it was not her doing the manifesting. You see, Satan was whispering in her ear, cautioning her to make sure it was the Holy Spirit speaking ... and not her. Satan had been taking advantage of her honesty and sincerity.

To this she agreed, and the weeping became more intense. Her introverted sobbing changed into uninhibited crying...face open and upward. Her sorrowful crying soon shifted to crying for joy, filled with words of praise and adoration in English. It was not long before passionate groanings blended with her glorious worship.

With encouragement to accept all that was happening as coming from the anointing of the Spirit, and believing that the groanings by the Spirit were as authentic as speaking in other tongues, and just as scriptural, syllables and phrases other than English began to intermingle with her words of praise, and she knew the utterances were coming forth by the Holy Ghost. Very shortly thereafter she was speaking fluently in some foreign language, while the whole church rejoiced in praises, shouts of joy, worship, and adoration for Jesus the baptizer, for the Holy Ghost, and for God the Father.

Hallelujah!!

# CHAPTER 15

# ALL CHRISTIANS SHOULD SPEAK IN TONGUES

Everyone should accept by faith and have no doubt that the Holy Spirit took up his abode within them at the time they received Christ and were saved. In fact, receiving the Holy Spirit is confirmation that one has been forgiven and adopted into the family of God.

- *ROM 8:14 For as many as are led by the Spirit of God, they are the sons of God.*
  *15 For ye have not received the spirit of bondage again to fear; but ye have received the Spirit of adoption, whereby we cry, Abba, Father.*
  *16 The Spirit itself beareth witness with our spirit, that we are the children of God:*

It is a perplexing dilemma that a person who was given the Holy Spirit at the time of their conversion would continue to seek for the baptism with the Holy Spirit as though he had not yet been given to them. Contrary to traditional Pentecostal theology one must believe by the same faith whereby they accept their personal salvation that the Holy Spirit is also received as a part of the gift of salvation by grace. After one's faith has accepted the fullness of the new birth as being *"born of the Spirit,"* it becomes less complicated to receive the manifestation of the gifts of the Spirit simply because one believes their body has become the temple – dwelling place – of the Holy Spirit.

Once one accepts the teachings of Paul regarding speaking in other tongues, they will welcome the experience as a supernatural sign and confirmation that the Holy Spirit does dwell within, just as occurred on several occasions in the book of Acts, and they will *"desire spiritual gifts"* (1CO 14:1), including speaking in tongues.

The idea of "saved...but not yet baptized in the Spirit" is being brought up for review by this book you are reading. In the same context the idea of "saved...but not yet sanctified" is also up for questioning. If these important issues are accepted as an **inseparable** part of regeneration and renewal as the Bible says we must say what the Bible says. If it is true that at the time of the new birth one becomes a new creature in Christ Jesus...cleansed, washed, sanctified by the blood...and their body becomes the temple of the Holy Ghost, this must be preached around the world. Sanctification is a work of the Holy Spirit that is an inseparable part of the cleansing process when one is saved and filled with the Holy Spirit.

- *TIT 3:5 Not by works of righteousness which we have done, but according to his mercy he saved us, **by the washing of regeneration, and renewing of the Holy Ghost;***

   *6 Which he shed on us abundantly through Jesus Christ our Saviour;*

   *7 That being justified by his grace, we should be made heirs according to the hope of eternal life.*

**This is all a part of being born again which Jesus explained to Nicodemus:**

- *JOH 3:3 Jesus answered and said unto him, Verily, verily, I say unto thee, Except a man be born again, he cannot see the kingdom of God.*

> *7 ... Marvel not that I said unto thee, Ye must be born again.*
>
> *8 The wind bloweth where it listeth, and thou hearest the sound thereof, but canst not tell whence it cometh, and whither it goeth:* **so is every one that is born of the Spirit.**

Being *"born again"* and being *"born of the Spirit"* is a simultaneous, synonymous divine action of God's grace through the operation of the Holy Spirit. At the time of the new birth washing, regeneration, renewing, is all accomplished by the Holy Spirit as one is *"born of the Spirit."*

Everyone must seriously consider important scriptures with this view in mind – while realizing there is a higher truth, that all Christians--Pentecostal and Non-Pentecostal--can joyfully receive that will be a major step toward unity and fellowship among the family of God, the church of God, the body of Christ. The truth will not hurt us, it will set us free. We must not be afraid of exploring the word of God...neither fearful, lest we might have to change a little.

If Christ perfects his church as he said he would, I am sure we all will change a lot. Of course, at this point none of us can see just where or how, because we all figure we are mostly right, and have no need to change. But, we have the promise of Christ that the Holy Ghost will *"guide us into all truth"* (JOH 16:13). All truth? That is what he said! *"Ye shall know the truth, and the truth shall make you free"* (JOH 8:32).

## Do all speak with tongues?

This question is the subject and substance of this book you are reading. The answer is YES!!!

... Because all born again believers should speak with tongues. Jesus said, *"these signs **shall** follow them that believe,"* and he emphatically said, *"they shall speak with new tongues"* (MAR 16:17). All Christians should speak with tongues of praise; all should speak with tongues of intercession; and all could, at some time or other, speak to the church in other tongues, with the awareness that it should be accompanied by the gift of interpretation of tongues so that everyone present would know what was said.

## Paul's question, *"Do all speak with tongues?"* Explained

When Paul asked, "do all speak with tongues?" by no means was he trying to discourage speaking in tongues, or make the point that some Christians do not speak in tongues at all. Don't forget that Paul said, *"I thank my God, I speak with tongues more than ye all"* (1CO 14:18). Therefore, it can be rightfully deducted that all Christians in the Corinthian church spoke in tongues; however no individual spoke in tongues more than Paul. I am sure he was constantly driven to his knees in his secret closet of prayer where he relied heavily on the intercession of the Holy Ghost regarding his many trials and spiritual battles which he sometimes enumerated.

When Paul asked the question, *"Do all speak with tongues?"* he was giving instructions to the church concerning how the ministries and gifts of the Spirit should function in the church...especially when the whole congregation was assembled in a meeting, and it would only be appropriate that the manifestation of speaking in tongues should occur in an orderly fashion. Therefore, even though they were all capable of speaking in tongues, it was only reasonable that all could not expect to speak in tongues in one service. I am sure they were all eager to be used of the Holy Ghost for the edification of fellow believers, but it was not practical for all to speak in tongues. Paul advised that two or three should speak in tongues, and then one should interpret. Paul certainly was not saying there will be some persons who would never speak in tongues because not all speak in tongues.

Later, in this fourteenth chapter, Paul gives specific instructions concerning how the worship is to be conducted, *"decently and in order,"* when the church comes together in a formal assembly.

Paul was explaining this same thing when he taught that, just as everybody could not be an apostle, or a prophet, or a pastor, even so every person could not expect to be used to speak in tongues within a given worship service.

- *ICO 12:29 Are all apostles? are all prophets? are all teachers? are all workers of miracles?*
  *30 Have all the gifts of healing? <u>do all speak with tongues?</u> do all interpret?*

Chapters 12 through 14 of First Corinthians must be taken together as one unit or one inclusive body of instructions from Paul. The things said in chapter 12 ties into that said in 14. After giving previous teachings in chapter 12 and 13, Paul makes this connection by asking the question, *"How is it then brethren? When ye come together ..."*

- *ICO 14:26 How is it then, brethren? when ye come together, every one of you hath a psalm, hath a doctrine, hath a tongue, hath a revelation, hath an interpretation. Let all things be done unto edifying.*
  *27 If any man speak in an unknown tongue, let it be by two, or at the most by three, and that by course; and let one interpret.*
  *28 But if there be no interpreter, let him keep silence in the church; and let him speak to himself, and to God.*

Here is an extremely important point. These instructions are given for the purpose of teaching the church how it is supposed to be when they come together. Verse 26 establishes this. Then they are instructed concerning the decent and orderly conduct of the service. While they all have the indwelling gift of the Spirit for potentially giving a message to the church in other tongues, Paul is instructing them to be aware that they can't all speak in one service, but some will need to hold their peace, keep silence in the church, and speak unto themselves, and to God.

In light of the above scriptures, no one should exclude themselves from the blessing of speaking in other tongues as the Spirit gives the utterance. Don't be misled by some misguided teacher who discourages others by telling them that not everyone speaks in tongues. Speaking in tongues is Biblical; it is Old Testament; it is New Testament; it is Pauline; it is doctrinally sound; it is God's will directly from Christ, and it is for all Christians. One must remember the context in which Paul asked the question, "do all speak with tongues?" The answer once again: "yes, all can speak in tongues of praise, in tongues of intercession, and in tongues for interpretation."

While the ministry callings are given to specific persons and not to everybody, the operation of the gifts of the Spirit are not reserved to only specific persons, but are given to every believer.

# CHAPTER 16

# SPEAKING IN TONGUES IS ONE AMONG NINE GIFTS

All of the gifts of the Spirit are important and have their place within the daily operation of the church. It is evident that those who discount or reject the manifestation of speaking in tongues also limit or even delete the true operation of the other gifts.

I was in a service in a church which had not allowed speaking in tongues, or any other manifestation of spiritual gifts. The pastor spoke apprehensively concerning his fear that someone might speak in tongues in one of their services. A lady spoke up from the congregation, "It would scare me to death! If they do, I will leave and never come back." Many gave consenting nods and "amens."

This is a good example of how the Spirit is suppressed in ways too numerous to tell in churches throughout the world…all in ignorance concerning what the Bible says.

The gifts of the Spirit were given so that man could profit by them. They were not given to hurt, but to help; therefore one should not be afraid of them.

- *ICO 12:7 But the manifestation of the Spirit is given <u>to every man</u> to profit withal.*

These are things which Paul thought to be normal and that should be expected in the church because they were given by God.

The word, *"withal"* in the above verse is interesting. It means "by means of this." Paul was saying the manifestation of the Spirit is given to every man to profit *by means of this*. Paul excluded no one because he said the manifestation of the Spirit is given to *"every man"* to profit.

## Discerning of Spirits

Discerning of Spirits is a gift that is given little attention and is practically ignored in most church circles. A minister told me about pastoring a country church where there was a man who held so much power in the church that it made pastoring difficult. The man probably had more money than anyone in the community, and he exercised control over everyone and everything, including the pastor.

They began a revival meeting with a minister who was acquainted with the manifestation of spiritual gifts, and very soon he began to discern by the Spirit the situation concerning the dominant church boss. The first night this person sat on the front row and said amen to everything the evangelist said. He even said amen to some things as a cover-up, because everyone knew the preacher was coming down on him pretty hard.

The next night he sat one row back, and his amens were fewer and not quite so boisterous. Each night he sat progressively farther back and his face took on expressions of scorn and irritation. Finally, he could stand it no longer. Right while the preacher was preaching, he jumped out in the center aisle and demanded the evangelist to stop. He turned to the people and said, "we need to stop this meeting right now. This is no revival. All this man is preaching is condemnation."

This happened to be a church that preached strongly against the use of tobacco. The minister stepped in front of the pulpit, squared off fearlessly in front of the man, pointed a finger into his face and began to prophesy.

He told him how he had lorded over the whole church, including the preacher. He then began to tell him evil things about his life. The man denied angrily with threats of reprisal. It appeared he might even attack the evangelist.

The evangelist then said, just to show this church and this community, which you have deceived for years, God is going to reveal you for who and what you are. He then pointed to a teen-aged boy near the door saying, "young man, go outside to the back corner of the church. Count so many bricks up and then so many bricks to the right and you will come to a loose brick. Pull it out and you will find a pack of cigarettes that belongs to this man. God has shown me that it will be a pack of Lucky Strikes."

You see, what had been happening was, the man had been going out to an outside toilet during every service. He was an addicted smoker and could not last through a service without a smoke, and yet he had carried on within the church as though he was living by the standards of holiness espoused by the congregation. I am sure he defended the obvious smell of tobacco which he carried as being from others who smoked around him throughout the day.

The young man soon returned with a pack of cigarettes in his hand, exactly like the evangelist had prophesied. When the evangelist explained what had been going on, the congregation was able to verify the behavioral pattern of going out during every service. They just thought he had a small bladder, not realizing he had a big habit... and that he was a deceiver.

The man fell on his face, wept bitterly, was truly repentant, and experienced a true new birth. The evangelist had spoken in his own language which was also the language of the people, but he had spoken by the utterance of the Holy Ghost.

It is true that preaching can be prophesying, but not all preaching is prophesying. Everyone attempting to preach should hope that soon after they begin, the Holy Ghost will take over and begin to speak through them, just as authentically as if they were speaking in tongues by a supernatural manifestation...but in their own language.

Not all prophesying is as secret-revealing as the above story. Not all prophesying is as personal, but is directed to the congregation in general. It can be just as exposing to sinfulness and spiritual weakness at times. I am sure that the spiritual gift of discerning of Spirits also was manifested in the above story.

- *1CO 14:23 If therefore the whole church be come together into one place, and all speak with tongues, and there come in those that are unlearned, or unbelievers, will they not say that ye are mad?*
  *24 But if all prophesy, and there come in one that believeth not, or one unlearned, he is convinced of all, he is judged of all:*
  *25 And thus are the secrets of his heart made manifest; and so falling down on his face he will worship God, and report that God is in you of a truth.*

It is quite obvious that Paul fully believed in, and expected the gifts of the Spirit to be manifested. He knew that when one was baptized into Christ by the Spirit, they became a part of a spiritual church body which is analogous to a human body with arms, legs, eyes, ears, etc.

The operation of the gifts of the spirit through each individual member was totally a sovereign act of God, who places the members in the body as it pleases him. In this analogy, it is the gifts of the Spirit that give animation and life to each single member of the body.

Since the subject of this writing is "speaking in tongues," it must be pointed out that tongues is listed with an impressive group of gifts, and every one has their individually useful function. Ignorance concerning these gifts is tragic beyond comprehension for the church.

To develop the philosophy that some gifts are unimportant, or have become obsolete, or are outranked by more important gifts...or by charity...is not in keeping with the emphasis Paul places on each one, illustrating their individual uniqueness and importance.

As I write I seek to be anointed as much as when I stand in the pulpit to preach. I am equally desirous to speak by the gift of prophesy through my fingers as I type this manuscript. I hope and believe that it is by the gift of the Holy Ghost that I utter these words, thoughts and ideas. As I write I am motivated by the desire to endeavor to keep the unity of the Spirit in the bond of peace.

## The best gifts

Paul concluded the twelfth chapter with these words:

- *1CO 12:31 But covet earnestly the best gifts: and yet shew I unto you a more excellent way.*

What did Paul have in mind when he used the term "best?" A close study will reveal that uppermost in his mind was the edification of the church. To *edify* means to strengthen, build up, help, encourage, etc. He definitely was not putting some gifts down while elevating others. In order to understand this we must ask, "best for what?" It is obvious Paul was interested in that which is *best* for edifying the church when they come together for an assembled meeting.

## Tongues is not a lesser gift

Let me say at the outset in our search for the best gifts that one must not take the position that tongues is a lesser gift. Paul was not creating a *value-comparison* among the gifts because they each have their unique function and purpose. None can replace the other; neither can one gift be left out without losing an important operation of the Holy Spirit. Paul was not saying that prophesy is of greater value than tongues. He was actually stressing the importance of a third gift--the gift of *"interpretation of tongues."*

There are those who contend that tongues is a "lesser gift," and use that term almost every time they mention tongues. They speak only disparagingly concerning tongues. They have nothing good to say about it, because in ignorance they reject it.

The Bible does not say that tongues is a lesser gift. Men have created this idea from a statement made by Paul when he was giving instructions concerning the best use of the gift of tongues: *"...greater is he that prophesieth than he that speaketh in tongues"* (1CO 14:5).

From this many jump to conclusions, and magnify prophesying

while belittling speaking in tongues. This admonition from Paul is to encourage individuals to serve the greatest or most edifying function possible for the church's benefit. There are times when prophesying is more appropriate and beneficial for the assembled church body. But, the truth is, **speaking in tongues has equal value to prophesy if it is accompanied by the gift of interpretation**. This enables those who hear the speaking in tongues to understand what was said, and therefore to be equally edified. That is the whole objective--that everyone in the congregation be edified, or helped. Listen to the rest of that verse:

- *ICO 14:5 ...for greater is he that prophesieth than he that speaketh with tongues, **except he interpret**, that the church may receive edifying.*

Therefore, when the church comes together in an assembled meeting, and both prophesying and speaking in tongues occupies the attention of the whole congregation, speaking in tongues should be accompanied by the gift of interpretation of tongues in order to be of equal value as prophesying. Just keep in mind that the Bible does not say that tongues is a lesser gift. It is misinformed people who say this.

## Fruit of the Spirit is primary

You see, possessing the *fruit of the Spirit* is a prime prerequisite to being able to experience and manifest the *gifts of the Spirit*. I learned this directly from the Lord. I was driving on my way to church and had planned to speak concerning the manifestation of the gifts of the Spirit. Suddenly, I heard in my spirit as distinctly as if a voice had spoken audibly, *"One cannot manifest the true gifts of the Spirit without first possessing the fruit of the Spirit."* I quickly brought my car to a halt next to the curb and sat there dumbfounded. I had never given thought to this in the way that it had just been revealed to me.

I knew the passage well from Galatians, chapter five, and could quote it verbatim. I could also quote the verses from the twelfth chapter of First Corinthians which lists the gifts of the Spirit. But it dawned on me that this was exactly what Paul was saying when he said that if one tried to exercise the gifts of the Spirit such as tongues, prophesy, or understanding all mysteries and knowledge without having charity, a fruit of the Spirit, the gifts were as void and meaningless as a sounding brass or a tinkling symbol.

As I sat there beside the road contemplating what I had just heard, the Lord spoke to me saying, *"tell the people that if they desire to be used in the gifts of the Spirit, the way to achieve this is to seek for the fruit of the Spirit. When God acknowledges that they have the fruit of the Spirit, he will seek them out to use them in spiritual gifts."*

It is not uncommon for zealous people to try to force the operation of the gifts of the Spirit. One must be aware of this in order to understand how to achieve the true manifestations of the Spirit in their own life, and how to recognize it in others. This is why Paul said, *"Now concerning spiritual gifts, brethren, I would not have you ignorant"* (1CO 12:1).

It must be true that the early church learned by doing when it came to the gifts of the Spirit, and it is still true today. Of course, we have the benefit of the Scriptures. Also, concerning the operation of the church, Paul had been given revelation knowledge directly from Christ when he was caught up into heaven. Paul's advice and counsel was valuable then, and still is today.

Now, let's take another look at the last verse of the 12th chapter of First Corinthians:

- *1CO 12:31 But covet earnestly the best gifts: and yet shew I unto you a more excellent way.*

*"Covet"* means to strongly desire. For the sake of the church and for the benefit and advancement of the kingdom of God, one must strongly desire that the gifts of the Spirit should be manifested in the best way possible … the most genuinely supernatural in the pureness of the Holy Spirit … totally free from fleshly influence … coming forth from a purged vessel.

## A more excellent way

The last verse of chapter 12 is an introduction to chapter 13; *"I show unto you a more excellent way."* That more excellent way is fully explained in chapter 13 where charity is revealed as the indispensable ingredient in the manifestation of all gifts of the Spirit.

Notice that Paul said covet earnestly the best *"gifts"* (plural). He had all the gifts in mind, and was aware that the *"best gifts"* must also be motivated by pure charity. In fact, without true charity the gifts are rendered void and worthless.

When Paul said, *"covet earnestly the best gifts"* he had just enumerated a list of nine gifts, and in Chapter 13, was about to explain the proper and correct (best way) each gift was supposed to operate within the church.

## Interpretation not always required

One must keep in mind that all speaking in tongues does not require interpretation. There are tongues of worship and praise when a group or congregation flows together in spontaneous united worship and adoration in tongues while magnifying and speaking of the wonderful works of God:

- *ACT 2: 8 And how hear we every man in our own tongue, wherein we were born?*
  *11... we do hear them speak in our tongues the wonderful works of God.*

In this situation no one is holding the attention of the entire congregation while they individually speak in tongues, but the entire audience is lifting a concert of praise in tongues to God. This is beautiful and glorious to behold and hear, and must raise to heaven the fragrance of a spiritual bouquet of worship that gets the attention of all the hosts of heaven.

Also, there are tongues of personal intercession which has to do with individual needs. This should not be done in such a manner that occupies the attention of the entire congregation because no interpretation is required.

But, when the attention of an entire meeting is focused on one, or two, or at the most three, who are speaking in tongues in turn, then it is appropriate for the gift of interpretation to follow as only one person interprets the meaning of the message, or messages given in tongues.

This is why it is important that speaking in tongues in a worship meeting be interpreted so it can have an impact comparable to prophesy because it is in a language that can be understood by all, and especially by unbelievers, and hopefully they will be converted.

## Spiritual worship is all inclusive

All fruit of the Spirit and gifts of the Spirit should be equally engaged within worship activities of the church. To capitalize on one or two manifestations falls far short of what God intended when he sent the Holy Spirit to dwell within all believers that make up the church. Placing over-emphasis on a single gift such as tongues, or prophesy, or healing, etc., creates an imbalance that will become top-heavy and cumbersome. There must be a balance which includes all the manifestations and operations of the Holy Spirit.

- *1CO 12:4 (NIV) There are different kinds of gifts, but the same Spirit.*
  *5 There are different kinds of service, but the same Lord.*
  *6 There are different kinds of working, but the same **God works all of them in all men**.*

# CHAPTER 17

# SHALL TONGUES CEASE?

Let's consider a verse that has been seriously misinterpreted:

- *1CO 13:8 ...whether there be tongues, they shall cease;*

This verse is often used to support the opinion that speaking in tongues is no longer a valid gift to be manifested in the church today. This is a good example of where it is important to stick with the text and the subject, which, in this case is "charity." Paul was dealing with the matter of attempting to manifest the gifts of the spirit while failing to possess true charity towards those to whom one is ministering. Charity is more than sympathy, or an emotion, but is love with something in its hand to give, to help, to share, to care. Charity is a supernatural endowment of love which can be shed abroad in one's heart only by the Holy Ghost. Charity in its Biblical form is to possess a genuine concern for the spiritual and material needs of others with a sincere desire to help in some way to alleviate those needs.

## Indispensable Charity

In the previous chapter (First Corinthians, Chapter 12) Paul enumerated the gifts of the Spirit. Chapter thirteen continues by pointing out the futility of trying to manifest the gifts of the Spirit, namely of tongues, or prophesy, or the word of knowledge, discernment, or philanthropy, or self-sacrifice, without being motivated by pure charity. The results will be a carnal, fleshly display, rather than a Spiritual manifestation of true charity. True love for those in need must accompany the benevolence.

When Paul speaks of charity he is describing a genuine love that comes from the heart which prompts a believer to truly care for others in their time of need. This same kind of love prompts efforts to aid and assist others, whether it is by items of monetary value, or words of advice and wisdom that comes directly from God. Knowledge and faith are rendered powerless and void if it is not motivated by a sincere love and concern for those to whom one is ministering. Even spiritual gifts fall into the void category when charity fails. It is under these conditions that prophesy fails and tongues cease to be genuine.

- *1CO 13:1 Though I speak with the tongues of men and of angels, and have not charity, I am become as sounding brass, or a tinkling cymbal.*
  *2 And though I have the gift of prophecy, and understand all mysteries, and all knowledge; and though I have all faith, so that I could remove mountains, and have not charity, I am nothing.*
  *3 And though I bestow all my goods to feed the poor, and though I give my body to be burned, and have not charity, it profiteth me nothing.*

Paul continues talking about *charity*. The entire dissertation which follows is about charity and its importance. When the statement is made, *"when that which is perfect is come,"* he is talking about perfected charity.

- *COL 3:14 And above all these things put on charity, which is the bond of perfectness.*

The point is, charity must be the compelling force in one's heart that motivates them to minister and render spiritual aid to others, and to be selfless in their commitment to others.

- *2CO 5:14 (NIV) For Christ's love compels us, because we are convinced that one died for all, and therefore all died.*
  *15 And he died for all, that those who live should no longer live for themselves but for him who died for them and was raised again.*

Paul then describes charity:

- *1CO 13:4 Charity suffereth long, and is kind; charity envieth not; charity vaunteth not itself, is not puffed up,*
  *5 Doth not behave itself unseemly, seeketh not her own, is not easily provoked, thinketh no evil;*
  *6 Rejoiceth not in iniquity, but rejoiceth in the truth;*
  *7 Beareth all things, believeth all things, hopeth all things, endureth all things.*
  *8 Charity never faileth ...*

In comparison to manifestations of tongues, or knowledge, or other gifts of the spirit which can easily be flawed by human weakness, true charity will never fail. Verse 8 continues:

> *...but whether there be prophecies, they shall fail; whether there be tongues, they shall cease; whether there be knowledge, it shall vanish away.*

Paul is candidly speaking in terms of human frailty and failure. Attempting to be spiritual without charity is compared by analogy to being a child before growing into adulthood. The lack of understanding which is characteristic of a child, the limited knowledge, the speaking on the level of a child, all describe the person in the flesh before they gain the ability to minister in the spirit, and most important of all is to be able to do so by the motivation of charity. Remember that Paul has never left the subject of charity.

> *9 For we know in part, and we prophesy in part.*

*10 But when that which is perfect is come, then that
which is in part shall be done away.*

Being a child certainly limits one's ability. Being a child
spiritually has the same effect. The following verses confirm that
this is what Paul is saying, and it is only when one is able to possess
and demonstrate true charity, that those limitations are removed or
"done away."

*11 When I was a child, I spake as a child, I understood
as a child, I thought as a child: but when I became a
man, I put away childish things.*

The phrase, *"when that which is perfect is come"* is not speaking
about when Jesus comes again, but when charity comes into the heart
and spirit of the believer. It is then, and only then, they put away
childish things, and begin to see clearly, and to know spiritual truth
even as it has been revealed to them by the one who knows them
thoroughly.

*12 For now we see through a glass, darkly; but then face
to face: now I know in part; but then shall I know even
as also I am known.*

Paul has never deviated from the analogy of being a child vs.
being a man. There is nowhere in the context of this passage that
one should think that he suddenly jumped from the subject of the
necessity of charity to the second coming of Christ, even though
this has been the most common interpretation of this passage. The
fact that he has never left the subject of charity is evident in the next
verse.

*13 And now abideth faith, hope, charity, these three; but
the greatest of these is charity.*

*"Seeing through a glass darkly," "knowing in part," "and
prophesying in part," "prophesies that fail," "tongues that cease,"
"knowledge that vanishes away,"* are all from *"speaking as a child,"*
and must be *"done away."* Perfected charity must come. One must
cease to be a child spiritually and become an adult. One must see

clearly--*"face to face"*--and know the mind and knowledge of Christ--*"know as we are known."* Perfected charity, which is the love of God, comes into us by the Holy Ghost:

- *ROM 5:5 And hope maketh not ashamed; because **the love of God is shed abroad in our hearts by the Holy Ghost** which is given unto us.*

Charity must be considered as an indispensable spiritual endowment so that spiritual gifts can be truly genuine and profitable. As the church grows in perfection, speaking in tongues shall not cease, but shall increase through growing in grace because of the increasing ministry of the indwelling Spirit.

In Chapter twelve, Paul had stated he did not want the church to be ignorant of spiritual gifts.

- *1CO 12:1 Now concerning spiritual gifts, brethren, I would not have you ignorant.*

In this chapter (12) he tells them what these gifts are and how one receives them. He explains that these gifts are manifested through those who have become a part of, or a member, of the body of Christ, having been baptized, or placed into that body by the Holy Spirit.

## A more excellent way

The last verse of Chapter twelve introduces Chapter thirteen:

- *1CO 12:31 But covet earnestly the best gifts: and yet shew I unto you **a more excellent way.***

Instead of predicting that speaking in tongues would cease, chapter thirteen shows the church the most excellent way to be used in the operation of the gifts of the Spirit through charity, and how worthless and powerless the gifts are if "not" prompted and motivated by true charity.

Paul did not say that he could manifest the gift without charity, but said, "Though I was to do these things and have not charity." He was speaking strictly in the sense of a supposition..." just suppose I were able to speak with the tongues of men and angels, etc., while doing it without charity."

Paul continues with his emphasis on charity in the next chapter. The first verse says:

• *14:1 Follow after charity, and desire spiritual gifts ...*

## The gift of Tongues did not cease

To take this teaching and advice from Paul and turn it around to destroy the very thing he was reinforcing is missing the mark drastically. There is no way that Paul was destroying in the thirteenth chapter what he had established in the twelfth chapter. One must keep reading, and include all he said in these three chapters (12, 13, and 14) before telling anyone that tongues have ceased to function in the church today. Why would he give instructions in chapter 14 concerning the proper and orderly use of tongues in an assembly of the church if they had been declared to cease in chapter 13?

Just as the ministries--apostles, prophets, evangelists, pastors and teachers-- that God has set in the church are still in effect today, even so are the gifts of the Spirit, and none of them have been excluded or eliminated. When perfect understanding and knowledge about a matter comes, it does away with ignorance and partial knowledge. *"When that which is perfect is come, that which is in part shall be done away."*

When true charity is the motivation behind bestowing all one's goods to feed the poor...instead of profiting nothing, it gains rewards in heaven. What God wants is the real thing. He wants that which is perfect to come into the midst of the church..."*charity which never faileth."* This is the more excellent way Paul had in mind. This is the most excellent way to operate in the gifts of the spirit. Do not let anyone convince you they have been done away with.

# CHAPTER 18

# DESIRE SPIRITUAL GIFTS

The first verse in Chapter 14 immediately connects with charity and spiritual gifts in Chapters 12 and 13.

- *1CO 14:1 Follow after charity, and desire spiritual gifts, but rather that ye may prophesy.*

Also, the outline of chapter fourteen is set out in the first verse.

**(1) Follow after charity.**
**(2) Desire spiritual gifts.**
**(3) Emphasize prophesying.**

The "golden text" for chapter 14 is found in the twenty-sixth verse: I want to take another look at this important verse.

- *1CO 14:26 How is it then, brethren? when ye come together, every one of you hath a psalm, hath a doctrine, hath a tongue, hath a revelation, hath an interpretation. Let all things be done unto edifying.*

The question which begins this verse is, "*How is it then, brethren? When ye come together ...*" This question summarized the things that Paul was teaching. He was asking, **"how is it supposed to be**

**when the church comes together for a meeting"?** He immediately answers how it is supposed to be by telling them every one should come to the meeting expecting to contribute something. Depending on what they contribute, this could be prepared beforehand, or might be spontaneous as the Holy Spirit chooses to use them in the manifestation of some spiritual gift.

## Stand on the Word

At age 30 my father was a young Christian of about two years when he attended a church service in Perry, Oklahoma. A very large lady was testifying when an unexpected anointing came upon her. She suddenly placed her Bible on the floor, stood on it with both feet, and began to forcefully repeat, "Stand on the word! Stand on the word! Stand on the word!"

When this surge of spiritual energy subsided, she became embarrassed at what she had done as she imagined how awkward she must have looked, a woman of her size, trying to balance her weight on that small Bible--approximately one-half of a square foot.

Throughout the rest of the service she felt quite foolish, not knowing that her words had penetrated my dad's heart like a dagger. That was exactly what he needed to hear at that precise moment, and those four words, repeated several times had done more to change his life, forever, than a great oratorical sermon could have done.

At the close of the service Dad approached the lady to tell her what her obedience had meant to him, but before he could say hardly anything, she began to apologize saying, "I don't know what made me act like that. I became so embarrassed, and I know I must have embarrassed others." Dad stopped her abruptly. "No! No, sister! You will never know what that meant to me. You did that just for me. God spoke to me through that."

My dad told me more than once, that was a life changing moment for him, and he caught a glimpse of the importance of basing everything on the word of God, and trusting in its truths regardless. Of course, most manifestations of the operation of the Holy Spirit in speaking to the church are not as dramatic as that, but this illustrates just how much we must be willing to allow the Spirit to bypass our mind and override our restricting intelligence.

The list of the gifts of the Spirit given in First Corinthians, chapter twelve, includes the following:

> *"The word of wisdom, the word of knowledge, faith, gifts of healing, working of miracles, prophesy, discerning of spirits, divers kinds of tongues, and interpretation of tongues."*

None of these can be left out without creating a void where they rightfully should be operating. These all bring into operation the one-and-only, same Holy Spirit. They are all manifestations of him, and he must have someone through whom to manifest these gifts.

- *ICO 12:11 But all these worketh that one and the selfsame Spirit, dividing to every man severally as he will.*

I have explained that the word *"severally"* means "individually." All these operate by that one and selfsame Holy Spirit, spreading out the manifestations <u>to (through) every member</u> of the body <u>individually</u> as it pleases him. No person should withdraw from the Holy Spirit, refusing to allow him to use them for the glory of God. In fact one should look forward with excitement to the possibility of being used by the Spirit. One should covet the gifts of the Spirit, hoping he would use them as an instrument of blessing for the best interest of the church. This gives motivation for one to dedicate and consecrate themselves to God to be cleansed, and ready for holy use.

- *2TI 2:21 If a man therefore purge himself from these, he shall be a vessel unto honour, sanctified, and meet for the master's use, and prepared unto every good work.*

All gifts play their part in this process of building up the body of Christ, and each one is singularly indispensable. But, Paul majors on the necessity of *prophesy* for establishing the church in truth, in doctrine, and in understanding the word of God.

## An instructional guide

With this background, the fourteenth chapter of First Corinthians becomes a verse-by-verse instructional guide concerning the proper use and manifestations of the gift of tongues, interpretation of tongues, and prophesying. The first verse ties chapter thirteen to the next chapter with these words:

- *1CO 14:1 Follow after charity, and desire spiritual gifts, but rather that ye may prophesy.*

This is a transition verse from the subject matter of the "charity chapter." into the fourteenth, the "spiritual worship chapter." This chapter gives instructions concerning "how it is supposed to be when the church comes together."

The reason for desiring spiritual gifts will be to edify and build up fellow-members in the body of Christ. The prominent gift for edifying the church is *"prophesy."*

Prophesy is speaking by the power, anointing and direct utterance of the Holy Ghost in one's own language. This can occur in any speaking situation ranging from ministering from a pulpit to teaching a class--or while speaking to one person.

The following verses explain what is happening when one prophesies:

- *1CO 14:3 But he that prophesieth speaketh unto men to edification, and exhortation, and comfort.*
  *4 He that speaketh in an unknown tongue edifieth himself; but he that prophesieth edifieth the church.*

Paul fully expected every single member of the body, the church, to be capable of being used by the Holy Ghost at any time the Spirit chose, with whatever gift the Holy Ghost sovereignly determined to operate, demonstrate, and administer through them (1CO 12:5-7). When one receives the Holy Ghost they have the potential to be used in any single gift, or all of them.

As the early church continued to worship in the new supernatural dimension that had been given, the joy and deep feeling of praise and adoration of Christ which accompanied the manifestation of the gift of the Holy Spirit was a welcome departure from the drab, melancholy rituals of the temple worship under the yoke of the law.

Once anyone experiences the gift of *"divers"* (various) kinds of tongues even today, it is virtually impossible to reverse their mind on the matter. Those who have not experienced it will never understand, and will often be opposed until they do. Then, they too will be a staunch, fundamental believer in that which is so obvious in the Bible.

Unequivocally, and scripturally, every saved person has received the Holy Ghost as a gift from God. This occurs as an integral part of the new birth, which was described by Jesus as being born of the Spirit. But, at the present time within Christianity, a high percentage of believers have compelled the Holy Spirit to remain dormant, or inactive, in the most important areas for which he was given.

## Millions speak in tongues

Many have never shared in the joyous chorus of corporate praise as I, and millions of others have. The truth is, millions around the world are hungry for true spiritual worship and millions more have already tasted of the heavenly gift (HEB 6:4).

The following is an excerpt copied directly from the Wikipedia Encyclopedia.

**Pentecostalism** is a renewalist religious movement within Christianity that places special emphasis on the direct personal experience of God through the baptism of the Holy Spirit.

It is estimated that of the world's 2 billion Christians, a quarter are Pentecostals or Charismatics.

Estimated to number around 115 million followers worldwide in 2000, Pentecostalism is sometimes referred to as the "third force of Christianity."

Pentecostal and charismatic church growth is rapid in many parts of the world. Jeffrey K. Hadden of the Department of Sociology at the University of Virginia collected statistics from the various large pentecostal organizations and from the work by

David Stoll demonstrating that the Pentecostals are experiencing very rapid growth.

In the late 1960s and early 1970s, Christians from mainline churches in the United States, Europe, and other parts of the world began to accept the teaching that the baptism of the Holy Spirit is available for Christians today.

Charismatics adopted as their motto, "Bloom where God planted you."

http://en.wikipedia.org/wiki/Pentecostal

## The Holy Ghost fell <u>on all them</u>

When Peter preached at the home of Cornelius, he began to lift up Jesus. No one who has read the story carefully could disagree that Peter must have been vibrating on the inside with the power of the Holy Spirit as he spoke about Christ. The main ministry of the Holy Spirit is to testify about Christ. Jesus said, *"he shall testify of me"* (John 15:26).

Right while Peter was speaking, the Holy Ghost took over. The entire group of people suddenly began to speak in tongues. What were they doing? Magnifying the Lord!

- *ACT 10: 44 While Peter yet spake these words, **the Holy Ghost fell on all them** which heard the word.*
  *45 And they of the circumcision which believed were astonished, as many as came with Peter, because that on the Gentiles also was poured out the gift of the Holy Ghost.*
  *46 For they heard them speak with tongues, **and magnify God**.*

Here, simultaneously--all at once – all speaking at the same time--the Holy Ghost fell on *"all of them."* And, the Jews which came with Peter were amazed *"for they heard **them** speak with tongues."* The idea that it is out of order for several to speak in tongues at the same time is not Biblical.

Here is what happened when Paul found twelve men who received Christ at Ephesus:

- *ACT 19:6 And when Paul had laid his hands upon them, the Holy Ghost came on them; and they spake with tongues, and prophesied.*
  *7 And all the men were about twelve.*

The best thing that could happen to someone who does not believe in such is that it would happen to them just once. It would create havoc with their intelligent rationalizing. It would devastate their formalities. But it surely would release them from a lot of bondage which has built up over the years by unscriptural brainwashing through well-meaning pulpit advisors, friends, and teachers who really knew nothing about the manifestations of the Spirit and spiritual worship.

Many years ago when the Holy Ghost began to fall on churches throughout the country, a story was told about a farmer who attended a Methodist holiness meeting where the Holy Ghost had fallen on a rural church group. Of course this became the talk of the whole area, especially after the Holy Ghost fell upon farmer Jones, a well known man in the community.

A lot of wild, exaggerated stories were fabricated about the worshipping and rejoicing that went on at the meeting. Not long afterwards farmer Jones was out plowing in his field when farmer Brown rode by on his horse. Suddenly farmer Jones stopped his mule, grabbed his hat, and started whooping and hollering, running, jumping and dancing in circles around his mule and plow, all the while slapping his legs and ankles with his hat.

Farmer Brown had been extremely critical of the revival meeting where the Spirit was falling on people. His immediate reaction was that farmer Jones' religion had finally got to his head. Farmer Brown raced off toward town a short distance away, and in a cloud of dust pulled his horse to a stop in front of the Sheriff's office.

"Sheriff, sheriff!" he cried. "Come quickly. Farmer Jones has gone crazy. His religion has finally gone to his head." He described all the jumping and hollering, and the sheriff rode off to rescue the poor man from his religious craziness.

When the sheriff arrived, farmer Jones was plowing away, normal as ever. The sheriff stopped him and told him about the report from farmer Brown. He said you were jumping, and hollering, and running around and around your mule and plow. He vowed that your Spirit religion had gone to your head, and it had made you go crazy.

Farmer Jones calmly wiped the dust and sweat from his forehead, and said, "well sheriff, farmer Brown just didn't see those bees."

While it cannot be denied that there have been excesses of exuberance at times, and sometimes people have gone beyond the moving of the Spirit, and have reacted in the flesh, one must recognize that it is Biblical for there to be times of great joy and rejoicing as a normal expression of praise and worship.

There are many who "just haven't seen the bees." They have not felt the anointing and power of the Holy Spirit within their inner man.

When the Holy Ghost was poured out on the day of Pentecost, the disciples acted in such a way that some accused them of being drunk. Can anyone imagine anything any greater than being so full of the Spirit that one would be so released from the cares, worries, and problems of life, and for a few moments be able to break away into delirious happiness, rejoicing laughter, praise, worship and sheer joy and peace…and speaking in seemingly non-intelligible utterances.

- *ACT 2:12 And they were all amazed, and were in doubt, saying one to another, What meaneth this?*
  *13 Others mocking said, These men are full of new wine.*
  *14 But Peter, standing up with the eleven, lifted up his voice, and said unto them, Ye men of Judaea, and all ye that dwell at Jerusalem, be this known unto you, and hearken to my words:*

*15 For these are not drunken, as ye suppose, seeing it is but the third hour of the day.*
*16 But this is that which was spoken by the prophet Joel;*
*17 And it shall come to pass in the last days, saith God, I will pour out of my Spirit upon all flesh: and your sons and your daughters shall prophesy, and your young men shall see visions, and your old men shall dream dreams:*
*18 And on my servants and on my handmaidens I will pour out in those days of my Spirit; and they shall prophesy:*

Immediately after the Holy Ghost was poured out on the day of Pentecost, Peter explained the joyous events by quoting David:

* *ACT 2:26 Therefore did my heart rejoice, and my tongue was glad; moreover also my flesh shall rest in hope:*
  *28 ... Thou hast made known to me the ways of life; thou shalt make me full of joy with thy countenance.*

Paul and other disciples ministered mightily in Antioch in Pisidia. As they left that city and were heading for Iconium, the following describes their happiness in the Lord:

* *ACT 13:52 And the disciples were filled with joy, and with the Holy Ghost.*

Is it any wonder that the contrast was drawn by Paul, using the extreme opposites and yet analogous likeness of being drunk with wine and being drunk on the Spirit.

* *EPH 5:18 And be not drunk with wine, wherein is excess;* *but be filled with the Spirit;*
  *19 Speaking to yourselves in psalms and hymns and spiritual songs, singing and making melody in your heart to the Lord;*
  *20 Giving thanks always for all things unto God and the Father in the name of our Lord Jesus Christ;*

It makes one not just want to see the bees, but to "wake up and smell the roses." This is exactly what Paul was saying in this same chapter:

- *EPH 5:14 Wherefore he saith, Awake thou that sleepest, and arise from the dead, and Christ shall give thee light.*

If one sees the light on the Holy Spirit, they will never be the same. They may think they have the light, but if they do not have the joy, the power, the manifestations, the anointing, and the gifts, it is more than likely they have seriously quenched the Spirit.

If their only mention of the Holy Spirit is in caution, or warning, or negative ways, it is certain they do not have the freedom, or fullness of the Spirit. They are not qualified advisors, and yet they will speak with pretense of great authority on the subject. How sad!

Now, listen carefully. The most important sign which has been given to believers so they can know without any doubt that they have been given the seal and earnest of the Holy Spirit is speaking in tongues which *"are for a sign"* that will transfer one from the ranks of the unbelievers to the camp of the believers forever. Read all the above verses again ... and again!

- *1CO 14:22 Wherefore tongues are for a sign, not to them that believe, but to them that believe not:*

Therefore, tongues are not an initial evidence that one has just received the Holy Ghost, but is a *"sign"* that the Holy Spirit was given to them when they were saved. Everyone who claims to have obtained salvation through faith in Christ must also accept by the same faith that Christ has, as a part of the salvation plan, baptized them with the Holy Ghost.

## Encouragement to those who should speak in tongues

Those who have been saved for a long period of time, but who have never experienced the confirming manifestation of the Holy Spirit through the gift of tongues should set their heart and mind on pursuing the fullness of the salvation experience as clearly outlined in the word of God. A great spiritual satisfaction will be obtained in actually tasting of the sign of confirmation as Paul said, *"Wherefore, tongues are for a sign"* (1CO 14:22).

## Move into the fullness

This is not saying they are not truly saved, but it does say they have additional important ground to cover regarding their walk with the Lord. One thing is for sure. Once they have experienced the miracle of speaking in other tongues as the Spirit gives the utterance they will have taken a giant leap into the confirmed camp of believers because they have received the Biblical sign.

There are millions of saved people who, for a multitude of reasons, have failed to move into the fullness of the salvation plan provided for them through the Holy Spirit. They must be encouraged to move into their rightful life and walk in the Holy Spirit which was provided for them when they were born of the Spirit.

A simple way to obtain this confirmation is to glorify and praise God in one's own language while expecting the Holy Spirit to add his anointing of praise and worship to their words, while being willing for the Spirit to magnify Christ as utterances begin to come involuntarily, to which they yield their soul, spirit, mind, and body … as they worship Christ their Lord in the Spirit.

One should worship, praise, and magnify God at every opportunity, not only when they are in church, but when away from church. One should kneel beside their bed when retiring and spend some time in praise and worship.

They should expect and anticipate that the Holy Spirit may intersperse utterances along with their words that are involuntary and without understanding on their part. They should go with the flow while accepting by faith that the word of God is coming alive within them. It is a time of total trust and surrender. One must not focus primarily on the utterances or analyze them, but should keep their mind centered on God and his word. While enjoying intense worship one should relax their control over their speaking, and make their lips, mouth, tongue, and voice available to the Holy Ghost for him to give utterance in worship and praise to God.

This can occur anywhere – while washing the dishes, doing house cleaning, raking the yard, driving the car, and especially when awaking in the middle of the night. Any person, saved or unsaved, should anticipate such an encounter with Christ and the Holy Ghost. They should *"desire spiritual gifts"* (1CO 14:1). They should appreciate the Holy Spirit as a Gift from Christ.

# CHAPTER 19

# CONTEMPORARY EXPERIENCES

While the title of this book asks the question, *"Should All Speak With Tongues?,"* emphasis cannot be just on speaking with tongues, but on the Holy Spirit, including all the fruit of the Spirit and all the gifts of the Spirit.

It does not take a deep study of the word of God to discover that speaking in tongues is only the beginning of living and walking in the Spirit, but those who receive the truth regarding speaking in tongues find that willingness to walk in truth discussed in this book leads to many open doors of spiritual power and knowledge, meaning all the *"administrations," "operations,"* and *"manifestations,"* of the Holy Spirit (1CO 12:5-7). Living and walking in the Spirit can become an exciting way of life for those who dare to take the word of God literally concerning the gifts and operations of the Holy Spirit.

## Leroy Butler

A remarkable event occurred when a dear friend of mine and I would go to a black neighborhood on the north side of our town. We would arrive early on Sunday mornings, before time to go to our church. We would go to the center of black businesses which had a couple of grocery stores, a restaurant, a few bars which had been filled until near dawn, and a barber shop which was the center of activity for several men who got out at an early hour.

On this occasion we first went into the barber shop, which we had done several times. I played my accordion and sang, and Leroy preached a short message. He had a remarkable ability to stir people into attention about heaven and hell. It was not uncommon for the Holy Spirit to convict men on the spot, unexpectedly, and sometimes against their will...but the power of God was strong, and several prayed fervently.

Next, we went across the street to a night club where we found numerous couples sitting in booths and at tables...sleeping off hangovers. A tired little lady looked through a serving window at us. Leroy asked her if it was OK for us to sing and preach to her customers. I suppose she was waiting for them to awaken so she could serve them breakfast, hoping to make a little money.

It was obvious by the way they were zonked out that they had partied all night, and I had little hope of arousing any interest among these near-dead folk. But Leroy, the most indomitable man I have ever known, said, "Brother, start playing your accordion and sing *Peace In The Valley.*"

When I began, it was hilarious as Leroy went around and began to shake them, telling them to wake up...that we were going to have church. They were so limber and lifeless, try as they might, most of them just could not make it, but would flop down again like a rag doll. Leroy gave me swirling hand signals to come on out with the singing...louder and louder. I responded and he kept going back, and around, until he had most of them sitting up and getting their eyes open a little. They all had such a hang-over, this was no easy task.

When they got awake enough to realize where they were, they began to look at each other in total disbelief. Leroy began to instruct them to look at me and listen to the words I was singing. He assured them that Jesus was coming, and they would be left behind if they did not pay attention. They tried their best, but sleepily, at best.

Leroy then asked me to sing, "It is no Secret What God Can Do." This song seemed to turn him on, and he took on an evangelistic fervor as though, if he did not get all these people saved, their blood might be on his hands. It was not long before he had every single person on their knees crying out to God for mercy. Several of them were there with someone who was not their marriage partner. It was a miracle how conviction gripped those people, and needless to say, I was singing under an anointing that I would have thought impossible at 7:45 A.M. Tears were flooding down my cheeks as I went from song to song, rejoicing as much as I was singing.

Finally, Leroy said to them, "you have been here committing sin against each other, against your husbands and wives, against your children, and against God. Now you leave this place and don't come back." Leroy knew the woman at the window might not like what he had said, and he turned to face her. Tears were running down her face, and she said, that is OK. I hope they all get saved, and you all come back anytime you want.

Everyone got up with tears in their eyes, hugging us, shaking our hands, and began going out the door. As the last woman started out the door, the power of the Spirit came upon Leroy and he stopped her as she stood against the half-opened screen door. He asked, "Sister, do you know anything about the Holy Ghost?" She replied, "no sir, I have never gone to church and I don't know anything at all about that stuff."

Leroy said to me, "Brother, let's lay hands on this woman. God wants to baptize her in the Holy Ghost." You can understand my amazement when we simply laid hands on her, and her hands flew into the air while she began to speak in a language which sounded perfectly foreign. This continued for several minutes. She actually did not know what had happened to her, but she knew it was divine. She had been sovereignly filled with the Holy Ghost just like those at Pentecost, at Cornelius' house, and at Ephesus.

We explained what had happened, wrote some scripture locations for her to read, and sent her away rejoicing. As she went across the street, through a vacant lot, and disappeared between some buildings, she was waving her hands to God and rejoicing for her new-found fellowship with God. I wished we could follow up more, but that was not possible at the time. We encouraged her to find some new friends who knew about Jesus and the Holy Ghost, and left her in God's hands ... and commended her to God ... much like Paul did at Ephesus:

- *ACT 20:25 And now, behold, I know that ye all, among whom I have gone preaching the kingdom of God, shall see my face no more.*
  *32 ... **And now, brethren, I commend you to God, and to the word of his grace, which is able to build you up, and to give you an inheritance among all them which are sanctified.***

## B. H. Clendennen

An interesting incident was related by Brother B.H. Clendennen, from Beaumont, Texas. He had the opportunity to minister in South Viet Nam, during the war. It was a miracle that he was allowed to go into secured governmental and military facilities which were highly restricted. It was his opportunity to speak to people who knew only about the religion of the Vietnamese, plus a few who had limited knowledge regarding Christianity. But, before the meeting he was warned that he could say nothing about the Holy Spirit in the Pentecostal sense. It would be permissible to make reference to the Holy Spirit, but not the baptism in the Holy Spirit. The religious leaders in charge said this would introduce confusion, and informed him that if he did so, there would be secret agents in the audience who would escort him out.

The night before the meeting, he was tempted to decline, rather than submit to such a limitation. He and his wife prayed in their hotel room for guidance, and he concluded that he had wondered at times if a lot of Pentecostalism, and particularly speaking in tongues was not a learned or programmed response. He concluded that he would do just as they asked. He would magnify Christ, and make references to the Holy Spirit in the context of his present-day work as the messenger of Christ, doing the work of Christ today through those who have received Christ.

He gave an invitation for those who wanted to be a person through whom Christ worked, but he said nothing about the gifts of the Spirit, especially speaking in other tongues.

I heard Brother Clendennen's wife relate the story, and how it changed her life to witness fifty-some people come forward. Brother Clendennen knew that the moment of truth had come. Could it be possible that these people who had come to make a commitment to Christ could be baptized in the Holy Ghost as sovereignly as on the day of Pentecost? Could they, or would they begin speaking in other tongues, just as spontaneously, without any knowledge of the phenomenon beforehand?

Suddenly, confusion began breaking out. It was evident that secret servicemen began to rise, but not knowing what to do. The interpreter turned to Brother Clendennen saying, "something is wrong…these people are acting strangely…they may be losing their minds." Brother Clendennen asked, "what's the problem?" It was obvious that they were all overwhelmed in ecstatic praise and worship, and Brother Clendennen suspected what had happened, but he asked again, "what's taking place?" The interpreter said, they are all talking, but not in their language. They are confused.

Every person in the line was sovereignly baptized in the Holy Ghost and began to speak in other tongues as the Spirit gave them utterance. There was no way Brother Clendennen could be blamed for it, nor held responsible for it…neither could he take credit. God did it. I have relayed this story from memory, after several years have passed, but I am sure a copy of the complete story could be obtained from Brother Clendennen, of Beaumont, Texas.

## Vessie Hargrave

There are continuous testimonies from somewhere in the world that speaking in other tongues is confirmed as being a supernatural utterance of a known language by someone who does not know the language at all. Vessie Hargrave was a man who gave his life to ministering in remote, mountainous jungles of Mexico. He was the first Caucasian they had ever seen. The son of American missionaries, he had been born in Mexico. He obtained his Doctorate from Trinity University in San Antonio, Texas. Having learned the language of Mexico as a child, he was very fluent in both English and Spanish which were both studied as part of his Doctoral Degree.

Early in adulthood he also ministered in Mexico. His desire was to reach tribes of people so far back in the mountains that they had never been contacted with the gospel of Christ. He pioneered such a successful work among the Mexican Indians that crowds of several thousand walked many miles to attend an annual conference. As the work grew, others from America traveled with him to the meetings. He told me personally that, on several occasions, he had heard native Mexicans speak beautiful English when they were filled with the Holy Ghost.

I personally heard Lee Watson, a very prosperous businessman from Atlanta, Georgia, as he spoke at a missionary convention in Memphis, Tennessee, attended by several thousand people. He gave a report on a trip he had taken with Vessie Hargrave. Mr. Watson said they traveled into the mountains as far as possible by truck then transferred to a Jeep because the road became so rocky and impassable by other vehicles. Finally, they changed to donkeys and traveled for many more steep miles and came to a remote tribal mountain village.

Vessie had been ministering to these people for a few years, and was the only white man, or American, they had ever seen before Lee Watson and a few others who came. These people had experienced a mighty move of God, and many miracles like those in the Bible had occurred in their midst. Blindness, deaf ears, crooked limbs, deadly diseases, etc., had been healed. Demons had been cast out of many, and the dead had been raised.

Many of these small statured, barefooted people had walked for days, bringing their sick, lame, and demented for help. This was an annual special meeting attended by several thousand natives. The crowd pressed right against the two white men as they began to pray and minister to the people's needs.

Suddenly a woman in the crowd began to speak quite loudly in beautiful, unbroken English, with no dialect...perfect English. She sounded like an ordinary, everyday American.

Lee Watson said he looked with startled amazement to Vessie Hargrave, and said, "I did not know there were any Americans here, or anyone who could speak English. Vessie replied, "there isn't." She has just received the baptism in the Holy Ghost. The woman who was obviously an uneducated Mexican Inca Indian continued for a long while in English, praising God and magnifying Jesus as Lord, Savior, Redeemer, and coming King. These are reputable men, and I heard the testimony from them personally.

## O. E. and Betty Waters

A long-time acquaintance and dear Christian brother and wife, O.E. and Betty Waters, who live in my hometown, felt a call to minister in Mexico, so they bought a passenger bus and had it converted to a motor home. They began to make frequent trips into Mexico taking food, clothing, Bibles and medical supplies.

They were at an age when normally they would be thinking of retirement, but here they were, keeping themselves exhaustingly busy. They were not sponsored by any organization, and did the entire ministry on their own. A few people would help them gather clothing and other items for Mexico, and some would give donations of money, but by-and-large, most of the items and money would come from their own pockets and self efforts.

Eventually, their married children, other relatives, close friends, and even church associates and ministers began to discourage them from making another grueling trip. They were also placed in grave physical danger at times. Their friend's reasons for why they should not go were realistic and their arguments persuasive, but, O.E. and Betty just could not be talked out of it.

Some of the church people became almost offensive as they began to tell them they were not authorized to do missionary work since they were not officially approved by the mission board of some church. This hurt, but they kept smiling and went on anyway, believing they were called of God to this work. Needless to say, Satan used this to his advantage because some had even slacked off from being supportive financially.

They found themselves asking God if they were in his will, and nagging doubts began to arise. They had just about decided to make their last trip when God gave them a miracle.

They had gone to a little country church deep into Mexico to help an aged lady missionary who had been there many years. She had started two churches, and they had finished service in one and were on their way to another. They followed the lady missionary who was driving her car ahead of the bus. Suddenly her car's engine stopped, and her efforts to restart the engine failed.

Finally, when O.E. tried to start her car, it started immediately, and he thought this was a little strange. He offered to drive the missionary's car the rest of the way, just in case it acted up again. Betty Waters was accustomed to driving the bus, so the missionary lady rode with her as they continued their trip.

There were several young Mexican men in the car with O. E. In their excitement over the car running again, they began to worship and sing as they went down the road. Their worship turned into praise and it seemed to O.E. that some were beginning to praise in other tongues, since O.E. had a limited knowledge of Spanish, and he realized it did not sound like they were speaking Spanish which was the only language they knew.

Suddenly, the one sitting next to O.E. turned to him, and began to speak in perfect English. He began to tell O.E. about those who had tried to discourage him from coming to Mexico, but assured him that he was in God's perfect will. He was told not to listen to men, but trust in God.

We can imagine O.E.'s reaction of amazement when something so supernatural like that happened. The truth is, it actually did occur. There was no doubt in O.E.'s mind that God had spoken to him directly and personally through that uneducated Mexican youth. It confirmed many things to O.E., one of which was the validity of speaking in other tongues as being literal human languages. O.E. and Betty wept as they related the story to me and my wife, Margaret.

## Thomas Ball Barratt

Thomas Ball Barratt who had founded the famous Filadelfia Church in Oslo, Norway, visited the Azusa Street Mission in 1905, and received the message concerning the Holy Spirit which was being poured out abundantly. He returned home and became known as the Father of the Pentecostal Movement in Europe. He also spent a year in India, during which time illiterate Indian girls who knew no English prayed and praised the Lord in perfect English. The same thing happened in China among ignorant Chinese who knew no English.

(Ref. "Warning! Do Not Seek for Tongues," Page 118, By Joe E. Campbell, Th.D.)

## C. B. and Lorell Anderson

I co-pastored for thirteen years with C.B. Anderson, and his wife, Lorell, who had been missionaries to India for seventeen years. I asked them if they had ever heard native Indians speak in English while they were speaking in tongues. They said they had heard this happen several times.

## My personal experience

When I was seventeen years of age, I experienced speaking in tongues for the first time while attending a rural church in Mount Olive, Tennessee. Immediately thereafter, I was bombarded with doubts concerning the experience. Prior to experiencing speaking in other tongues, I had resolved in my mind that, if I ever spoke in tongues, it would be the real thing…and not done by me. I guarded against being prompted by such a strong desire that I would help the Holy Ghost a little. Nevertheless, after it happened, I was still challenged by Satan who accused me of being over-anxious.

It happened as follows: I had gone forward to the altar in response to an invitation. A couple of dear farmers who were real prayer-warriors knelt with me and began to encourage me to submit to the Holy Ghost and let him baptize me. I had come to the altar just to pray…not to get involved in seeking for the infilling of the Holy Ghost…but they were persistent. I began to feel guilty for my lack of interest, and through a prayer of confession for this attitude, I sensed a deep, warm, loving presence of God overtake my spirit in a special way.

As I had done many times before, I began intently seeking to be filled. Of course, I expectantly wanted to speak in other tongues, but was at a total loss as to how to submit, or allow the Holy Spirit to baptize me. Several things these men said helped me greatly. I knew they were rough, hard-working, sincere men who loved God with all their heart. Their diamond-hard qualities and value would not be recognized by most churchmen, or ministries, but I recognized that God knew them, and they were anointed to pray with me.

One said to me, "son, don't pray with your lips, pray with your heart." That struck home, and immediately I began to sense my prayer, and praises coming from my innermost being. I began to wait until genuine, heart-felt praises would spring forth like a geyser. In a few moments I felt a praise begin to surge forth like a soft, moving rumble, deep in my spirit, and I just held back, suppressing it a little.

Tears of joy and praise filled my dry eyes, gushing forth like tiny flowing streams tracing their way down my cheeks. The hot tears flowed over my lips and splashed onto the altar below my face.

At this point, I must relate that one dear brother must have loved garlic and onions. While he was helping me, the devil was using his garlic breath to hinder me. I backed away, and finally put my face down beside the altar to get away from his ever-increasing "hallelujahs" and "amens."

My legs began to hurt from kneeling for so long, and as I attempted to change positions to sitting sideways, somehow I turned a little too far, and wound up in a painfully twisted position, hanging onto the heavy wooden altar bench for support. In desperation I turned the altar loose and could not keep from going flat on my back alongside the altar. The dear farmer could now reach right over the altar with his face right above mine. I thought I could not take this, but the spirit of prayer, worship, and praise was on me so mightily that I was more interested in keeping the momentum of the spiritual flow; therefore, I slid my face right under the bench-type altar and kept praising God with great joy.

I reached the point that my praise was no longer a mental or intellectual effort, and I would wait upon the words to come from the depths of my innermost being. I had the sensation of a spontaneous, free-flowing artesian well swelling up from within, and I just waited. I could hold it back no longer, and the word "hallelujah" came slowly rolling out in a deep, crying, rejoicing expression of praise.

But, I got only a couple of syllables out when the last two did not fit the word. My mind suddenly reasoned that I had become so ecstatic in praise that I had got mixed up, so I thought about that a few seconds when, here came that deep, wonderful feeling of praise again. I determined that I would take care not to help the Holy Ghost, meticulously avoiding going into gibberish, or non-intelligible utterances on my own, to avoid thinking I was speaking in other tongues when I was not.

But the same thing happened again, even with my trying to say "hallelujah" carefully and precisely. Those last two syllables came again, exactly as the first time. The inner-explosion of praise became stronger and my ability to hold it back became less as the urge came in the form of the words "glory to God."

Needless to say, it was as though an involuntary speech force would finish my words, superimposing its will over mine, causing me to say sounds that did not come from me at all--not my mind, or my will--and yet it soon became obvious as I continued from various words and phrases, that my heart was sensing the very close presence of God.

I began to wonder why this was coming forth, half English, and half something else. Once again God used one of the farmers who said, "the devil is a tricky old fellow. He will take advantage of you through your honesty and sincerity. He will try to convince you that it is you getting your tongue tangled up right while the Holy Ghost is helping you turn your speaking over to him."

I thought that over a little, and, hey! I felt that deep moving of the Spirit in my soul again and I determined I would not try to hold back. I relaxed and the praises began to flow, but not in my language, but quite soon I began to take back over with my sincere logical reasoning…"It will not be me when I speak in tongues."

Then the devil began to whisper in my ear, "that cannot be God…there was such a little of it." About that time God used one of the farmers again, who said, "Accept by faith whatever God gives you. If he gives you a spoonful, accept it. Don't refuse it because it is not a shovelful. God has more, and if you do accept the spoonful, it will be easy to believe for the shovelful. Don't worry! God has a tubful."

I suddenly realized that I must accept by faith what God had given, and even if it was seemingly a small quantity, that was not what mattered. It was the substance that was important. I found myself momentarily believing that I had spoken in tongues, at least a little.

Once I began to accept this gift of God by faith, I found it easier to shove Satan's suggestions and doubts into the background. The Holy Ghost truly took control, and it was almost like listening to someone else speaking through my vocal cords. The sounds began to take the form of a foreign language, and by an utterance that came from within without any prompting from my mind or intellect, I worshipped and praised God for several minutes. I was refreshed, relaxed, overcome with joy and felt pleasant inner peace…and I was satisfied that I had truly spoken in other tongues as the Spirit gave the utterance.

But, as I said, on the way home, the devil jumped on me with all four feet. My rational mind began to convince me that I had, after all, maneuvered myself into an emotional release to satisfy a spiritual longing. Several days of frustration followed, and I hardly had the spirit to pray, let alone expect to speak in tongues again.

At that time I was a student at Lee College in Cleveland, Tennessee, where, a week later I had another outstanding encounter with the Holy Ghost. Following a student assembly and chapel service, a few students lingered in the main auditorium. They began to talk about God and started praying. I was so miserable, confused, and unsure of my experience that I said, "God, I am going backstage and get between those heavy velvet curtains and stay there until I settle this issue. Either I received the Holy Ghost and spoke in other tongues, or I did not. I have got to know, and I will settle this issue, or stay there until my bones bleach." I knew no one would know I was there, and it would be several days before the auditorium would be used again. The huge backdrop curtains were spaced about two feet apart and would give me an excellent place to hide away with God.

I slipped around through a side door, making sure no one saw me. I knelt and began to explain my plight to God. Almost before I could get started, that well of water began to flow, first like an artesian spring, then like a fountain, then like a geyser--splashing, gushing, overflowing, lifting high in praise, then subsiding in soft worship. Ecstatic rapid words would rush forth in utterances unfruitful to my understanding. Then slow, rolling words filled with emotions of sheer worship and adoration would swell forth.

Then praises in English would lavish the Holy One, yet in eloquence and expressions that were beyond me in literary style and excellence, comparable to Shakespearean quality. I knew that God was showing me that the Holy Ghost was able, not only to speak in other languages through me, but he was able to speak through my own language, yet under his control, and not mine. This went on for several minutes and I was totally satisfied and convinced, because all doubt had been removed, and remains removed to this day. God had been gracious to me to give me such a convincing experience, and I loved him for it.

But, I had no idea what was about to happen next. I was surprised to find that the other students were still in the auditorium. Several thicknesses of heavy velvet curtains had made the space around me practically soundproof. I sat down with the group who were singing some songs. We began to softly sing, "Search me, oh God, and know my heart today." It suddenly dawned on me that, without realizing it I had switched to singing in the Spirit.

## Jean Suliman

About that time, a foreign student named Jean Suliman, said,

"Listen! Mac is singing in French! I kept on singing … just submitting … not trying to keep on…but not trying to stop either … just singing, and worshipping to the depths of my soul.

I was not out in a trance, but fully conscious, sitting in a theatre-type auditorium seat. I had my eyes closed and my face looking upward. I could hear their discussion of what was happening. Jean began to interpret everything I was singing, and for several minutes I sat spell-bound by what was coming out of my mouth. It was literally beautiful. Jean had the natural French accent that can make English so beautiful. French was her native language.

The praise was all about Jesus…who he was…his involvement in creation…his relationship to the Father…his Godhead… his mission to earth…his glorious ministry, suffering, death, resurrection, ascension, his future reign as King-of-Kings and Lord-of-Lords, his kingdom, and…on and on. The phraseology was so far beyond my ability that it was unbelievable. Things came forth about his kingdom that I did not even know, but learned later through study--His heavenly Priesthood, his anticipated Millennial Kingship.

All those around me were softly weeping, praising, speaking in tongues, and listening at the same time, as they listened to the Spirit as he used me to bring forth supernatural anthems of praise that moved in and out of unbelievable poetry…to prose…in eloquent descriptive phrases and adjectives…all conforming to the beautiful melody of the song, *"Cleanse Me."*

After the power and unction of the Spirit subsided within me, excited discussions began with all sorts of questions and answers. These kids--my friends--knew me, and they knew I could not do that on my own. Jean Suliman was disbelieving, and yet she had heard it for herself, in her own language. The others questioned her thoroughly. They questioned me: What was it like? How did you feel? Were you in a trance? Could you hear us? Could you hear Jean as she told us what you were saying? What were you thinking? Did the thoughts come and then you sing them? Were you thinking in English as you were singing in tongues? Was it hard to keep going for so long? Were there any momentary hesitations in your mind? Was God speaking to you? Did it feel good?

I recall the experience as vividly as if it were yesterday. I remember the inner peace and pleasure I experienced as I listened to the obviously French sounding vowels and consonants formed involuntarily. I knew there had to be a supernatural source for what I was doing because there was no way under the sun that I could even pretend to speak in French and make it sound like the language. It was obvious that I was actually singing in a foreign language the same way as on the day of Pentecost.

I will never forget when I looked straight into the eyes of Jean and asked her intently, "Jean, are you sure?" She looked back at me with even deeper intensity as she replied, "If you heard someone speak in English, wouldn't you be sure?"

We all knew that we were not lying to each other. This was real. This was Biblical. Something had happened to us that would never be taken out of our hearts. Faith in Jesus as the baptizer in the Holy Ghost was confirmed beyond any doubt. Resolve broke into fervent flames within all of us as we determined to find those who were being robbed of this miraculous truth and help them to understand the reality and importance of this beautiful and marvelous gift.

We suddenly understood why Satan would fight it so hard. We had tasted; we had felt; we had seen! And, Satan does not want that. He does not want us to experience the real, true, authentic, spiritual power of God. He works through neighbors, friends, relatives, and even preachers, to prevent anyone from moving into the realm of the Spirit to this extent.

Everyone has the power to choose what they want to believe. One must choose to believe the Bible just as it is without limiting the truth of God's word contained therein. God can, and will confirm his word to those who hunger and thirst after righteousness.

- *MAT 5:6 Blessed are they which do hunger and thirst after righteousness: for they shall be filled.*
- *MAR 16:20 And they went forth, and preached every*

*where, the Lord working with them, and confirming the word with signs following. .*

- *ACT 5:32 And we are his witnesses of these things; and so is also the Holy Ghost, whom God hath given to them that obey him.*

## Paul and Delores Blissett

I led a Bible Study in the home of the Blissetts for several months. We would close each session with prayer. Usually we would form a circle and various ones would pray as they felt led. Normally I allowed others to pray, but on occasion I chose to pray the dismissal prayer, and while doing so I began to pray in tongues, and when I finished Paul said, "Mac, you prayed in perfect Spanish."

Paul and Delores had been directors of a Bible College in Mexico for many years, and they both spoke Spanish fluently. Paul was a very honest and humble man who would not have said such a thing before his wife if it were not true.

A few weeks later at the close of another meeting the same thing happened again. Naturally, I was thankful to God for the experience. Since I was working on writing this book, it bolstered my faith and confidence that I was pursuing a course that pleased God and hopefully would bless others.

Needless to say, I firmly believe that God has anointed me heavily at times while writing these things which I believe are taken straight from the word of God.

## Jack Smith, Oakwood, Texas

An amazing encounter with the Holy Ghost was experienced by Jack Smith, Sr., who lived in Oakwood, Texas. Jack had been appointed as the Wednesday evening devotional leader of a Baptist church a few miles out of Oakwood. It was his duty to moderate the Wednesday evening services. He made announcements and then gave a limited devotional. Jack took this responsibility seriously because he had a deep commitment regarding the spiritual care of the Lord's sheep that had been placed upon him. His daily life took on a deeper level of commitment to prayer, Bible reading, and guarding his thoughts, words and actions as he went about his daily activities.

His secular job was to drive a bulldozer clearing land of trees and brush, building dams for stock ponds, and preparing building sites. One morning he felt a strong urge to pray while he worked. There were other workers in the area, but he knew they could not hear him praying because of the noise of the bulldozer's diesel engine. Much to his own surprise, when he began to pray he began to cry, shedding a flood of tears. An overwhelming emotion of worship and praise to God came over him and the feeling was like divine electricity. His intention was to pray to God regarding his Wednesday evening responsibilities, but instead, his focus centered on God and what he was experiencing in his spirit for the first time.

He said his praises became so loud that he shoved the throttle to full open to drown out his voice, and let the praises flow. He knew he was not going to do anything to turn off this heavenly waterfall that was bathing his soul with ecstatic joy. He was using every praise word he knew, and some that were not his common prayer vocabulary. Hallelujah, glory, praise God, thank you Jesus, amen, wonderful Lord, and my Savior, plus more seemed to roll off his tongue and out of his mouth fluently. This had never been his nature, or religious personality, and never had he experienced anything like it. This went on for a large part of the day. He was amazed at what he had experienced, and also what he had done. He had trees and brush scattered everywhere.

The next day as he started the engine of his machine he began to thank God for yesterday's blessing. When he got into full swing of roaring into trees and pushing them down he said, "God let it happen again." He put the throttle wide open because he felt another wave coming. Tears of joy gushed out of his eyes. A torrent of praise even more powerful lifted his soul into a realm of heavenly adoration of the great God he served, and that had become so close and personal to him.

In fact, as he bathed his God with floods of praise, he finally could not even say the words, the current was flowing too fast, and he was being swept along with the tide. He reached a point where all he could do was jabber and try to speak intelligently, but he was so enraptured with the divine presence that had engulfed him, he quit trying to say his own words, and enjoyed the moment without understanding why such was happening to him.

Well, this went on for a few days more, and then came Wednesday evening. When it was time for his devotional he decided to tell the people what had happened to him. He told how he had started to pray to God asking for his help and guidance regarding his duty as Wednesday evening devotional leader. He went into detail describing how he had been so overcome by a spirit of praise and worship, and how it had happened repeatedly. He then recommended that every one of them go out into the woods and pray to God while hoping the same thing would happen to them.

On a Sunday morning thereafter, the pastor spoke privately with Jack accusing him of trying to be Pentecostal. Jack was dumbfounded because he knew absolutely nothing about the Holy Ghost or speaking in tongues. He told the pastor he did not know what he was talking about, but his words fell on deaf ears. That Sunday evening several came to Jack and Dianne's house because they were hungry to hear more. They knew they wanted more than they were getting, and also knew their church would not accept their hunger for what even they did not understand.

There were a few people among them who knew more about the Holy Ghost than Jack did. They began a diligent search to see what information they could find in the Bible on the subject. Their number was growing and they decided to meet in homes until something else was shown for them to do.

Eventually a visiting minister came who preached on the Holy Ghost. As the preacher prayed for Jack he received a glorious liberty to worship and praise in other tongues. Jack realized this was what he had experienced on the bulldozer. Jack became the pastor of the flock which, to date, has grown to a dynamic local church where many people have been enlightened regarding the infilling of the Holy Spirit. I was privileged to participate in the early days of this move of God, and preached and held a revival where gifts of the spirit were manifested in undeniable infallible proofs.

Acquaintance with the church and area-wide fellowship among surrounding churches developed. I was one of the speakers for several annual conventions sponsored by the church, and was invited to minister during a weekend of special services. While I was driving to Oakwood, I began to sing a song which I had recently written. I had received the song while reading where Peter said to the lame man at the gate of the temple, "such as I have give I to thee," then took him by the hand and told him to stand up (ACT 3:6). The words to the song are as follows:

## SUCH AS I HAVE

*Verse 1*
*The beggar so low, deep in despair*
*Sat by the gate with no one to care*
*He looked with delight when Peter stooped low*
*Only to say, "No silver or gold"*
*Verse 2*
*The beggar I know could have been me*
*Lost and alone, deeply in need*
*When Jesus bent low and lifted me up*
*What silver and gold he placed in my cup*
*Verse 3*
*No silver or gold I hold in my hand*
*But treasures untold I command*
*My Father owns all on a thousand hills*
*He left it to me, It's all in the Will*

Chorus
*Such as I have, give I to thee*
*Such as I have, t'was given to me*
*Freely received, freely to give*
*In Jesus' name, stand up and live!*

I intended to sing the song that evening before I preached. I felt that God had assured me that he would bless the song as I sang it as a means to bless his people. When I ended the song with the last phrase, *"In Jesus name, stand up and live,"* the whole congregation leaped to their feet and began to praise God.

It was obvious that a mighty outpouring of the Holy Spirit was sweeping the place. Numerous testimonies came regarding wonderful things that had occurred at that glorious moment.

The pastor's wife, Dianne, testified that she had been suffering from a terrible back problem for a long time. She declared mingled with excited praise, that when she leaped to her feet, the back pain completely left.

It was reported that twelve people experienced speaking in other tongues for the first time when the Holy Spirit fell upon the congregation as they spontaneously jumped to their feet in glorious praise.

There was a group of teenaged young men that came forward and kneeled at the front of the church. I later learned they had not accepted the Holy Spirit move which had overtaken their parents, and they were embarrassed among their friends, because it had created quite a stir throughout the community and especially among their friends at school. But, this night God spoke to them by the Holy Spirit and they came forward and repented. Needless to say, I did not get to preach that night because there was such joy in the camp over these sons who had kneeled at the foot of the cross.

Several times throughout the following weeks and months I called Jack and Dianne, and learned that the back pains which had been a frequent problem had not returned. There were also other testimonies where God had miraculously given a divine touch of healing.

## Supernatural dentistry

A lady in the church gave an amazing testimony. I do not recall if she was one who leaped to her feet when so many were touched, but soon thereafter she said she had gone to the dentist with a pounding toothache. He drilled out the decay and filled the cavity with a temporary filling because he doubted the tooth could be saved.

She returned to the dentist in a few days, and when he looked in her mouth he asked who had filled her tooth. She replied that she had not been to any dentist, but at church she had asked God to heal her tooth.

He told her that he had drilled an irregularly shaped cavity, but there was a perfectly round filling in a perfectly round cavity, and it looked like a pure silver filling. He took some more x-rays to compare to his file and sent her on her way rejoicing. The dentist acknowledged that it had to be a miracle.

## A child healed of asthma

Some time later I went with Jack and Diane to a church a few miles away from Oakwood. I had been invited to preach, and in the middle of my message I noticed a commotion a few rows back. Since several were standing and obviously praying over a couple, I asked if there was a problem. They both stood up. The father was holding a baby boy which had leaned backwards over his arm. The mother said, I believe our baby has just died. She explained that he frequently had acute asthma attacks, and the doctor had described the case as being so severe that they could expect a fatal attack at any time. She said he had just suffered probably the worst attack ever, and had stopped breathing.

I could easily see the seriousness of the situation because the child had already turned blue, his eyes were rolled back in his head, and he was totally limp on his father's arm. I told the church we were going to pray and ask God to bring the child back to life and heal him.

As we prayed the child raised up perfectly erect, looked around at his surroundings, as though he was wondering what was going on. His color returned to normal, and his father and mother hugged and embraced him as they both cried in amazement and disbelief.

I asked the parents if they knew Jesus as their Lord and Savior. They said they were only visitors to this church with some friends who had invited them. They explained they were Catholics and had never been in a church like this. It was so strange to them, but all their defenses were broken down because they had just witnessed a miracle. They were humble and willing to learn, and you can guess that I did not get to finish my sermon because the church was energized with praise as the parents were gloriously born again by the Holy Spirit as they confessed Christ as their Lord and Savior. As before, I called Dianne and Jack numerous times, and they reported the little boy had no more asthma attacks.

I am telling these things to encourage anyone and everyone to believe in the Biblical truth regarding the Holy Spirit. One can know that if they will dare to believe what the Bible says, they will experience many amazing blessings. By taking the first few steps regarding the fruit of the Spirit, and by embracing the truth of the gifts of the Spirit and regarding the sign of speaking in other tongues, this will open heaven's door to the manifestation of all the gifts as they are operated by the Holy Spirit.

## My personal healing at Oakwood

From childhood I had suffered frequent sickness from what I learned was esophageal reflux disease. Sometimes I would have a sick spell almost weekly, and frequently twice a week. The attacks would be accompanied by severe headaches, acidic regurgitation, and prolonged vomiting. I would be about as sick all over as one could get.

This continued throughout my life and resulted in many days of lost time. I carried on as best I could, in spite of the frequent attacks. I was careful to control my diet, took over-the-counter medicines of various kinds, but obtained little relief from the inevitable spells of sickness.

I was invited to be the morning speaker at an annual convention held by the Oakwood church. My wife and I stayed in a nearby motel. About two A.M. I awoke knowing an esophageal reflux attack was coming on strong. A splitting headache, upset stomach, and up-chucking ensued, and by daylight I could hardly hold my head up, and I was supposed to preach at 10:00 A.M.

There was a restaurant associated with the motel. My wife

encouraged me to try to eat something, and hopefully I might be able to hold something on my stomach. This I did, and slight relief came, but I was still very ill when I entered the pulpit. I persevered and delivered the message which I had received a few days earlier.

To say the least, I was very perplexed concerning why I had not been healed. In fact, I had prayed for the healing of others while I was seriously ill. On one occasion, I was preaching while enduring a severe headache which I knew would lead into a severe bilious attack. A lady named Sister Suggs interrupted my preaching, and while coming forward toward me said, Brother Symes, I have got such a terrible migraine headache that I must leave if I am not healed.

I thought, who am I to be praying for her healing while I also have a debilitating headache? I was about to confess to her and to the church that I was not qualified to pray for her because of my own need for healing. I intended to call for some of the church folk to gather around her for prayer when the Lord spoke to me, clearly saying, "Divine healing is not dependent upon the condition of your physical body, but on the stripes Jesus bore on his body for healing."

With that word from God I anointed Sister Suggs with oil according to the scripture and she was instantly healed, and so was I. But I was not permanently healed at that time. God had something else in mind.

Now, back to Oakwood. I made it through the 10:00 A.M. message, and went back to the motel bed. A young Pastor from Louisiana was to minister in the evening service. I very much wanted to attend, but was weak from the lingering effects of my sick spell. I went anyway, and at the conclusion of his message he invited anyone needing prayer to come forward. Over the years I had responded to almost every such invitation hoping my time would come for healing. In fact I had almost become discouraged from trying again, but I went anyway.

A line formed and I was the last in line. Almost every person ahead of me fell out when they were prayed for. This had become almost a spectacular phenomenon throughout the land as many would fall out and line the floor like cordwood. I was finding it hard to reconcile this with scriptural events recorded in the New Testament. In spite of this I was attempting to curb any critical spirit that might impede the flow of the Spirit, and most of all, I wanted to be healed.

I was willing to fall out if this is what God wanted, but I assured him that if I did fall, it would be by his power, and not by my help in any way. I knew there were scriptural instances where people fell under the power of God, and that is what I wanted, pure and simple.

When my time came, with people lying all around me, I stood erect, but mentally submissive to whatever God wanted. The minister placed his hands firmly on my head and began to move it around, forward and backward, side to side, and in a circular motion.

I am an instrument rated pilot, having owned my own aircraft, and in my instrument training the instructor had attempted to induce vertigo in my head while I was under the hood. He did all sorts of dips and dives, spins and stalls, but to no avail. My vision was blocked by the hood and the only thing I could see was straight ahead at the instrument panel. He finally gave up and said I was very resistant to vertigo which was a good thing.

As the minister was moving my head around this came to my mind, while I recalled that many people become dizzy from such gyrations of the head. I resisted any attempt to rationalize the situation and kept telling God that if he wanted me to go down, it would have to be him because I was not going to help him.

The preacher became more aggressive as he pushed my head to the side and bent me sideways until my head was around waist level. The strain on my spine became almost unbearable as it seemed the preacher intended for me to go down. I said, "God, what am I supposed to do?"

Suddenly, a surge of divine virtue flowed through my entire body. My head whipped out from under his hands, and I stood with my hands raised, as I began loudly praising God with an overflowing force of joy.

God spoke to me clearly saying, "I have healed you because you were willing to stand for a truth."

When I returned to my seat I told my wife that God had healed me of the reflux disease. The church had prepared a fabulous dinner for the noon meal, and served another meal for just the ministers and their wives after the evening service. I went into the dining hall and loaded my plate with everything I should not eat. My wife went along cautioning me with every big helping I took.

I assured her I had heard from God, but she was not convinced. She said, "We'll see." She had nursed me through my bouts of sickness for years and knew what the normal results of a big nighttime meal would be.

After the evening service we intended to make the ninety-minute drive home. She warned me that I would never make it without needing to stop on the way and lose all that I had eaten. She said, "you know what happens when you eat a big meal before going to bed."

All the way home she kept asking me how I was feeling, and I assured her I was doing fine with no sick feeling coming on. I made it without a problem. That night I awakened frequently, surprised that my morning hours were not accompanied by a building headache.

That occurred over twenty years ago, and I have never had another esophageal reflux attack, accompanied by the painful headache, extreme nausea, and daylong hangover. God completely and thoroughly healed me.

My wife, Margaret said, "We'll see," and we did. God did it!!

I do not have time or space to relate all the many miracles God has performed over the years, and Oakwood is certainly a memorable highlight, but there are many, many more just as spectacular. I hope to attempt to record most of them someday.

I have given the above testimonies to emphasize the truth regarding the gifts of the Spirit, and to encourage everyone to *"live in the Spirit,"* and to *"walk in the Spirit."*

- *GAL 5:25 If we live in the Spirit, let us also walk in the Spirit.*

Jack Smith Senior has graduated to Glory and his Son, Jack Junior and his wife, Tina, carry on pastoring a thriving and growing New Testament Church.

## Emphasis on the Holy Spirit

A close observer will discover an obvious association and correlation between speaking in tongues and all the other gifts. Those who accept and manifest the gifts of the Spirit are mainly those who also embrace speaking in tongues which is listed with the other gifts of the Spirit. Endorsing the gift of tongues opens the door to all the spiritual gifts. The motivation is to strongly desire spiritual gifts.

- *1CO 14:1 Follow after charity, and desire spiritual gifts ...*

Besides the oral gifts, namely speaking in tongues, interpretation of tongues, and prophesy, the other supernatural gifts are essential for a fully rounded life in the Spirit. All the gifts are listed as follows:

- *1CO 12:7 But the manifestation of the Spirit is given to every man to profit withal.*
  *8 For to one is given by the Spirit **the word of wisdom**; to another **the word of knowledge** by the same Spirit;*
  *9 To another **faith** by the same Spirit; to another **the gifts of healing** by the same Spirit;*
  *10 To another **the working of miracles**; to another **prophecy**; to another **discerning of spirits**; to another **divers kinds of tongues**; to another the **interpretation of tongues**:*
  *11 But all these worketh that one and the selfsame Spirit, dividing to every man severally as he will.*

It is God's will that every believer should speak in tongues. Paul said,

- *1CO 14:39 Wherefore, brethren, covet to prophesy, **and forbid not to speak with tongues.***

Paul also said,

- *1CO 14:18 I thank my God, **I speak with tongues more than ye all:***

I was sitting by a Christian Brother in a Non-Pentecostal church. He asked me what I had been doing to keep busy. I told him I was working on a book getting it ready for publication. He immediately asked about the title of the book. I was a little apprehensive concerning his reaction, not knowing where he stood on the subject. I said, "you may not like it, but the title is *Should All Speak With Tongues?"*

He sat silent for a moment, and then he said, "Well, there is a lot in the Bible about it." I was surprised by his answer because he was a staunch member of his Non-Pentecostal church where we were sitting.

He continued, "I have a son-in-law who is Pentecostal, and I have a son who attends a Charismatic church." He went silent, as though he was in deep thought, and it was evident he had acknowledged the Biblical authenticity of the subject, even though he was avoiding receiving the truth personally. I sensed God was dealing with him about the matter, and he was able to at least recognize there was a lot in the Bible about speaking in other tongues.

From his response I believe the Holy Spirit will prevail with him because Jesus said,

- *JOH 16:13 Howbeit when he, the Spirit of truth, is come, he will guide you into all truth: for he shall not speak of himself; but whatsoever he shall hear, that shall he speak: and he will shew you things to come.*
  *14 He shall glorify me: for he shall receive of mine, and shall shew it unto you.*

I hope he will be able to read my book, and when he fully comprehends that the Holy Spirit already dwells within him, he will burn with desire to experience the fullness of all the gifts of the Spirit including worshipping and praising God in other tongues.

## The author's statement

I have never pursued or sought after manifestations of the gifts of the Spirit, but have simply walked in the full belief of the scriptural truth regarding the fruit of the Spirit and the Gifts of the Spirit. I believe that if I had stopped short of embracing the gift of tongues as the Spirit gives the utterance, I would have failed to experience the abundant manifestation of wonderful experiences such as I have related above. These are only a few of the many that could not be told within the limitation of these pages. I am sure that if we humbly and repentantly draw nigh to God through believing his supernatural word, he will draw nigh unto us in the demonstration of his power.

- *JAM 4:8 Draw nigh to God, and he will draw nigh to you. Cleanse your hands, ye sinners; and purify your hearts, ye double minded.*
  *9 Be afflicted, and mourn, and weep: let your laughter be turned to mourning, and your joy to heaviness.*
  *10 Humble yourselves in the sight of the Lord, and he shall lift you up.*

# CHAPTER 20

# TURNED ON BY TRUTH

Sensitivity to the moving of the Spirit is interwoven with our human spirits and emotions because we are emotional beings. "Emotion" is not a bad word, but is good. The Holy Spirit uses human beings in which to dwell, and through which to express himself. This is the means by which he brings forth his ministry in the earth generally, and in the church specifically.

Normal human emotions such as laughing, enthusiasm, encouragement, extolling praises, exuberance, joy, happiness, cheering, victorious rejoicing, exclamations of delight, affirmation of confidence, acknowledgment of truth, and delighting in good news are in order. Other normal emotions include sorrow, lamenting over defeat, remorseful resolve, repentant confession, defiant standing, defense of truth, and almost any other emotional position have their place in the heart and spirit of the church as believers meet together for preaching, singing, prayer, worship, praise, exhortation, reproof, Bible study, and fellowship…in the Spirit.

Why allow the free spirit of emotions in sports and worldly entertainment, and then restrict them at church? Imagine someone going to a game involving their hometown team, and jumping, shouting, clapping their hands, waving banners, and hugging their friends and neighbors at every score, and finalizing by a whoop and a holler with a little victory dance upon winning the game.

Now, imagine this same person going to church, and further imagine true New Testament operations and manifestations of the Spirit are occurring, and they are not allowed to express great joy at seeing a manifestation of the gift of healing, or a sinner converted, or witness an infilling of the Holy Spirit. Furthermore, when truly anointed ministries open the word of God, showing promises and rewards of eternal life, they are to keep things respectable...claiming to keep the worship "decent and in order."

Paul said, charity <u>rejoices</u> in the truth. When truth is declared to the church they have a right to rejoice in that truth. Any church which has been in bondage to traditional religious limitations regarding spontaneous worship would be revolutionized if they were allowed to rejoice in the truth. I mean rejoicing when truth is brought forth regarding the goodness of God, the gift of his Son, the deliverance from sin, the hope of eternal life, the gift of the Holy Spirit, the overcoming life – the list is endless. This should bring joy to the soul and food to the spirit.

Jesus agrees with this for he said:

- *MAT 5:12 <u>Rejoice, and be exceeding glad</u>: for great is your reward in heaven:*
- *LUK 10:20 Notwithstanding in this rejoice not, that the spirits are subject unto you; but rather rejoice, because your names are written in heaven.*
  *21 In that hour Jesus rejoiced in spirit, and said, I thank thee, O Father, Lord of heaven and earth, that thou hast hid these things from the wise and prudent, and hast revealed them unto babes: even so, Father; for so it seemed good in thy sight.*

The New Testament is filled with rejoicing, beginning with the disciples who followed Jesus:

- *LUK 19:37 And when he was come nigh, even now at the descent of the mount of Olives, the whole multitude*

> *of the disciples began to rejoice and praise God with a*
> *loud voice for all the mighty works that they had seen;*
> *38 Saying, Blessed be the King that cometh in the name*
> *of the Lord: peace in heaven, and glory in the highest.*
> *39 And some of the Pharisees from among the multitude*
> *said unto him, Master, rebuke thy disciples.*
> *40 And he answered and said unto them, I tell you*
> *that, if these should hold their peace, the stones would*
> *immediately cry out.*

I am a Dallas Cowboys fan, and every time I see those big, husky men dancing and embracing with full hugs, celebrating some great play, I cannot help but claim the right to such free expression of joy for the church...because we are on the winning team and have a right to celebrate in a purely human fashion. It becomes extremely exciting when the *"joy of the Lord"* fills one's spirit and becomes their strength.

- *NEH 8:10 Then he said unto them, Go your way, eat the*
  *fat, and drink the sweet, and send portions unto them*
  *for whom nothing is prepared: for this day is holy unto*
  *our Lord: neither be ye sorry; **for the joy of the LORD***
  ***is your strength**.*

If Israel could rejoice over victory, why can't the church. The formal church world has traditionally been critical of any show of emotion...especially among those who rejoice in the Holy Ghost. To suppress the joy of the Lord is comparable to suppressing the excitement and spontaneity of love in a marriage. Satan has been so successful at this that public amens are considered inappropriate in many religious circles. I am sure it was not this way in the early church, and should not be so today. The Holy Spirit expresses himself audibly in spoken languages, both foreign and domestic, in singing in the Spirit, in Psalms and hymns...and these should rightly convey normal human emotions and joy.

It is a mistake to put the activities of the Holy Spirit in a closet, as though it is embarrassing. The whole world needs to see, and hear, and know. This is certainly what happened in the book of acts. As the church comes together to sing, and pray, and rejoice, and exhort, and speak in tongues, and interpret, and pray for the sick, and to cast out devils, and to prophesy, one must not impose the "decent and in order" rule so as to quench the Spirit. It is not "decent and in order" to suppress responses of praise and worship that should come as a natural reaction to the Holy Spirit's work in the lives of grateful humans.

When the scripture is fulfilled literally, it is not "indecent and out of order" for the following to happen:

- *ICO 14:24 But if all prophesy, and there come in one that believeth not, or one unlearned, he is convinced of all, he is judged of all:*
  *25 And thus are the secrets of his heart made manifest; and so falling down on his face <u>he will worship God</u>, and report that God is in you of a truth.*

When this happens, don't take them to the back room. The whole church needs to experience and see the moving of God's Spirit as men and devils are brought under the power of the Holy Ghost. The workings of the devil are not taken to the back room, but are being brought right into the living rooms of every home through TV, so why take the manifestations of God to a back room in the church. The truth is, if we will be up front in joyful praise and worship, we will see more manifestations of the power of God in the home and in the church.

Parents walk right past the television as their children are spellbound by watching teen idols scream ungodly lyrics to demonic acid rock music, and their bodies become distorted and twisted by evil orgasmic surges of Satanic power. The parents will even stop and watch a while themselves, then walk on with no concern for what is happening in the soul of their child.

Our children need to be exposed to the manifestations of the power of God as these evil forces scream and protest their being exorcised from the bodies and lives of people who are helplessly bound by sin and iniquity. The church must be the place where deliverance can be found. It is the only place within God's rightful order where it is expected to be commonplace. Many people who resist the operation of the gifts of the Spirit would actually like to change their Bibles to read like what one sees in their churches.

Youth are turning to the occult because they possess an innate need for experiencing the supernatural manifestations of the power of God. Many who have turned to Satanism would not have done so if they had been given the true power of God.

When the true New Testament church exists--which is prophesied to be fully operational in the last days before Christ's return to set up his kingdom--social formality common to refined ceremonial church liturgy will lose its strangling grip. It will not be something to be whisked to the back room when someone rushes forward tormented by condemnation, falls headlong in the midst of the church, and begins to pour out their heart and soul before God and man. The church in the last days will experience great joy as the Holy Spirit works in their midst.

- *ACT 8:5 Then Philip went down to the city of Samaria, and preached Christ unto them.*
  *6 And the people with one accord gave heed unto those things which Philip spake, hearing and seeing the miracles which he did.*
  *7 For unclean spirits, crying with loud voice, came out of many that were possessed with them: and many taken with palsies, and that were lame, were healed.*
  *8 And there was great joy in that city.*

The church will respond with anointing, power, and authority. Satan's power will be bound and men will be set free. Abundant rejoicing will fill the air. Victorious rejoicing will abound more at the church over spiritual battles won, than at the sports stadium where a touchdown is scored.

The primary objective of the church is not to come together just for the purpose of rejoicing and having a high time spiritually. The purpose is to give God a time and place to move in the midst of his people collectively. It is a time for men in bondage to be set free, and for men who have been set free to move on out into the deeper things of God...a time of ministry to the body...a time for sinners to have an encounter with the power of the Holy Spirit.

Nothing can be greater than for sinners to come out of curiosity, and for saints to come out of excitement, to a gathering around Jesus. When things are being done decently and in order in the mind of the Holy Spirit, it might seem like pandemonium to some who are less informed.

Great power and spiritual authority will be given in a dimension never dreamed as the church comes into unity in the last days. Signs and wonders will confirm the word preached, just as in the early church, and more so...because it is the last days. People will come streaming out of the church pews which have held them in bondage to their Spirit-less (void of the Holy Spirit) formality.

This can come about only by the demonstration and manifestation of the same Holy Spirit which anointed Jesus.

- *ACT 10:38 How God anointed Jesus of Nazareth with the Holy Ghost and with power: who went about doing good, and healing all that were oppressed of the devil; for God was with him.*

It was this same Holy Ghost in which Paul trusted to confirm the word he preached by supernatural demonstrations.

- *1CO 2:4 And my speech and my preaching was not with enticing words of man's wisdom, but in demonstration of the Spirit and of power:*
  *5 That your faith should not stand in the wisdom of men, but in the power of God.*

After the truth is preached, it is the Biblically authorized ministry of the Holy Ghost to confirm the word with supernatural manifestations.

- *MAR 16:20 And they went forth, and preached every where, the Lord working with them, and <u>confirming the word with signs following</u>.*

Jesus said these words:

- *MAR 16:15 And he said unto them, Go ye into all the world, and preach the gospel to every creature.*
  *16 He that believeth and is baptized shall be saved; but he that believeth not shall be damned.*
  *17 And these signs shall follow them that believe; In my name shall they cast out devils; they shall speak with new tongues;*
  *18 They shall take up serpents; and if they drink any deadly thing, it shall not hurt them; they shall lay hands on the sick, and they shall recover.*

This can easily be summarized by saying that supernatural signs and manifestations...including speaking with new tongues...shall follow them that believe. The church shall experience great joy... and it will all be done "decently and in order," in keeping with Paul's instructions to the Corinthian church.

## Put to the test

I was invited to be the speaker for a men's retreat sponsored by a church in a nearby town. The men attending were from a variety of denominational backgrounds...some were staunch old-line Pentecostals, and others called themselves Charismatics. The pastor had been an ordained Southern Baptist minister, but he had embraced the doctrine of the Holy Spirit and the contemporary operation of the gifts of the Spirit.

Several days before the retreat was to begin, I felt a leading of the Spirit to teach concerning the concepts set forth in this book. Up to that time I had not discussed these matters with anyone--partly because of the reaction I might get from the staunch Pentecostals who believed that when one gets saved they probably will not receive the Holy Ghost at that time.

I was also aware that most of the Charismatics had allowed themselves to be convinced that they had been saved for years... without having been filled with the Holy Spirit...and only recently had they received the baptism. It was obvious they believed their denominational contemporaries were also lacking the baptism in the Holy Spirit, but had experienced salvation only. This newly-found light concerning the Holy Spirit was so precious to them; therefore, they were not likely to question the doctrinal platform to which they had subscribed.

I approached the meeting very apprehensively, not knowing what would be the outcome or reaction. I intended to go right into the subject the first evening, and as I prepared to do so, the gift of wisdom began to function. The Spirit began speaking to my mind in ways I had learned to hear and understand. He said, the first night, do not go into the subject, but give the scriptures only.

That evening I taught on a related subject but did not go into the question, "does one receive the Holy Ghost when they are born again?" At the end of my teaching session, I wrote a list of scripture references on the blackboard, asking them to copy the list. These passages all had one thing in common; they indicated that, at the moment of conversion the Holy Ghost is given as a seal, or a sign, or proof and confirmation that one has been saved. This means that God has accepted them into his family, the body of Christ, the church. This means their name has been written in the Lamb's book of life, and their sins had been deleted from the books which hold such records, and which will be opened at the white throne judgment... the judgment of sinners. These scriptures state that the way one can know they have been saved is because God has given them the Holy Ghost as proof of his acceptance and his adoption of them as his children.

I asked all the men at the meeting to copy each scripture reference. I then gave them an assignment to read each one before they retired for the night. They were not given a hint about what I was going to teach the next morning, but I stressed the importantance of their reading the scriptures beforehand. I warned them that I might shock them a little with what I would have to say. They all agreed enthusiastically that they would read the assignment.

That night I prayed for wisdom and anointing to teach--for my first time--the things that had been building in my spirit for several years. Since I have felt a calling to help bring unity and fellowship to the body of Christ, I have had things quickened to me concerning the doctrines that have divide Christians into factions and denominations. To me the subject I was approaching was one of the worst causes for disunity.

The next morning, all my fear of men was completely gone, and I knew God had prepared me for the task. When I asked how many had read the scriptures, all had done so. There was an air of excitement and suspense, because they still had no clue which direction I would go in the teaching.

I began something like this, "these scriptures all have something in common, which is 'the Holy Spirit.' This morning, I am going to show you by these verses where almost all of Christianity has been wrong in one way or another concerning the baptism in the Holy Ghost. This is true on both sides of the Pentecostal fence. Now I am assuming that most in this group claim to have received the Holy Ghost with the evidence of speaking in other tongues. You all believe that you were filled with the Holy Spirit subsequent to, or after you were saved." To this they all agreed.

I continued, "I am sure most of you have friends and relatives who are saved, but have not yet been filled with the Spirit." They all affirmed heartily. "How many of you previously believed that you received the Holy Spirit at the time you were saved?" The response was probably seventy-five percent. Did any of you believe the gifts of the Spirit, especially speaking in tongues were not essential?" Several hands went up. "But, you changed, believing you had not received the Spirit, but must do so…confirmed by the manifestation of tongues." They nodded affirmatively.

"Several of you, from old-time Pentecostal backgrounds have positive beliefs that one does not receive the Spirit at the time of salvation, but receives him only after one's vessel has been cleansed through the new birth, and sanctification." Amens punctuated the point.

I then said, "now, brethren, I am going to ask you all to stay with me, and don't form any final opinions until I am through.

Please don't pitch me out until you hear me out." It was obvious that tension was beginning to build a little...and needless to say, I had their attention.

I then said, "Brethren, I am going to propose to you that both sides have been partly right...and partly wrong. It is my intention to show you how the scripture says that one *does* receive the Holy Spirit at the time of conversion, and that the gift of the Spirit is a sign, or seal from God as evidence that one has been born again. Furthermore, I plan to show from the scripture that everyone who is saved should expect--and want--the manifestation of the gifts of the Spirit immediately thereafter, especially the gift of tongues which has been designated as a *'sign,'* or miracle from God to forever transfer them from the ranks of unbelievers into the fellowship of believers...becoming one who is eternally convinced concerning the validity of the Holy Spirit and the gifts of the Spirit."

## Sealed with the Holy Spirit

I began with Ephesians 1:13-14, which says that after one believes the word of truth, the gospel of their salvation, and have trusted in Christ, they are sealed (like a king's seal of approval) with the Holy Spirit.

- *EPH 1:12 That we should be to the praise of his glory, who first trusted in Christ.*
  *13 In whom ye also trusted, after that ye heard the word of truth, the gospel of your salvation: in whom also **after that ye believed**, ye were sealed with that holy Spirit of promise,*
  *14 Which is the earnest of our inheritance until the redemption of the purchased possession, unto the praise of his glory.*

(This scripture gives no indication of any time lapse between trusting in Christ, believing the word, and being sealed with the Holy Spirit).

## After that ye believed

I explained that the Holy Spirit was not given after they were saved but *"after that they **believed**."* Believing is the key which unlocks the door to God's response and blessings. After one believes they are ***"sealed with the Holy Spirit"* (V. 13).** It is the coming in of the Holy Spirit that brings about the new birth, the washing by the Spirit, the baptism in the Holy Ghost, the regeneration, being born of the Spirit, salvation, adoption, and many other words that describe being saved. Yes, after one **believes** according to God's requirement, they are given the Holy Spirit, and the regeneration that results entitles those thus converted to live and walk in the Spirit. This includes manifesting all the fruit of the Spirit and all the gifts of the Spirit. This renewing is why all Christians should speak in other tongues as the Spirit gives the utterance.

- *TIT 3:5 Not by works of righteousness which we have done, but according to his mercy he saved us, by the washing of regeneration, and renewing of the Holy Ghost;*
*6 Which he shed on us abundantly through Jesus Christ our Saviour;*

Without doubt, one is given the gift of the Holy Spirit as an integral part of the salvation process.

## Witness of the Spirit

I pointed out that God is no respecter of persons, and this same seal which confirms one's acceptance into the family is like a legal adoption document which is signed and sealed by God, with the Holy Spirit as his witness. The gift of the Holy Spirit is this witness, or seal that confirms one's new birth.

- *ROM 8:15 ...but ye have received the Spirit of adoption, whereby we cry, Abba, Father.*
*16 The Spirit itself beareth witness with our spirit, that we are the children of God:*
*17 And if children, then heirs; heirs of God, and joint-heirs with Christ...*

The men that I was teaching began to acknowledge that proof we are the children of God is confirmed by the seal of the Holy Spirit attesting that one has been saved. A great unity began to develop as I continued to open confirming passages of scripture that they had read the night before. Scriptures such as the following:

- *2CO 1:21 Now he which stablisheth us with you in Christ, and hath anointed us, is God;*
  *22 Who hath also sealed us, and given the earnest of the Spirit in our hearts.*
- *1JO 3:24 ...And hereby we know that he abideth in us, by the Spirit which he hath given us.*
- *1JO 4:13 Hereby know we that we dwell in him, and he in us, because he hath given us of his Spirit.*

I can tell you that fellowship was sweet that day as brethren from both sides of the theological fence came together in love around the word of God. They all agreed that their church environment and upbringing had influenced them in various ways, and they realized that the church had been severely divided--and was still severely divided--over the Pentecostal differences.

They all agreed that in spite of what they had previously believed regarding when they had received the Holy Spirit, it was accepted that the true Biblical position was that when they were saved Christ had baptized them with the Holy Ghost. Their varied doctrinal positions had been based on the influence of church environments that had programmed them to believe according to their traditions.

But, they enthusiastically accepted the challenge to search the word intently with the purpose of enlightening those who claimed to be saved, but say they had not received the gift of the Holy Ghost to change their claim. It was agreed that this could be a major step in the right direction toward helping people receive the fullness of the Spirit and to encourage them to live in the Spirit and walk in the Spirit. This removes a major barrier to accepting the manifestations of the gifts of the Spirit, and will make it easier to trust Christ to lead them into the experience of speaking in other tongues as the Spirit gives the utterance.

Those who were formerly Non-Pentecostals who had experienced speaking in tongues thought they had received the Holy Spirit when they spoke with tongues for the first time. But, during this retreat they came to understand that they had been baptized in the Holy Spirit at the same time they were saved. Therefore when they spoke in tongues they had already received the Holy Spirit before they spoke in tongues, and he was finally allowed to manifest the *"sign"* (the gift of tongues) through them.

This changes the way Pentecostals and Non-Pentecostals approach each other. Instead of Pentecostals telling them they have not received the Holy Ghost until they have experienced the initial evidence of speaking in tongues, it confirms that if they have been born again, they were given the Holy Spirit when they were saved; therefore they have the potential for manifesting all the fruit and gifts of the Spirit.

Non-Pentecostals who understand this truth must acknowledge that if they have been saved according to the word of God, they have the indwelling of the Spirit, even though they have quenched him. Non-Pentecostals who claim to have received the Holy Spirit when they were saved must be loved into longing for the manifestation of that Spirit in their spiritual lives, and to desire all the gifts of the Spirit, including receiving the *"sign"* of speaking in other tongues.

Pentecostals who have been teaching that one does not receive the gift of the Spirit when they are saved must stop teaching receiving the Holy Spirit is a second, or subsequent work of grace. I have found it to be a powerful truth to tell sinners and new converts that when they are born again it is a birth by the Holy Spirit, at which time he takes up his abode within them. Jesus himself acknowledged that being born again is a birth by the Holy Spirit:

- *JOH 3:6 That which is born of the flesh is flesh; and **that which is born of the Spirit is spirit**.*
  *7 Marvel not that I said unto thee, Ye must be born again.*
  *8 The wind bloweth where it listeth, and thou hearest the sound thereof, but canst not tell whence it cometh,*

*and whither it goeth:* __*so is every one that is born of the*__
__*Spirit.*__

I find that it is much easier for people to enter into the gifts of
the Spirit, such as speaking in other tongues when they do not have
to tarry, and pray, and beg the Holy Spirit to come into them. When
they believe--based on the word of God--that he came in when they
were saved they have less difficulty going deeper into the gifts of
the Spirit. And, this is exactly what the word of God says regarding
when the Spirit moves into a person.

One must think twice before telling a saved person that they
do not have the Holy Spirit, regardless of how it bends or breaks
one's theology. On the other hand, one must also think twice before
claiming to be saved, while discrediting the necessity for being
filled with the Spirit...the same as occurred on the day of Pentecost.
Similarly, one must take caution in claiming to be filled with the
Spirit while rejecting the full operation of all gifts and fruits of
the Spirit, including speaking in tongues. Jesus warned about
blaspheming the Holy Ghost who is an important person within the
Trinity of the Godhead. His ministry among believers within the
church is currently of extreme importance to Christ.

The profound truth that leaps off the pages has to do with the deep
involvement the Holy Ghost shares in all aspects of New Testament
theology regarding salvation and eternal life.

# CHAPTER 21

# CONFIRMATION OF OUR SONSHIP

In Chapter Seven I covered the matter that the gift of the Holy Spirit was God's official seal upon his Son, Jesus Christ. In this chapter I am elaborating more regarding God's confirmation of our personal Sonship.

Immediately after the Holy Ghost came upon Jesus as he was standing in the Jordan River, God spoke from heaven, *"This is my beloved Son."* Even as it was necessary for the sonship of Jesus to be confirmed by baptism with the Holy Ghost, so is it necessary for believers today to receive the Holy Ghost as confirmation of sonship. The doctrine that this confirmation may come later as a second experience--maybe months or years later--is not consistent with the word of God. It happens up front as an immediate sign to the unbeliever confirming them as a believer.

How does one know they are saved? Is it because they feel saved? Or, apart from feeling, do they, just by resolute believing achieve a positive affirmation of salvation? Or, do they go by a required score-card, checking off a list of qualifications they have met...

sorrow for sins, confession, repentance, denial of self, acceptance of forgiveness, etc.?

No! We must go by the scriptures which relate to this matter of confirmation of sonship, and we must stand on the word.

## Affirmation of our sonship

There are many scriptures regarding the Holy Spirit as the proof and confirmation of being born again, which Jesus called being *"born of the Spirit."* There is a definite Biblical way that one knows with a positive affirmation that they are saved and have been **adopted** into the family of God. The proof positive is that God gives the Holy Spirit to every person he adopts into his family.

- *ROM 8:14 For as many as are led by the Spirit of God, they are the **sons of God**.*
  *15 For ye have not received the spirit of bondage again to fear; but ye have received the Spirit of adoption, whereby we cry, Abba, Father.*
  *16 The Spirit itself beareth witness with our spirit, that we are the children of God:*
  *19 ... For the earnest expectation of the creature waiteth for the manifestation of the **sons of God**.*

This is the Biblical confirmation which must be accepted by faith...the same way one accepts the matter of their forgiveness and salvation. Sad to say, ignorance of this truth has prevented many sincere people from enjoying the fullness of the Holy Spirit.

The apostle John was very positive on this matter and clearly stated twice that one knows they dwell in Christ because he has given them the Holy Spirit.

- *1JO 3:24 And he that keepeth his commandments dwelleth in him, and he in him. And hereby we know that he abideth in us, by the Spirit which he hath given us.*
- *1JO 4:13 Hereby know we that we dwell in him, and he in us, because he hath given us of his Spirit.*

Paul stated it like this:

- *2CO 1:22 Who hath also sealed us, and given the earnest of the Spirit in our hearts.*

Peter acknowledged the authenticity of the Gentiles' salvation experience by the fact they had been given the Holy Ghost as a witness.

- *ACT 15:8 And God, which knoweth the hearts, bare them witness, giving them the Holy Ghost, even as he did unto us;*

The scripture clearly states that one does, in fact, receive the gift of the Holy Spirit as the seal of adoption into the family of God. While tongues are definitely given for a sign, one does not have to wait until they have spoken in tongues to accept by faith the transaction of grace which converts them to being a temple in which the Holy Ghost dwells. On this basis one should expect and want the sign of tongues to be manifested. If the manifestation of tongues is not forthcoming, ministry by the elders is in order for this purpose, such as happened at Samaria.

The Holy Ghost is received on the same basis as one receives salvation...*by faith.* Just as one must accept all the requirements and stipulations having to do with regeneration and the new birth, namely the new creature, even so one must accept by faith all the Biblical stipulations having to do with being a dwelling place for the Holy Ghost.

As this truth is fervently taught, it will become commonplace for believers to speak in other tongues as the Spirit gives the utterance almost simultaneously with being born of the Spirit. They will be expecting it, and will have little or no barriers or resistance to speaking in tongues. Sound preaching and teaching is vital to the revelation, understanding, and acceptance of this truth.

One should not wait until they have spoken in tongues before accepting by faith the experience described by Jesus to Nicodemus... that of being born again, or, as Jesus said, being born of the Spirit. While there should be little or no delay in the manifestation of tongues, a thorough study of the passages having to do with the experience should build one's faith to accept the word of God on this subject at face value. Sound teaching and doctrine by helpful and supportive brothers and sisters in the family of God should be effective as the ministry of evangelists, pastors, and teachers bring forth the word in such power and anointing that an outpouring of the Holy Spirit will flood the church, and reach sinners outside the church.

It is amazing how much easier it is to believe, and to receive the manifestations of the Spirit, when one accepts by faith that the Holy Spirit has already come in at the time of being born again. Knowing this, one must submit to him in a gentle, sweet, non-struggling way, expecting him to confirm his entrance through speaking in other tongues. One can also expect him to manifest himself through every gift and fruit, not just tongues…but also in prophesying, discernment, wisdom, knowledge, faith, miracles, healing…prefaced with love, joy, peace, longsuffering, gentleness, goodness, faith, meekness, and temperance.

I have ministered on this basis to candidates for salvation and for the infilling with the Holy Spirit, and I can witness to the obvious ease with which people move into regeneration and being filled with the Holy Spirit…with the sign of speaking in other tongues as the Spirit gives the utterance. A scriptural explanation which shows that the Holy Spirit comes as a part of the new birth transaction gives hungry souls a solid basis for faith to submit to the Holy Spirit and to receive the manifestation of praise and worship in other tongues.

## Personal confirmation

Those who have been born again for a long period of time, but have never spoken in tongues should study the word until they are overtaken with an intense desire for the Holy Spirit to manifest himself through spiritual praise of Christ in other tongues. Jesus has given the following promise:

- *MAT 5:6 Blessed are they which do hunger and thirst after righteousness: for they shall be filled.*

Sound teaching and preaching must be done from the housetops around the world. Ministers of Christ must keep the truth concerning speaking in other tongues before the church at all times. In these last days all believers must know about the reasons and benefits for speaking in tongues. As times get harder, persecution increases, and Satan fights harder, one will need the comfort and power of the Holy Spirit.

It is necessary that all Christians--both Non-Pentecostal and Pentecostal--agree that the Holy Spirit does, in fact, take up his abode within a newly born again believer immediately upon their believing, repentance, confession, justification, regeneration, new birth, and adoption.

There is absolutely no time delay, or reason for the Holy Spirit to refuse, refrain, retard, or otherwise delay his beginning to dwell within the new creature in Christ Jesus. He is needed immediately as the teacher, the guide, the comforter, the reprover, the giver of spiritual strength, the guardian of the mind, and the mortifier of the carnal flesh. The new babe in Christ needs him immediately. The Holy Ghost is the sanctifier, the one that uses the blood of Christ to wash and cleanse the sinner. He cleanses as he comes in. His is the Purifier and Perfector.

One must *"receive"* (accept) the Holy Spirit without question. Receive him in child-like faith. One must receive the Holy Ghost just like they receive Jesus. Jesus sent him to continue his ministry in the earth. He gives the followers of Christ the power to be witnesses for Christ. All Christians are the disciples of Christ; therefore they should accept Christ's provision of the Holy Spirit. Jesus breathed on his disciples and said, *"receive ye he Holy Ghost."* In reality, many who profess to follow Christ have rejected the Holy Spirit in a day of Pentecost format, while claiming they received him and have knowledge of him, but to them he is dormant, inactive, and inoperative.

This book is talking about an entirely different relationship to the Holy Spirit than has been experienced by the "Non-Pentecostal" Christians. One thing I can guarantee, based on the word of God: that all Non-Pentecostals who have been born again were given the indwelling of the Holy Spirit when they were saved, but they have not allowed him to manifest himself in his fullness...or not at all.

This might not seem like an appropriate analogy, but it makes the point so well that I beg for understanding. The Non-Pentecostal religious world has kept the Holy Spirit like a Genie in a jug, and has not let him out to help them.

On the other hand, the Pentecostals have been telling Non-Pentecostals that they did not receive the Holy Spirit at salvation, and now must seek to receive the Holy Spirit as a second or third work of grace.

Sad to say, both have been errant...and even though it seems that the twain should never meet...this does not agree with the word of God. I am telling you that unity among the family of God is coming in a supernatural way far beyond what one could even ask or think. It is God's will and plan that we all speak the same thing, and with the same mind and mouth glorify God. One of the things that will bring this about is that the same truth will be spoken by believers on both sides of the Pentecostal fence. That fence must be abolished and disappear.

## Discard divisive identities

The time will come, prior to the second coming of Christ, when one will have to hunt far-and-wide to find Christians who classify themselves as either Pentecostal or Non-Pentecostal. The Holy Spirit is revealing just how "man-made" this division is. I strongly state that believers should not identify themselves as "Pentecostal" or "Non-Pentecostal." It is not Biblically sound.

In writing this book I have used the terms *Pentecostal* and *Non-Pentecostal* in order to identify the problem and to communicate the message of the *"one faith"* contained in this book, but my use of the two terms does not reflect my support for them. I never refer to myself as a *Pentecostal*, but as a *Christian*. Neither do I refer to myself as a *Spirit filled Christian* because this would infer that some Christians are Spirit filled, and some are not. The Biblical fact is, if one is a Christian, they are Spirit filled...meaning he came into them at the time they were born again. What they have done with him since that time is a different matter.

No sincere Christian would want to remove the events that happened on the day of Pentecost from their Bible. Neither would they do away with what happened at Cornelius' house, or at Samaria, or among the twelve brethren at Ephesus.

Some theologians who resist the doctrine of the baptism of the Holy Ghost say that only the twelve apostles received the Holy Ghost on the day of Pentecost. But, the Bible does not say this at all. It is simply a man-made doctrine. The record says there were one hundred and twenty people present and tarrying for the promise of the Holy Ghost.

- *ACT 1:15 And in those days Peter stood up in the midst of the disciples, and said, (the number of names together were about an hundred and twenty,)*
- *ACT 2:4 And they were **all** filled with the Holy Ghost, and began to speak with other tongues, as the Spirit gave them utterance.*

After they were baptized with the Holy Ghost, later that same day three thousand were also baptized with the Holy Ghost. And, the numbers grew exponentially in succeeding days to include multitudes.

- *ACT 2:41 Then they that gladly received his word were baptized: and the same day there were added unto them about three thousand souls.*
- *ACT 4:4 Howbeit many of them which heard the word believed; and the number of the men was about five thousand.*
- *ACT 5:14 And believers were the more added to the Lord, multitudes both of men and women.)*

## Discard false doctrine

Forget all the *junk-mail* the devil has sent in opposition to the truth concerning the reality of the Holy Ghost, and glorify God in your spirit because of this truth. The Holy Ghost will make himself real and personal to anyone who desires to know that he abides within. Everyone who is saved should thank him for abiding within.

- *JOH 14:16 And I will pray the Father, and he shall give you another Comforter, that he may abide with you for ever;*
*17 Even the Spirit of truth; **whom the world cannot receive**, because it seeth him not, neither knoweth him: **but ye know him**; for he dwelleth with you, and shall be in you.*

Bring him into the living room of your life, rather than keeping him hidden in a closet. It is a privilege and an honor. The sinner, the worldly, the unsaved, cannot receive him. The world does not receive him, see him, or understand him. *"But, ye know him"* (v 17).

## Full of the Holy Ghost

It is obvious that some Christians are *full* of the Holy Ghost, while others are *partly full.* When dependable men were needed in the early church to oversee some phase of the church business, *"full of the Holy Ghost"* was an important factor in selecting persons for the job.

- *ACT 6:3 Wherefore, brethren, look ye out among you seven men of honest report, **full of the Holy Ghost** and wisdom, whom we may appoint over this business.*

The first mention of being *"full of the Holy Ghost,"* related to Jesus after he had been baptized in water by John the Baptist.

- *LUK 4:1 And Jesus being **full of the Holy Ghost** returned from Jordan, and was led by the Spirit into the wilderness,*

Jesus was about to go into a severe round of temptations at the hand of Satan himself. The strength and comfort of the Holy Spirit was crucial, even to Jesus, because he had taken upon himself human flesh, and was subjected to human limitations and temptations. It was therefore necessary and essential that he be *"full of the Holy Ghost."*

There are other references to being full of the Holy Ghost. One had to do with Stephen as he preached in the face of death, and then was actually stoned to death because of his faith in Jesus.

- *ACT 7:55 But he, being **full of the Holy Ghost**, looked up stedfastly into heaven, and saw the glory of God, and Jesus standing on the right hand of God,*

When the church at Jerusalem needed someone to send to Antioch where many were becoming believers in Christ. Barnabas was chosen because *"he was a good man, and **full of the Holy Ghost**, and of faith."*

- *ACT 11:22 Then tidings of these things came unto the ears of the church which was in Jerusalem: and they sent forth Barnabas, that he should go as far as Antioch.*
  *23 Who, when he came, and had seen the grace of God, was glad, and exhorted them all, that with purpose of heart they would cleave unto the Lord.*
  *24 For he was a good man, and **full of the Holy Ghost** and of faith: and much people was added unto the Lord.*

This should inspire every Christian to want to be *"full of the Holy Ghost."* Without doubt, as God is searching for persons he can use in his church, this is one of the most important criterion for being chosen of God.

## Live in the Spirit daily

One must emphasize the importance of the Holy Spirit in their daily life...to walk in the Spirit, to pray in the Spirit, to quench not the Spirit, to grow in the Spirit, to read the word of God while relying upon the gift of knowledge to be imparted by the Spirit, to think in the Spirit, to talk in the Spirit...giving one's self to the indwelling and empowering of the Spirit for service and ministry.

- *ROM 8:9 But ye are not in the flesh, but in the Spirit, if so be that the Spirit of God dwell in you. Now if any man have not the Spirit of Christ, he is none of his.*

*10 And if Christ be in you, the body is dead because of sin; but the Spirit is life because of righteousness.*

*11 But if the Spirit of him that raised up Jesus from the dead dwell in you, he that raised up Christ from the dead shall also quicken your mortal bodies by his Spirit that dwelleth in you.*

*12 Therefore, brethren, we are debtors, not to the flesh, to live after the flesh.*

*13 For if ye live after the flesh, ye shall die: but if ye through the Spirit do mortify the deeds of the body, ye shall live.*

*14 For as many as are led by the Spirit of God, they are the sons of God.*

A sober, committed, dedicated lifestyle, following in the footsteps of Christ is a happy life. Refraining from the revelries of sin and carnality is the path to being *"full of the Holy Ghost."*

- *EPH 5:17 Wherefore be ye not unwise, but understanding what the will of the Lord is.*
  *18 And be not drunk with wine, wherein is excess; but* ***be filled with the Spirit;***
  *19 Speaking to yourselves in psalms and hymns and spiritual songs, singing and making melody in your heart to the Lord;*
  *20 Giving thanks always for all things unto God and the Father in the name of our Lord Jesus Christ;*
  *21 Submitting yourselves one to another in the fear of God.*

The way to live a victorious life over the flesh is by walking and living in the Spirit.

- *GAL 5:16 This I say then, Walk in the Spirit, and ye shall not fulfil the lust of the flesh.*

## The works of the flesh

The works of the flesh will dominate one's life, unless they are *"full of the Holy Ghost."* A long list is given:

> *19 Now the works of the flesh are manifest, which are these; Adultery, fornication, uncleanness, lasciviousness,*
> *20 Idolatry, witchcraft, hatred, variance, emulations, wrath, strife, seditions, heresies,*
> *21 Envyings, murders, drunkenness, revellings, and such like: of the which I tell you before, as I have also told you in time past, that they which do such things shall not inherit the kingdom of God.*

## The fruit of the Spirit

Notice what a difference the Holy Spirit can make in one's life. The contrast found in the very next verse is remarkable.

> *22 But the fruit of the Spirit is love, joy, peace, longsuffering, gentleness, goodness, faith,*
> *23 Meekness, temperance: against such there is no law.*
> *24 And they that are Christ's have crucified the flesh with the affections and lusts.*
> *25 If we live in the Spirit, let us also walk in the Spirit.*

If one has been baptized in the Holy Spirit, they might as well take advantage of the fullness of the Spirit. Anyone who claims to have received the Holy Ghost when they were born again should not only claim him, but should walk in him. If they do not, they are living beneath their privileges.

## Where to from here?

Do not let anything hinder you from living and walking in the Spirit. If anyone forbids you to speak in tongues, do not let this hinder you from experiencing the fullness of the Spirit. Do your best to get information to them such as is included in this book. Love them, especially because of their need for the truth. Never give the impression that they are sub-standard Christians because of their lack of knowledge or understanding.

Search out believers with whom you can enjoy fellowship in the Holy Spirit and get together with them when possible for prayer, worship, and Bible study. Desire spiritual gifts and learn together in group situations where everyone is willing to allow babes in Christ to develop in the operation and manifestation of the gifts of the Spirit. Seek for the genuine supernatural administration of the Spirit through prophesy, tongues, interpretation of tongues, miracles, gifts of healing, faith, discerning of spirits, wisdom and knowledge.

Pray much when at home, in your car, at work, or wherever you may be. The Holy Spirit will pray through you without any prompting on your part. You will learn to allow the easy transition from praying with your mind to utterances coming from the Holy Spirit. At times it will be audible, and sometimes under your breath.

It may be that you are the one God has called to bring truth to your local church fellowship concerning the gift of the Holy Ghost. If so, hang in there with tenacity. Do not put your light under a bushel. Do not be afraid of criticism. Do not keep silent at the expense of refusing to humbly speak concerning the truth. Sow seeds of truth wherever and whenever you can. Always remember that an important message to everyone who is saved is, they must be aware of the Holy Spirit which they have received, and must learn how to allow him to manifest his gifts and fruits in their life.

You are called to be a seed sower, so spread as much seed as you can...while you can. The response will sometimes be good and hopefully some others will also learn to walk in the Spirit. Sometimes others will come along and water the seeds you have sown. You must leave all this to God. One thing to remember is that God is the only one who can make the seeds grow. Paul knew this, so when he got beaten or run out of town for sowing seed, he just praised God all the way to the next town. Always remember that you are laboring together with God. What could be greater than working together with him for the causes that are dear to his heart?

- *ICO 3:6 I have planted, Apollos watered; but God gave the increase.*
  *7 So then neither is he that planteth any thing, neither he that watereth; but God that giveth the increase.*
  *8 Now he that planteth and he that watereth are one: and every man shall receive his own reward according to his own labour.*
  *9 **For we are labourers together with God:***

All does not always go well, and circumstances vary from place to place. It may be that you will need to worship with a different body of believers in order to fellowship in the fullness of the Spirit...while you wait on the seed to flourish elsewhere. This is between you and God as you function under the Good Shepherd, Jesus Christ, who is the head of the church, and the head of your life. Do not allow men, or the devil to put you on a guilt trip over where you worship. This comes under the headship of Christ and not man. He will reveal the will of God concerning where you worship if you seek his will in the Spirit.

- *ICO 12:18 But now hath God set the members every one of them in the body, as it hath pleased him.*

Always keep in mind and practice the rule that all believers are in one church, the body of Christ. If you worship with one group of people and others worship in another group, they may claim to be in a different church, but you will know better because this is not true. God has only one church. We are all one in Christ. He has only one body...one church. If you worship in a different local church, that does not place you in a different church, but just in a different local fellowship of that one church. The ultimate goal is for every local fellowship to see and embrace the truth, and to agree on the baptism in the Holy Ghost as the universal gift from God that seals, signs, and identifies those whom he has received into his family. Whatever the church does, or whoever the Holy Spirit uses, it is all done by the same one-and-only Holy Spirit which is in us all.

- *1CO 12:11 But all these worketh that one and the selfsame Spirit, dividing to every man severally as he will.*
  *12 For as the body is one, and hath many members, and all the members of that one body, being many, are one body: so also is Christ.*

One can pray in the Spirit daily. One can worship and magnify God and Christ in the Spirit daily. While doing chores or housework is an excellent time for personal praise and worship. While driving the car is a choice time for private fellowship and worship. Turn the radio off and listen to God. He will bring important thoughts to your mind. He will speak to your spirit, and you will learn to know when he speaks to you.

Just think of all that was going through Jesus' mind when he breathed on his disciples and said *"Receive ye the Holy Ghost."* He was thinking of all that would happen on the day of Pentecost, during the great outpouring that followed, and that continues to happen throughout the world...and will yet happen...especially in the last days.

## Submit to the Holy Spirit NOW!

If you have never spoken in other tongues as the Spirit gives the utterance, just begin right now to worship God in your own language. Begin telling God how great and wonderful he is. Tell him that, even though there are many who do not believe in him, you wish to go on record as being one who believes in him with all your heart.

Thank God for giving his Son, Jesus, to the world. Magnify Jesus in every way you can imagine...for his life, death, resurrection, ascension, intercession, and his soon coming. Thank him for the hope of eternal life. Thank him for the Holy Spirit which was given to you when you were born again. Acknowledge the ways you know that the Holy Spirit has been with you as a comforter, guide, and teacher. Thank him for a conscience that is alive and alert because of the reproof of the Holy Spirit. Paul said *"my conscience bearing witness in the Holy Ghost"* (ROM 9:1). Be thankful that John the Baptist said Jesus is the one who baptizes with the Holy Ghost.

Tell Jesus that you want to experience all the manifestations of the Spirit that are available to you, and that you know these must be accompanied by the fruit of the Spirit in order to be effective (1CO 13). As you pray be willing to allow utterances to come forth that do not fit the words you are saying. Do not think this is strange, but rather, expect it. Allow the Spirit to interject his syllables, phrases, groans, crying, and praises that are not understandable to you. Enjoy the deep emotions of joy and worship as your eyes are bathed with tears of love and appreciation that come forth from deep within your innermost being. You need not attempt to speak in tongues. Just allow whatever utterances that come forth from your lips to swell up from your heart, and don't be ashamed to bask in the profound feeling of love for God and man that exceeds anything previously experienced.

- *ROM 5:5 And hope maketh not ashamed; because the love of God is shed abroad in our hearts by the Holy Ghost which is given unto us.*

The Holy Ghost is well able to speak through you as he gives the utterance. Do not attempt to intellectually analyze everything that happens, or comes out of your mouth. Do not try to figure out what the Spirit is saying, but simply rest assured that he is praising God, magnifying Christ, or making intercession for you. Do not stop speaking and start over when it seems you may have not spoken a word properly, or got your tongue tangled. The Holy Spirit may merge his utterances in with yours at first. That is the moment to stop trying to say anything on your own, and one will usually be amazed that the utterances will continue, only in words that are not understandable to the person speaking.

- *1CO 14:2 For he that speaketh in an unknown tongue speaketh not unto men, but unto God: for no man understandeth him; howbeit in the spirit he speaketh mysteries.*
  *14 ...For if I pray in an unknown tongue, my spirit prayeth, but my understanding is unfruitful.*

One can actually listen as the Spirit speaks through them. That is the moment to totally trust in, and rely on, and believe in the reality of the Holy Spirit, and accept with full assurance that he dwells within.

Your praying may go back and forth from praying in tongues to your own language, and back again. This is normal, and it should not cause questions in your mind if you do not speak in tongues continually. If the Spirit stops speaking in other tongues continue on your own in prayer, praise, and worship until the Spirit chooses to pray more.

Singing in the Spirit is also very scriptural. When Paul said he would pray and sing in the Spirit and with *"the understanding also,"* he meant in the Spirit and in his own understandable language. Paul prayed and sang both ways

- *15 What is it then? I will pray with the spirit, and I will pray with the understanding also: I will sing with the spirit, and I will sing with the understanding also.*

This is the time to drink, and drink, and drink!

- *JOH 7:37 ...If any man thirst, let him come unto me, and drink.*
  *38 He that believeth on me, as the scripture hath said, out of his belly shall flow rivers of living water.*
  *39 (But this spake he of the Spirit, which they that believe on him should receive ...)*

- *2CO 3:6 Who also hath made us able ministers of the new testament; not of the letter, but of the spirit: for the letter killeth, **but the spirit giveth life**.*

**PRAISE HIM NOW--AND RECEIVE AND EXPERIENCE THE FULLNESS OF THAT WHICH HAS BEEN GIVEN TO YOU.**

God bless you as you go in the Spirit!

Written by Mac Ward Symes
A Minister of Christ

*1CO 4:1 Let a man so account of us, as of the <u>ministers of Christ</u>, and stewards of the mysteries of God.*

Mac Ward Symes and wife, Margaret Elizabeth Symes work together as a ministerial team. Their ministry is channeled through a nonprofit corporation named **Mac & Margaret Ministries, Inc**. All publications (Books, Songs, CDs, DVDs, Videos, etc.) by Mac and Margaret are produced under the umbrella of the above nonprofit corporation. Their website is www.MandMMinistries.org. Information regarding available publications and products can be obtained through this website.

Email contact: MacWardSymes@MandMMinistries.org.

# APPENDIX

(Book No. 2020-1)     312 Pages     $22.95
**SHOULD ALL SPEAK WITH TONGUES? (Published 2013)**
     (Publisher--WestBow Press, Division of Thomas Nelson, 1663
Liberty Drive, Bloomington, IN 47403)

**Order online from WestBow Press**
**Log onto** www.westbowpress.com

Soft Cover Book:     [ISBN: 978-1-4497-6800-3 (sc)]
E-Book:     [ISBN: 978-1-4497-6801-0 (e)] $3.99
Order by Phone: 1-(866)-928-1240 (Order by ISBN Nunber)

*A scholarly textbook dealing with all aspects of the baptism in the Holy Spirit. Answers are given to long-standing differences between Pentecostals and Non-Pentecostals. Truth given in this book can help bring God's people together around the "faith once delivered to the saints" (Jude 1:3). Vital information in this book can help bring about an outpouring of the Spirit in these last days. This book will surprise many...and challenge all believers-- regardless of background--to walk in the Spirit.*

Soft Cover Book and E-Book May also be purchased from Barnes & Noble and Amazon;
Order through All Christian Bookstores;
Request from Wal-Mart, K-Mart, Target, Costco, and Sam's Club (plus other Book Retailers)
Available as E-Book;

Also order from the Author – (See Below)

Additional Books in Manuscript Form (To be published)
Written by Mac Ward Symes, Author
Unpublished Books are neatly bound in Manuscript form and are available only through the author.
(See below for contact information)

Suggested
Donation

(Book No. 2020-2)      190 Pages      $19.00

## ADDED TO THE CHURCH BY THE LORD

*This book challenges the deeply rooted tradition of church joining that is practiced by almost all segments of Christianity that has been highly divided by the man-made doctrine of joining the church as though such joining is scripturally required before one can be considered as a valid member of the local church somewhere and wherever they might be. Strong emphasis is placed on scriptures which say that the Lord adds immediately everyone whom he saves to his church when he saves them. "Receiving" and "acceptance" by the local church body of those who God has added (adopted) into the family is a higher truth than joining.*

*ACT 2:47 ... And the Lord added to the church daily such as should be saved.*

*Therefore, instead of requiring that one must join the church of their choice, a responsibility is placed upon the existing local churches to receive everyone whom the Lord receives as part of the household of God when he adopts them into his family. It is the practice of joining that has divided God's people into more than 38,000 denominations around the world. See proof of this along with information sources given in this book. Receiving is a higher truth than joining.*

> *ROM 15:7 Wherefore receive ye one another, as Christ also received us to the glory of God.*

**(Book No. 2020-3)      134 Pages      $13.00**

## THE MINISTRY OF APOSTLES

*This book shows in the scripture why the ministry of apostles did not cease with the first century church, and why apostles are needed today to bring about the perfection of the church in the last days.*

**(Book No. 2020-4)      218 Pages      $21.00**

## THE ORIGIN AND DEITY OF GOD'S BEGOTTEN SON CREATOR OF ALL THINGS

**A deep and thorough study of two important issues regarding the Son of God: First, that he is actually the begotten Son of God...a little-known Biblical fact; and second, that the Son actually created the universe, worlds, and all that are therein-- under the command of his heavenly Father.**

> *HEB 1:1-2 God, who at sundry times and in divers manners spake in time past unto the fathers by the prophets, Hath in these last days spoken unto us by his Son, whom he hath appointed heir of all things, by whom also he made the worlds;*

**A real eye-opener that powerfully confirms the deity of the Son of God.**

**(Book No. 2020-5)**      76 Pages      $8.00

## THE ERROR OF JUDAISM IN THE CHURCH
**Why the Church Does Not Observe Jewish Feasts, Sabbaths, and Holy Days**

*Must reading for anyone questioning if the New Testament church is supposed to observe the feast of tabernacles, the feast of trumpets, Passover, as well as Sabbaths and Jewish dietary laws. The answer is definitely No. The reasons are clearly shown in systematic scriptural detail.*

**(Book No. 2020-6)**      170 Pages      $17.00

## GIVING VS TITHING--GOD'S FINANCIAL PLAN FOR THE CHURCH

*Jesus taught "giving" out of a heart of love. This information can bring a financial breakthrough for the church and for those who make up the church as the body of Christ. This is probably the most complete and exhaustive book available for explaining why tithing was a commandment given to Israel, but not to the New Testament church. According to Malachi 3:7-8, tithing and temple offerings were an ordinance of the law of Moses. According to Ephesians 2:15-16 All Mosaic ordinances of the law were nailed to the cross. Christ sealed the New Testament with his own blood which clearly outlines God's plan of giving with no percentage attached. I urge every believer to read this book. It will amaze you.*

**(Book No. 2020-7)**      183 Pages      $18.00

## GOLD, SILVER, AND PRECIOUS STONE
**(Building the Church With Truth and Grace)**

*A hard hitting message to the church which reveals some inferior doctrines and practices which are compared to wood, hay and stubble. This is a book with answers for the church regarding doctrines that are durable, comparable to gold, silver, and precious stone. A message for the church today.*

**(Book No. 2020-8)**   373 Pages   $35.00

## CALVINISTIC CLICHÉS

### *"once in grace - always in grace"??*

*A thorough resource for understanding why the doctrine of eternal security has so many little clichés which are so easy to memorize, and on which so many depend to prove their theory of once saved - always saved. This is not a critical attack, but a compassionate and loving study of the doctrine of unconditional security to which millions have subscribed. The author asks that no one judge this book by its cover, but to read it just in case it contains information that could be beneficial because of the truth it might open to review.*

**(Book No. 2020-9)**   142 Pages   $14.00

## THE DOCTRINE OF BAPTISMS

*Six principles of the doctrines of Christ are listed in Hebrews 6:1-2. One of these principles is "the doctrine of baptisms." Five different definitions of the word "baptism" are outlined in the New Testament. They are: (1) To be placed into; (2) Jesus' baptism into death; (3) Baptism in water; (4) Baptism into Christ; (5) Baptism in the Holy Spirit. Most of the time when people come across the word "baptism" in the Bible, they think of water baptism, but the truth is, many of the scriptures are not remotely speaking of water baptism, but of one of the other baptisms. Therefore, serious doctrinal confusion results when each passage is not properly associated with its proper meaning. An enlightening and enjoyable book to read.*

**(Book No. 2020-10)**   178 Pages   $18.00

## TO THE JEW FIRST
## THE TRUE MESSAGE OF THE CHURCH TO ALL MEN

*A truly fascinating book which begins with a sermon preached by the author at the funeral of a dear Jewish friend who he led to Christ after twenty-five years of witnessing to him. It digs into the real message of unity that the church should be preaching to Israel. It magnifies the truth that Jesus died in order to bring into existence a church wherein both Jews and Gentiles have been brought together into one church body. The central text of this book is taken from the following passage:*

- *EPH 2:11 (NIV) Therefore, remember that formerly you who are Gentiles by birth and called "uncircumcised" by those who call themselves "the circumcision" (that done in the body by the hands of men) -*

  *12 remember that at that time you were separate from Christ, excluded from citizenship in Israel and foreigners to the covenants of the promise, without hope and without God in the world.*

  *13 But now in Christ Jesus you who once were far away have been brought near through the blood of Christ.*

  *14 For he himself is our peace, who has made the two one and has destroyed the barrier, the dividing wall of hostility,*

  *15 by abolishing in his flesh the law with its commandments and regulations. His purpose was to create in himself one new man out of the two, thus making peace,*

  *16 and in this one body to reconcile both of them to God through the cross, by which he put to death their hostility.*

  *17 He came and preached peace to you who were far away and peace to those who were near.*

  *18 For through him we both have access to the Father by one Spirit.*

  *19 Consequently, you are no longer foreigners and aliens, but fellow citizens with God's people and members of God's household,*

*20 built on the foundation of the apostles and prophets,*
*with Christ Jesus himself as the chief cornerstone.*
*21 In him the whole building is joined together and rises*
*to become a holy temple in the Lord.*
*22 And in him you too are being built together to become*
*a dwelling in which God lives by his Spirit.*

**(Book No. 2020-11)**     322 Pages     $32.00

## THE RAPTURE THEORY, THE GREAT TRIBULATION, AND THE SECOND COMING
### Subtitle: WIFE OF CHRIST--BRIDE OF CHRIST

*Very revealing information about the bride of Christ. It will excite anyone who is interested in the second coming of Christ, the end time and the great tribulation, the millennial kingdom, the new heaven and earth, the bride of Christ, and eternal life in the heavenly Jerusalem. Fresh and new facts that will challenge one to think...and study the word on the subject of the rapture and the second coming of Christ. This book systematically proves why and how the rapture doctrine is a fable that came out of the wishful thinking of those who feared the thought of living and going through the great tribulation. Almost everyone who reads this book comes from the experience rejoicing that the greatest revival that Christianity has ever experienced will occur right while they are enduring severe persecution such as there has never been. Please do not judge this book without reading it. Read the last chapter because the church wins, Jesus wins, heaven wins... and Satan and the antichrist lose.*

**(Book No. 2020-12)**     203 Pages     $20.00

## WHAT ARE THE COMMANDMENTS OF CHRIST?

*Jesus said, "If you love me, keep my commandments." This is a deep study explaining why the church today is supposed to teach and keep the commandments of Christ rather than the* commandments of Moses. *This is one of the most fundamentally Christian books ever written and is filled with doctrinal truth that is vital to the church. A rock-solid foundation is built that is New Testament to the core. It helps one understand the foundation on which the church is built. That foundation is "Jesus Christ, the Righteous."*

> *1CO 3:10 According to the grace of God which is given unto me, as a wise masterbuilder, I have laid the foundation, and another buildeth thereon. But let every man take heed how he buildeth thereupon.*
> *11 For other foundation can no man lay than that is laid, which is Jesus Christ.*

## CD MUSIC ALBUMS

**(CD No. 2021-1)**        $10.00
**Title: The Splendor of God**
    **11 Original songs written and**
    **Sung by Mac Ward Symes**

**(CD No. 2021-2)**        $10.00
**Title: Such as I Have**
    **8 Original songs written by Mac Ward Symes**
    **Sung by Mac and Margaret Symes**

    **The suggested donations are to help defray costs in providing these Manuscripts and CDs.**
    **Add 20% for postage, shipping, and handling.**
    **Note: Any of these books which have not been published by a standard book publisher are neatly bound in manuscript form, and are available only from the author.**

**Your comments, feedback, and suggestions are welcome.**

**(Contact us for Bible Study Group Discount).**

## AUTHOR CONTACT INFORMATION

Mac Ward Symes
Mac & Margaret Ministries, Inc.
6002 Foxcroft Road
Tyler, Texas 75703
Home Phone: 903-581-3708
Cell Phone: 903-520-0522
Fax: 903-581-2357
Email: MacWardSymes@MandMMinistries.org

## ORDERING INFORMATION

Order by Phone [(903-520-0522) using Credit Card listed below.
Order by Mail (M & M Ministries, Inc., 6002 Foxcroft Road, Tyler, Texas 75703).
**To order by mail:** Make checks payable to M & M Ministries, Inc., or give full credit card information (Name on Card, Card Number, Expiration Date, CID No., Billing Address, Phone of Cardholder).
**(Call 903-520-0522 for assistance).**
To Place Online Orders for Books, E-Books, Manuscripts, and CDs, Order from Website (www.MandMMinistries.org) using one of the following Credit Cards.

## *VISA* - MasterCard - DISCOVER
## - AMERICAN EXPRESS

The above manuscripts will eventually be published in Soft Cover Books as funds are available.

If you feel led to do so, donations to help in publishing all these books in regular book form would be greatly appreciated. Use the above author contact information.